SAGE was founded in 1965 by Sara Miller McCune to support the dissemination of usable knowledge by publishing innovative and high-quality research and teaching content. Today, we publish over 900 journals, including those of more than 400 learned societies, more than 800 new books per year, and a growing range of library products including archives, data, case studies, reports, and video. SAGE remains majority-owned by our founder, and after Sara's lifetime will become owned by a charitable trust that secures our continued independence.

Los Angeles | London | New Delhi | Singapore | Washington DC | Melbourne

Quality Management in Higher Education

Quality Management in Higher Education

Marmar Mukhopadhyay

Los Angeles | London | New Delhi
Singapore | Washington DC | Melbourne

First published in 2016 by

 SAGE Publications India Pvt Ltd
B1/I-1 Mohan Cooperative Industrial Area
Mathura Road, New Delhi 110 044, India
www.sagepub.in

SAGE Publications Inc
2455 Teller Road
Thousand Oaks, California 91320, USA

SAGE Publications Ltd
1 Oliver 's Yard, 55 City Road
London EC1Y 1SP, United Kingdom

SAGE Publications Asia-Pacific Pte Ltd
3 Church Street
#10-04 Samsung Hub
Singapore 049483

Published by Vivek Mehra for SAGE Publications India Pvt Ltd, typeset in 10.5/12.5 pts Times New Roman by Zaza Eunice, Hosur, India and printed at Chaman Enterprises, New Delhi.

Library of Congress Cataloging-in-Publication Data
Name: Mukhopadhyay, Marmar.
Title: Quality management in higher education / Marmar Mukhopadhyay.
Description: Thousand Oaks, California : SAGE Publications, 2016. | Includes
  bibliographical references and index.
Identifiers: LCCN 2016014125| ISBN 9789351509967 (hardback : alk. paper) |
  ISBN 9789351509950 (epub) | ISBN 9789351509974 (ebook)
Subjects: LCSH: Education, Higher—India. | Educational leadership—India.
Classification: LCC LA1153 .M85 2016 | DDC 378.1/010954—dc23 LC record
available at https://lccn.loc.gov/2016014125

ISBN: 978-93-515-0996-7 (HB)

The SAGE Team: Shambhu Sahu, Isha Sachdeva and Rajinder Kaur

At the altar of
Our Creator
and
My Peers
in the colleges and universities

Thank you for choosing a SAGE product!
If you have any comment, observation or feedback,
I would like to personally hear from you.
Please write to me at **contactceo@sagepub.in**

Vivek Mehra, Managing Director and CEO, SAGE India.

Bulk Sales

SAGE India offers special discounts
for purchase of books in bulk.
We also make available special imprints
and excerpts from our books on demand.

For orders and enquiries, write to us at

Marketing Department
SAGE Publications India Pvt Ltd
B1/I-1, Mohan Cooperative Industrial Area
Mathura Road, Post Bag 7
New Delhi 110044, India

E-mail us at **marketing@sagepub.in**

Get to know more about SAGE

Be invited to SAGE events, get on our mailing list.
Write today to **marketing@sagepub.in**

This book is also available as an e-book.

Contents

List of Tables

List of Figures

Preface

Indian higher education is experiencing phenomenal expansion and diversification. The system now comprises 36,000 colleges and more than 700 universities, hosting more than 23.5 million students—the third largest system in the world. However, the quality of higher education is a matter of serious concern, especially in the colleges and state universities where it actually matters. A few globally comparable higher education institutions indicate the potentialities of Indian institutions of higher education. However, such institutions are far too few to steer India to become a knowledge superpower. Central institutions support education of only 2.6 per cent higher education students; 38.6 per cent by state institutions and almost 58.9 per cent by private institutions in 2011–2012 (MHRD-CII, ASHE 2013). The state colleges and universities that actually carry the national burden of equity and access in higher education are in a state of utter deprivation. The focus of quality improvement, hence, must be on those colleges and universities that actually deal with Indian higher education. Quality initiatives in higher education must be inclusive.

I have had serious engagement in the capacity building of college principals and senior executives of universities over more than last 30 years. The concern for quality is consistent. What is missing is the wherewithal—tools, techniques and strategies for quality improvement. This book is an effort to respond to this challenge. The focus of this book is on enhancing quality of higher education institutions. It is not a generic macro-system discourse on higher education. The book has been styled to serve as a handbook of quality management in higher education institutions with concrete suggestions backed by well-tested tools and techniques.

I have derived significantly from my research on leadership and management of quality in authoring this book. I have also derived from my experience of heading/leading major Indian national institutions and a few international organizations. This book, if read in conjunction with my book *Leadership for Institution Building in Education*, would add value.

I am grateful to many individuals for their contribution in authoring this book. Professor Madhu Parhar helped me with research and review of the chapters. Professor Swati Basu and Ms Sharadha Ramanthan meticulously went through the manuscript for copyediting. Sri Sabyasachi Panja did the graphic designs. I thank them all with all my sincerity. I am equally thankful to SAGE Publications for undertaking this publication; and my special words of appreciation for the members of the SAGE Team who worked on the manuscript.

Marmar Mukhopadhyay
January 2016

Front Piece

1

In Search of a Philosophy of Quality Higher Education

Introduction

Quality is the buzzword in education, especially in higher education. With increasing demand for globalization, the noise has become louder. There is, hence, a need to set in a discourse on the nature and philosophical underpinning of quality in higher education.

The graduates of higher education not only shape their personal lives, but also provide leadership to people in all walks of community and national life. With increasing globalization, these higher education graduates determine the quality of life of the global community. Higher education graduates are the torchbearers of economic, political, cultural and moral life of the national and global societies. On the other side, higher education graduates also lead in demeaning social and moral values all around with greed, violence and strife, threatening the very existence of human civilization on the planet earth. They are the leaders in whatever field they are engaged in.

Quality education is almost mindlessly interpreted as cognitive and intellectual prowess without reference to moral and ethical values, without relating it to 'discriminating intelligence'. Nuclear warheads and nuclear medicine are contributions of nuclear scientists—one for destruction and another for resurrecting human life. It is the higher education that will shape the quality of life on the earth. This is especially true at a time when weapons of mass destruction are within the reach of many countries, and when spying and sale of defence secrets are far too common. Hence, there is a need to define what we mean by quality of higher education. We need to define what kind of people are to be cultivated with what kind of intellectual and emotional skills and human values. We need to construct a philosophy of quality that defines the outcome as well as the process. This chapter proposes to address this issue of philosophy of quality of higher education. We shall deal with the issue under a few heads, namely, idea or nature of human beings, purpose of education, concept of quality, educational paradigms and quality parameters in higher education.

Nature of Human Being

Of the several discernible sources revealing the nature of human being, the religious literature is, probably, the most important and authentic one. The *Mundaka Upanishad* articulates about the wisdom of *para vidya* or revealed knowledge. The Al-Quran was revealed to Prophet Mohammad. The Vedas were revealed to the saints and seers. Gautam Buddha's self-realization was the source of his prophetic wisdom on human nature. There are interesting points of convergence on the issue of nature of human beings:

- Human being, in Hindu religious tradition, has been described as Child of God (*Amritasya Putraha*).
- According to Islam, 'Man is God's Viceroy on earth'.
- 'God is the soul of man, his eternal nature', says Sikhism.
- According to Christianity, 'Man is God's workman on earth'.
- 'The Wise One created man to be like Him', contends Zoroastrianism.
- According to the Baha'is, 'Man is the supreme Talisman'.
- Jainism contends: 'Man is creation of God, made in the likeness of God'.
- 'Heaven has made man good. His original nature is good...' is the contention of Confucianism.

It would be evident that, in all religions, human beings have been defined, in one way or the other, with reference to God—as child or representative of God. Kahlil Gibran, in his famous poetic work *The Prophet*, told the parents that 'The child is *through* you' and *from the God*. Ibis indicates the essential unity of all religions—*Ekam Sad Vipraha Bahudha Vadanti* (Rig Veda) or 'Wherever you turn, there is the face of God' (Quran; Singh 2003).

The major implication of accepting the proposition that human is indeed the child of God is that every human being has the potentiality of achieving immortality, that is, the attribute of God himself/herself. Leonard Orr, the Christian spiritual leader, in his interesting treatise *Breaking the Death Habits*, argued that humans are basically immortal, that is, the attribute of God. He, however, added that humans develop the habit of dying.

This divinity in humans is, however, not apparent. Coats and coats of colours and habits hide the propensities. In view of Baha'i faith, 'lack of proper education hath, however, deprived him of that which he doth inherently possess'.[1] Thus, in the real world, we experience human beings positioned on a continuum between beastliness and divinity, the two ends of the continuum. In social terms, beastliness is indicated by the instinct of acquisitiveness—tendencies of acquisition of material wealth and comfort. Religious scriptures also describe excessive hunger, sleep, procreation, fear, anger and so on as indicators of lower order beings among the human beings.

Divinity, on the other hand, is indicated by renunciation—giving away for the benefit and happiness of others. The saints and seers are characterized by their nature of giving away all that they have. Sadhu Vaswani's life is an instant example where he gives away his meagre belongings to others in need. The crucifixion of Jesus, martyrdom of Guru Tegh Bahadur and innumerable instances of Hindu saints like Paramahansa Sri Ramakrishna relieving sufferings of fellow beings by taking away their diseases on to themselves are some of the outstanding examples where life itself was given away for the benefit of others. In poetic expression:

> *When you see a thorn on path lies,*
> *Take it up, and a flower let there be;*
> *A thousand thorns you will have thus uprooted,*
> *The road with flowers strewn smiling stand.*
> *(The Muse* by N.P. Mukherjee)[2]

---

[1] www.reference.bahai.org/en/t/c/BE/be-5.html (accessed on 20 April 2014).
[2] This is an extract from my father Late Sri N.P. Mukherjee's book.

In reality, it is not difficult to pick up the thousand thorns and leave the road smiling with flowers. It is a matter of value. The beastly behaviour is indicated by picking up the flowers, leaving the road strewn with thorns for others to walk on, whereas divinity is in picking up the thorns despite the risks of getting hurt. Humans move, across births, from one end of the continuum to the other. Importantly, every human being has the potentiality to move from where he/she is towards the ultimate destination—the divinity. Shri Aurobindo's contention of movement towards the superman and supramental with every birth also supports this hypothesis.

Should this interfaith proposition be conceded, the nature, rather quality, of human beings will be determined much more by the values rather than by the amount of information one has mastered. Wisdom that was the prerogative of the saints and seers of all religions is the information and knowledge tested out and purified on the fundamental values. Carrying the argument forward, human beings are essentially value configurations, not knowledge configurations. Whether a nuclear scientist applies his/her knowledge and expertise in creating a nuclear arsenal or nuclear medicine depends upon his/her value system; knowledge is a mere instrumentality. It is education that provides and strengthens the value aspect of humans to optimize their potential. Thus, women and men with higher moral values are higher in the continuum of evolution of human beings.

Purpose of Education

Throughout human history, experts all over the world have pointed out that the education of young human beings should involve much more than simply moulding them into future workers or citizens. The Swiss humanitarian Johann Pestalozzi, the American transcendentalists,[3] Upanishadic thinkers of India and many stalwarts of the 'progressive'

---

[3] Emerson wrote in his 1837 speech 'The American Scholar': 'We will walk on our own feet; we will work with our own hands; we will speak our own minds.... A nation of men will for the first time exist, because each believes himself inspired by the Divine Soul which also inspires all men'. Emerson closed the essay by calling for a revolution in human consciousness to emerge from the brand new idealist philosophy. http://en.wikipedia.org/wiki/Transcendentalism (accessed on 3 April 2014).

education movement insisted that education should be understood as the art of cultivating the moral, emotional, physical, psychological, artistic and spiritual—as well as intellectual—dimensions of the developing child (Scott and Martin 2004). An emerging body of literature in science, philosophy and cultural history provides an overarching concept to describe the purpose of education as holistic or all-round development of young people. As expressed in these works, holistic education facilitates a student's identity, meaning and purpose in life through connections to the community, to the natural world and to spiritual values such as compassion and peace. Besides, holistic education also aims to call forth an intrinsic reverence for life and a passionate love of learning from the learners. This cannot happen through an academic 'curriculum' that condenses the world into instructional packages, but through direct engagement with the environment (Miller 2000).

The *Taittiriya Upanishad* instructs learners at their graduation ceremony in the following words that can be interpreted as the purpose of education:

Speak the truth. Practise virtue. Make no mistake about study. There should be no inadvertence about truth. There should be no deviation from righteous activity. There should be no error about protection of yourself. Do not neglect propitious activities. Do not be careless about learning and teaching. There should be no error in the duties towards the Divine and the humanity. Let your mother be a goddess unto you. Let your father be a god unto you. Let your teacher be a god unto you. Let your guest be a god unto you. The works that are not blameworthy are to be resorted to, but not the others. The offering should be with honour; the offering should be in plenty. The offering should be with modesty. The offering should be with sympathy. Then, should you have any doubt with regard to duties or customs, you should behave in those matters just as the wise men do, who may happen to be there and who are able deliberators, who are adepts in those duties and customs, who are not directed by others, who are not cruel, and who are desirous of merit. (*Taittiriya Upanishad*, I. xi.1–4, cited in Radhakrishnan 2007)

Just as human beings have been defined with reference to God, implying potential for perfection *(purnam),* the purpose of education has also been defined universally as holistic development. Swami Vivekananda defined purpose of education as 'manifestation of perfection already in man'. Please mark, 'perfection' is the attribute of God. But, how does this apply to higher education?

We need to understand the nature of higher education and the idea of a university. John Henry Newman (1854: 1) is often quoted for the most authentic definition of a university:

> If I were asked to describe as briefly and popularly as I could, what a University was, I should draw my answer from its ancient designation of a Studium Generale, or 'School of Universal Learning.' This description implies the assemblage of strangers from all parts in one spot; (from all parts;) else, how will you find professors and students for every department of knowledge? and in one spot; else, how can there be any school at all? Accordingly, in its simple and rudimental form, it is a school of knowledge of every kind, consisting of teachers and learners from every quarter. Many things are requisite to complete and satisfy the idea embodied in this description; but such as this a University seems to be in its essence, a place for the communication and circulation of thought, by means of personal intercourse, through a wide extent of country.

Newman continued: 'But I have said more than enough in illustration; I end as I began;—a University is a place of concourse, whither students come from every quarter for every kind of knowledge'.

Mitra and Mandke (2004) offered another contemporary description of institutes of higher education—higher education as a knowledge enterprise. The Mitra model, as it is called, paints higher education to be the basis of knowledge engineering. Business of universities and other higher education institutions is an entrepreneurship in knowledge—implying knowledge creation through research and development, and not just transaction of knowledge. This spirit can be found in the recommendations of the Yashpal Committee that all universities should be teaching-cum-research institutions.

Quality Education

Generally speaking, there is no accepted definition of 'quality' as a concept in education. Some scholars have taken a bypass—'defining quality is not particularly important and useful' (Sallis 1996, 2002). Some have resorted to poetic refuge, 'as beauty lies in the eyes of the beholder, quality lies in the eyes of the customer'. Also, like beauty is inherent in the object of the beholding eyes, quality is also inherent in the perception of the customer/consumer and not in the product. Because of ambiguity in the customer perceptions, what is a great quality for one may not be enough for another. This 'tolerance for ambiguity' makes conceptualizing and managing quality a challenging creative process (Mukhopadhyay 2004a).

What is, however, universally acceptable are the following:

- Quality is relative, not absolute.
- Quality is dynamic, not static.
- Quality is a journey, not a destination (especially in education).

There are wide divergences in the concept of quality. What constitutes quality for one may or may not be relevant for another. For example, for some, quality is largely a functional concept. In the domains of consumer products as well as in education, quality is something that works and serves the purpose for which it is meant (Navaratnam 1997). For Indian scriptures, quality is a metaphysical concept. It is functionality and beyond. Quality is inclusive, not exclusive. Such conceptualizations are determined by the thought attributes of Western and Eastern minds.

There is an overwhelming influence of Western functionalism on contemporary Indian and Eastern education, particularly since the establishment of universities in the Western traditions and models (establishment of universities in Kolkata, Mumbai and Chennai in 1857 on the model of London University). The following statement by Lord Macaulay is an interesting example of functionalism in education:[4]

> We must at present do our best to form a class who may be interpreters between us and the millions whom we govern—a class of persons Indian in blood and colour, but English in tastes, in opinions, in morals and in intellect. To that class we may leave it to refine the vernacular dialects of the country, to enrich those dialects with terms of science borrowed from the Western nomenclature, and to render them by degrees fit vehicles for conveying knowledge to the great mass of the population.

---

[4] http://www.columbia.edu/itc/mealac/pritchett/00generallinks/macaulay/txt_minute_education_1835.html (accessed on 20 April 2014).

Functionalism as the blueprint for quality education is all pervasive. The difference between the Eastern and Western cultures in terms of conceptualization of quality of education has narrowed down. Globalization is facilitating and catalyzing this process of creating a common definition of quality of higher education. However, this exclusive emphasis on functionalism gives rise to the paradox or conflict between the potentials of human beings and limited purpose of education as enunciated earlier. The functionalist paradigm of quality is one-dimensional and, therefore, it bypasses/overlooks the holistic development model. Education becomes meaningless as it loses its connectivity to the ultimate—potential nature of human beings. Discourse on educational quality is of no consequence if it does not nurture human beings to actualize their full potential. The human beings stand minimized as the short-term goals and personal gains block the vision of the ultimate. Education gets discarded for a social good in favour of personal benefits (human capital formation) and commodity.

Let us go little beyond and examine a few more descriptions of quality in education. 'Quality in education' has been variously defined as:

- Excellence in education (Peters and Waterman 1982)
- Value addition in education (Feigenbaum 1951)
- Fitness of educational outcome and experience for use (Juran and Gryna 1988)
- Conformance of education output to planned goals, specifications and requirements (Crosby 1979; Gilmore 1974)
- Defect avoidance in the education process (Crosby 1979)
- Meeting or exceeding customers' expectations of education (Parasuraman et al. 1985)

For contextualizing quality education, it is important to understand the changing nature of social goals. American priority on human rights and personal freedom in the 1960s has changed due to success in the global economy in the 1990s; Britain's current emphasis is on what the students 'know and can do' rather than on numinous goals (Holt 2000). Japanese White Paper on education in the 1980s changed the focus to invention rather than on adaptation of technology. The Indian social goal has also changed from exclusive manpower planning to inclusive higher education for the transition from a literate society to a knowledge-based society aspiring to be a knowledge superpower. The emphasis is shifting from the previous value-neutral education to the value-oriented education. Empirical research in education raises a few major issues vis-à-vis quality in education. The most prominent among them is the concept of institutional effectiveness. The contention is that the effectiveness is the indicator of quality. The second major debate has been around the concept of accountability. Higher education institutions have been established and run at public cost either through government funding or through tuition fees. Hence, they ought to have social accountability. The institutions that set the benchmark, relentlessly work towards the achievement of targets and fulfil the expectations of students and the community are thus accountable and, hence, imparts quality education.

Educational Paradigms

For constructing a philosophical basis for quality higher education, we shall review a few paradigms.

Four Planes of Living and Four Pillars of Learning

Interfaith research concludes that human beings are made in the image of God; hence, its full potential is divine or completeness (Mukhopadhyay 2002). This metaphysical concept has been given a functional modality in Indian scriptures. Human beings live in four planes—physical, mental, intellectual and spiritual. This can be plotted in the form of a concept map (Figure 1.1).

Physical Plane

Physical domain is the body—something concrete that can be seen and felt. From the standpoint of education, it comprises, in most simple terms, external and internal health. Internal health is indicated by freedom from diseases and a long life. External health is indicated by physical strength, kinaesthetic skills as depicted by skills in dance and drama, sports and games and so on. Its importance is well articulated as *shariram adyam khalu dharma sadhanam* (The

Figure 1.1:
Four Planes of Living: Concept Map

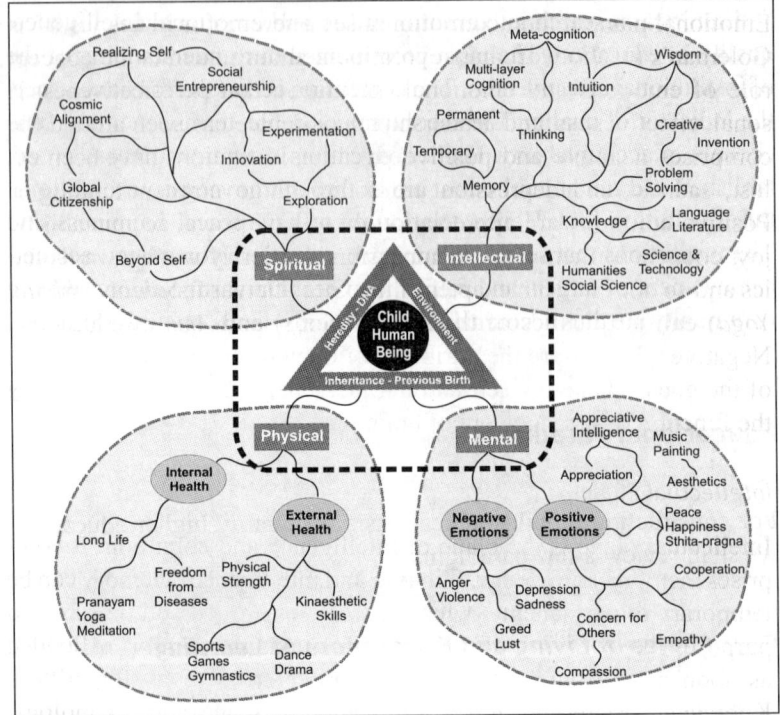

Source: Author.

Gita, Ch. 17 'Sraddha-traya-vibhaga Yoga'; the body is the basis of dharma—the ultimate.) Swami Vivekananda exhorted the youth to be strong: 'First of all, our young men must be strong. Religion will come afterwards. Be strong my young friends, that is my advice to you. You will be nearer to heaven through football than through study of Gita'[5].

Quality of the physical domain is indicated by posture, gestures, speed and dexterity, flexibility and attire.

---

[5] https://en.wikisource.org/wiki/The_Complete_Works_of_Swami_Vivekananda Volume_3/ Lectures_from_Colombo_to_Almora/Vedanta_in_its_Application_to_Indian_Life (accessed on 7 June 2016)

Emotional Plane

Emotional plane refers to emotional life and emotional intelligence. Goleman's (1995) work has revolutionized our understanding of the role of emotions and emotional intelligence on performance, personal effectiveness and leadership. In simple terms, mental plane comprises negative and positive emotions. Anger, violence, greed, lust, sadness and depression are some of the negative emotions. Positive emotions are appreciation of others, peace, happiness and joy, cooperation, empathy, compassion, concern for others, aesthetics and so on. The 16th chapter of the Gita (Daivasur *Sampad Vibhag Yoga*) enlists qualities of the *Devas* (Gods) and *Asuras* (Demons). Negative qualities are the attributes of demons and positive qualities of the gods. Managing self and intrapersonal relationships is largely the function of management of emotions.

Intellectual Plane

Intellectual plane is the plane of intelligence and cognition. It comprises memory, knowledge, thinking and intelligence. Memory can be temporary or permanent—what we store for limited and time-bound purposes like for writing examination is temporary and is offloaded as soon as the purpose is over (often referred to as forgetting). Knowledge represents information about science and technology, language and literature, humanities and social sciences and so on. Thinking is problem solving and invention, critical and creative thinking, multilayer cognition, intuition and wisdom. Intelligence is the backbone of both memory and knowledge and the ability to learn. The issue of values—right or wrong, good or bad and so on—is attributable to discriminating intelligence, a dominant concept in the Gita. With growing obsolescence of knowledge, the premium for the intellectual domain is shifting towards thinking and learning to know (UNESCO 1996).

Spiritual Plane

Spiritual plane can be referred to as spiritual intelligence according to the contemporary theory of Danah Zohar (or existential intelligence by Howard Gardner). The concept of spiritual plane is also linked to religious practices. I prefer to define spiritual plane with respect to the concept of spirit, for example, spirit of exploration, reaching out to people and so on. Accordingly, spiritual plane implies spirit of expanding and reaching beyond self (*udara caritanantu vasud-haiba kutumbakam,* and not *ayam nijah paro veti gananaa laghu-chetasaam*—for large-hearted people, the entire world is a family and not for the chicken-hearted who count 'this is mine, and that is others')—global citizenship, cosmic alignment on the one hand, and exploration, innovation and experimentation leading to social entrepreneurship, on the other hand. These are two paths leading to optimizing and realizing the self (self-actualization).

From this paradigm, quality higher education implies education for optimizing developments in all the planes. Thus, this provides an important framework for holistic quality.

Through the 'four pillars of learning', the International Commission on Education in the 21st century offers yet another framework for holistic quality (UNESCO 1996).

1. The first pillar 'learning to know' simultaneously exhorts higher order learning and learning to learn.
2. Concern of the second pillar, 'learning to do', is functional application of knowledge.
3. The third pillar, 'learning to live together', brings in the social and human concern.
4. The focus of the fourth and the final pillar, 'learning to be', is the self-actualization, emergence of the total being or being educated.

Educatedness

The *Taittiriya Upanishad* instructs learners, mentioned earlier, which can be construed as the qualities of an educated person: 'Speak the truth. Practise righteousness... (I.xi.1–4).

My philosophical proposition for quality in education is the concept of educatedness (Mukhopadhyay 1999). What constitutes educatedness? Who can be called educated? Can anyone with a degree be called educated? The fundamental hypothesis is: If education is expected to cultivate all four planes of living, whether just a qualification is enough to be called educated? A qualified person is at best informed about a structured set of knowledge. In popular parlance also people who are fully qualified but do not fulfil their family and social obligations are looked down upon as uneducated.

In this paradigm, educatedness is conceptualized as a four-tier hierarchic paradigm inspired by the question—who is an educated person or what is educatedness? The negative question is whether all qualified people are educated?

Educated individuals can be placed on taxonomy of educatedness: informed, cultured, self-actualized and emancipated (Figure 1.2). Let us examine each of these levels in little details.

Figure 1.2:
Taxonomy of Educatedness

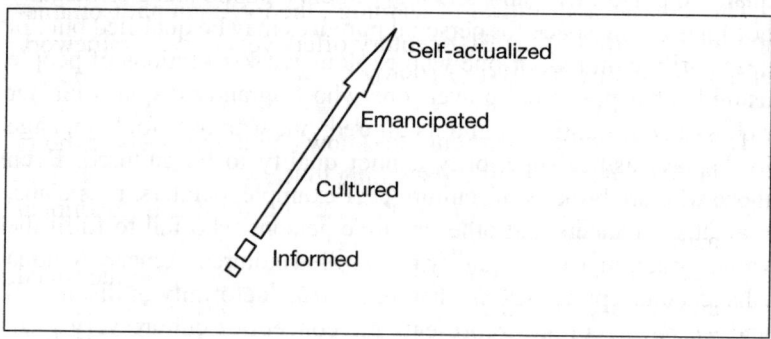

Source: Author.

Informed

The lowest in the hierarchy is being informed—either through formal or informal educational processes or through incidental learning. Information is bits of facts, figures, concepts and so on. These bits are not necessarily interrelated. Knowledge is in the organized form where information is woven into a meaningful pattern, a configuration. Hence, one and the first purpose of education is informing and processing information into the form of organized knowledge. A formal qualification indicates that the person is likely to possess knowledge of the concerned subject. There are two implications. First, this also means that those who are not qualified may not necessarily be 'un-informed', although their knowledge may not fit into known structures of knowledge. Second, being qualified does not also guarantee knowledge in the concerned subject since knowledge could be fragile due to cramming without going into the deeper understanding. In any case, being informed is just the first stage towards achieving educatedness.

Cultured

The second level is being cultured. Culture represents the style of the person—his/her warmth and the human values. It is manifested by one's style of interaction with self (e.g., self-esteem and self-concept), other human beings, animals, plants, places, objects and the like. It is the totality of the person. For example, an otherwise qualified person who unhesitatingly litters a public place or illegally occupies public space for personal purposes may be qualified but not necessarily cultured; or one who exploits weaker sections of people using his/her positional power; one who fragrantly displays his/her riches may be qualified but not cultured; one who uses foul language to display his/her superiority cannot qualify to be cultured. Even those who are brokers of 'culture', for example, painters, musicians, dramatists, dancers and other creative persons who fail to fulfil the value paradigm, cannot qualify to be called cultured. Acharya Vinoba Bhave's concept of *prakriti* (nature*), vikriti* (deformity or distortion) and *sanskriti* (culture) represents the concept of culture very well. The purpose of education is to culture the individual—develop the *sanskriti.* According to Vinoba Bhave, one eats when hungry is *prakriti,* when one eats though not hungry is *vikriti,* and when a hungry person gives away her/his food to the hungry is *sanskriti.*

Emancipation

One level ahead of culture is emancipation, where individuals rise above the smaller identities by their known artificial boundaries of religion, caste, creed, gender, and linguistic and geographic belongingness. A person can be proud of his or her mother tongue and heritage with equal respect and appreciation for the other languages, heritages and diversities of other countries. One can simultaneously be a proud Indian and member of the international community, for example, a Christian with respect (tolerance is not enough) for Islam or Buddhism (Singh 2003). This is basically achieving freedom from the strangleholds of ignorance, intolerance and so on. The purpose of education is to liberate—*Sa Vidya Ya Vimuktaye* (what liberates is education). A beautiful expression of this concept is, as mentioned earlier:

> *Ayam nijah paro veti ganana laghu chetsam*
> *Udar charitanam tu vaisudhaiva kutumbkam*

(This is mine; that is somebody else's, is the thought of narrow-minded people. For wise this whole world is a family.) Emancipation is breaking these narrow boundaries.

Self-actualization

The last and the final attribute of educatedness is self-actualization where emphasis is on achieving the best of the potential already in the individual. Emphasis here is on holistic development—the way Swami Vivekananda defined education—'manifestation of perfection already in man'. Self-actualization also appears in Maslow's hierarchy of needs. Maslow[6] defined it as

> What a man *can* be, he *must* be. This need we may call self-actualization.... It refers to the desire for self-fulfillment, namely, to the tendency for him to become actualized in what he is potentially. This tendency might be phrased as the desire to become more and more what one is, to become everything that one is capable of becoming.

In Maslow's model, the emphasis is on 'becoming'. My emphasis in self-actualization is on 'being'. In this model, self-actualization implies achieving full potential in the physical, intellectual, emotional and spiritual planes. For example, a brilliant scholar or a musical genius but not emotionally rich who shares his/her resources with others is less than self-actualized.

Holistic quality, thus, implies 'educatedness'; being informed or qualified even at the highest level of excellence is not enough, at best the first step is in being educated.

---

[6] http://psychology.about.com/od/theoriesofpersonality/a/hierarchyneeds.htm (accessed on 22 April 2014).

Life and Employability Skills

Life skills and employability skills are important indicators of quality education. Stated differently, quality higher education should develop life skills and employability skills among the students. Life skills enrich life—personal life and life at home and community. Employability skills are a subset of life skills.

Employability skills are directly related to individual's ability to get an employment, retain and progress on the job and earn as well as contribute to national economic growth. Immediately after the economic recession, a number of studies were conducted to figure out the ways of resurrecting the economy, especially in Europe and the United States. These studies converged onto employability skills as the solution to reconstruct the economy. In other words, employability skills were found to be an essential requirement for national economic growth. At the individual level too, employability skills open gateways to jobs and career advancements. In this context, the recent findings of the Aspiring Minds (2013) are worth consideration.

- Less than 10 per cent Masters of Business Administration (MBAs) are employable.
- More than 47 per cent graduates are unemployable.
- Among the technical graduates (a) 4.2 per cent are employable in information technology (IT) product; (b) 9.5 per cent are employable in knowledge process outsourcing (KPOs); (c) 17.8 per cent are employable in IT services; (d) 25.9 per cent in technical support services and (e) 38.2 per cent in business process outsourcing (BPOs).

There are several lists of employability skills proposed by different institutions and individuals. However, there are common elements in these lists.[7]

Table 1.1 presents a list of employability skills that is most relevant for contemporary Indian education.

---

[7] www.nationalstemcentre.org.uk/elibrary/ (accessed on 22 April 2014); http://www.fremont.k12.ca.us (accessed on 20 April 2014).

Table 1.1:
Employability Skills for Graduates

Employability Skills	Explanations	Component Skills
Initiative and enterprise	• Taking initiatives • Contribute • Entrepreneurial ideas	• Risk taking • Innovativeness • Exploring and experimenting
Self-management	Constructive vs. destructive behaviour	• Problem solving • Win–lose • Confirmation • Rejection • Perspective taking • Avoidance • Understanding and rewriting • Life scripts
Learning (to learn)	Skills of learning to learn and know	• Reading • Observing • Listening • Consulting • Thinking • Reasoning • Internet surfing
Communication	Communicating ideas, information and feelings	• Oral, written and non-verbal communication
Teamwork	Ability to work in teams	• Joining teams • Contributing ideas and efforts • Forming teams and providing leadership

(Continued)

Table 1.1:
(Continued)

Employability Skills	Explanations	Component Skills
Problem solving	Solving problems	• Anticipating problems • Constructing solutions • Weighing pros and cons of every solution, Choose one and implement Assess impact
Planning and organizing	Planning and organizing events, and leadership	• Personal • Family related • Social groups
Technology (ICT)	• Technology awareness • User skills	• Technology resilience
Using information	Appropriate use of information at appropriate time and occasion	• Identifying, sourcing, collecting and processing Information
Mathematical skills	Ability to compute and calculate	• Orally, on paper, with calculators
Body management	Health and attire management	• Managing food, physical exercises and medication, whenever necessary for good health • Managing attire for hygiene, smartness and presentability

Source: Author.
Note: ICT, information and communications technology.

The philosophical consideration is whether employability should be considered as outcome of quality education. There is wide divergence of views between academicians and employers. Academicians usually take the position that universities are to educate people and not train people for jobs and employment. The employers, of course, expect employability skills among the job seekers (Mukhopadhyay et al. 2015).

Institutional Quality

Quality is an experience. It is a holistic experience. Like human beings, educational institutions are also 'dynamic beings' and live in four planes.

1. The campus—buildings and land with all its components, such as classrooms, laboratories and libraries, corridors, staffrooms, conveniences and so on represent physical plane of an institution—a college or a university. Whereas the adequacy and functionality indicate the external health, aesthetics, beauty and ambiance represent the inner health of the institution.
2. Curriculum development, teaching–learning process, examinations, certification and so on are the indications of intellectual life of an institution. Students, teachers and their day-to-day interaction, research, publications, seminars and conferences represent the intellectual life of an institution.
3. Satisfaction of the students, the staff, their joy and happiness, their mutual concern and interpersonal relationships, their sense of pride and belongingness, organizational concern for the employees and so on are the attributes of the emotional life of an organization.
4. The spiritual plane of the organization is its continuous striving for excellence, research and experimentation to explore and extend the boundaries of frontiers of knowledge, its concern for the society, nation state and the human civilization.

Higher education creates, preserves and disseminates knowledge. The knowledge creation through research and experimentation is the spiritual component of an institution, whereas knowledge preservation and dissemination are the intellectual components of an organization.

Yet another dimension of holistic quality of higher education is the resonance between goals of education of the individual and the institution. Only an institute with holistic quality can offer holistic (quality) education. A one-dimensional institute that does not nurture holistic quality, total quality of life in the institution, cannot impart holistic quality education. This is an in-equation. The holistic quality framework warrants total reconsideration of educational goals, contents and processes; in effect, policies, planning and management of higher education.

There are eight distinct functional areas of an educational institution, namely

1. Academic
2. Infrastructure
3. Personnel
4. Finance
5. Student services
6. Linkage and interface with outside agencies
7. Office management—rules, regulations and protocols
8. Leadership and managerial excellence.

Each of these areas comprises several subcomponents. For example, academic area comprises curricular planning, designing instruction and preparation, course delivery and student evaluation and assessment. We argue that unless quality is assured in each component of these areas, an institution cannot ensure quality in academic dimension.

Quality education is the product of quality institution. Quality institution, according to this holistic philosophical proposition, is one that plans quality, implements quality, assesses and assures quality and celebrates quality in all dimensions and departments of the institution. According to this paradigm, as mentioned earlier, quality is to be a holistic experience. For example, quality of infrastructure should be evident in terms of adequacy, functionality and aesthetics in every nook and corner—corridors and conveniences, staffrooms, classrooms, laboratories, private and public spaces in the institutions, and not restricted only to the offices of heads of institutions. Quality must be evident in the teaching–learning process through preparedness of the teachers, planning for course delivery, communication, punctuality and regularity, concern for students, mentoring and so on. Quality of leadership should be visible through the process of institution building. Serious consideration is the optimization of organizational potential—developing and enhancing the process capabilities of the organization for continuing self-renewal for holistic quality. The leadership efforts for institution building should be evident from the participative processes in the organization for building shared vision, strategic plans with milestones and quality benchmarks and techniques and schedule of assessment.

Conclusion

Conventionally, quality education has been seen through the prism of student performance in examination. In quality assessment, every other item is seen as a factor to student performance and academic achievement, often unrelated to life. It often fails to see education as an instrument of self-actualization. Philosophy of quality higher education demands a paradigm shift from academic quality to holistic quality.

This new paradigm proposes defining quality of higher education to start with the nature of human beings, especially accepting the huge gap between the actual potential (perfection already in man/woman) and perceived potential in terms of intelligence in conventional sense of performance in examination. Holistic quality asks us to redefine the purpose of higher education beyond academic domain to include all the planes in which human beings live, namely physical, emotional, intellectual and spiritual; it thereby specifies the qualities of individuals coming out of higher education institutions that should include cognitive skills, emotive skills, life skills and employability skills and the like.

Instead of taking on the face value, the new paradigm warrants defining parameters of quality higher education. Such definitions would also need to be complemented with quality inputs, processes and output of the higher education institutions. Quality should be inclusive, covering all the departments of the institution. Quality is something that must be felt in every walk of the institution; quality is to be a living experience.

Each higher education institution must decide its quality policy. Each institution has to decide the constituents of quality—whether only academic excellence or values, employability skills, educatedness attributes of the students; also, total quality in all aspects of the institution.

SECTION I

Methods of Quality Management

2

Quality Circle

Introduction

The search for quality has been a passion, rather an obsession, of the human mind. The journey through the corridors of history of human civilization from the prehistoric era to the modern days is indeed the story of quest for quality. It is characterized by continuous innovation and creation of new methods and approaches for improving quality of products and processes that ultimately contribute to the quality of life.

The new generation quality management movement dates back to the 1920s when Frederik Taylor was credited with the creation of a scientific management system; to be more precise, the quality-control systems were put in place by the 1930s. As the movement on quality management moved forward, there was increasing search for alternative ways to achieve quality. This quest for quality was seriously influenced by a brighter assumption about the human beings in general and the workforce in particular. Quality circle is the evolution from quality control through quality-control circles.

Genesis of Quality Circle

As mentioned above, there are a few landmarks in the development of the quality management movement throughout the world. Although it now stands rejected, scientific management propounded by Frederik Taylor in the 1920s was one of the important landmarks in the history of the quality movement. The 1930s witnessed a march of quality control, primarily depicted by the selection and rejection of products that do not fulfil the quality criteria and the benchmark. The obvious implication was that the people in the production line were not involved in checking the quality. Quality control was the job of the 'quality policeman' in the organization. The major issue, other than human dignity, was enormous amount of wastage due to rejection of products, enhancing the cost of production.

In the meanwhile, the human relations movement, particularly human motivation as the alternative way of achieving success and productivity in the industry, was gaining ground. This movement was gaining momentum with the contributions of Mayo and Maslow. There emerged a great debate whether Frederik Taylor's control-oriented scientific management or human motivation-based approach provides better alternative to achieve quality.

The movement witnessed a massive shift particularly after the Second World War. Japan, then known as a junk producer in the world with shoddy, cheap and poor quality products, was devastated in the war. It had to rebuild itself. She turned around looking for methods and mechanisms for quality improvement in management.

A large number of Japanese companies adopted statistical quality control as the primary methodology for quality management in production lines. Dr Deming, later known as total quality management (TQM) guru, was invited to Japan for conducting courses on students' quality circle (SQC). It was during this period that the Japanese Union of Scientists and Engineers (JUSE) was organized to promote quality control in Japanese industries. It was a tremendous success. And, JUSE still continues to be active. Despite the success, SQC was not found a panacea for all ills. The ownership of quality tended to stay with the quality-control department rather than with the people in the production line. Also, the commitment of the top management, as well as that of the workforce, did not come through.

The next phase of the movement started with the visit of Dr Juran to Japan in 1954. Juran's primary argument was that quality has to be seen as a management task, rather than task of the quality policeman in the organization. By implication, it meant that quality is everybody's business. Culturally congruent, this had the widespread acceptance in the Japanese industries and the workforce. This led to the emergence of the concept and practice of total quality control. In this new approach, every employee and the organization as a whole participated in quality management, and this required intensive on-the-job education of the workforce. As Robson (1985) points out, the last link of Frederik Taylor's scientific management was questioned on the grounds of manageability of a literate and educated workforce 'whose aspirations and expectations, depending on how the workforce was treated, could be directed either towards the achievement of company goals or away from them'. It was necessary to encourage the workforce to use the brains as well as hands (Robson 1985). It had to be democratized. Total quality control was a response to the new challenge.

There is another version of the birth of quality circles. In the magazine *Quality Control* by Japanese Women, Dr Ishikawa suggested creation of book reading circles. 'These book reading groups soon began to change from mere theoretical study, and became problem-solving groups. Individuals encourage their staff to join in, and quality circles are born'.

Quality circle, thus born, was an evolution over the years towards developing a participative model of management of quality. Unlike other similar initiatives like management by objectives[1] pioneered by Odiorne and Humble, the quality circles approach to quality management has survived the test of time. The first circles were established at the Nippon Wireless and Telegraph Company, which then spread to more than 35 other companies in the first year. A total of 75,000 circles were registered with JUSE in the mid-1970s, and by 1978 it was claimed that there were more than one million quality circles involving some 10 million Japanese workers. They are now in most East Asian countries; it was recently claimed that there were more than 20 million quality circles in China.

Quality Circle Defined

The literature on quality circles does not seem to be particularly rich with definitions, although there have been some meaningful efforts in capturing the spirit of the quality circle, describing what it is and

---

[1] The term 'management by objectives' was first popularized by Drucker (1954).

what it is not. Certain other efforts have tried to put all the components of quality circle together into one sentence. Let us examine a few available descriptions.

A quality circle consists of a small group of people who perform the same job or tasks. This group meets voluntarily, on a regular basis, to discuss problems, seek solutions, and cooperate with management in the implementation of those solutions. Quality circles operate on the principle that employee participation in decision-making and problem-solving improves the quality of work. Through the circle, members generate mutual respect and trust as they work on solutions to common, on-the-job problems. (*ERIC Digest*).

A quality circle is a volunteer group (composed) of workers (or even students), usually under the leadership of their supervisor (or an elected team leader), who are trained to identify, analyze and solve work-related problems and present their solutions to management in order to improve the performance of the organization, and motivate and enrich the work of employees. When matured, true quality circles become self-managing having gained the confidence of management.[2]

A quality circle is a participatory management technique that enlists the help of employees in solving problems related to their own jobs. Circles are formed of employees working together in an operation who meet at intervals to discuss problems of quality and to devise solutions for improvements.[3]

Quality circle is a small group of employees in the same work area or doing similar type of work who voluntarily meet regularly for about an hour every week to identify, analyze and resolve work-related problems, leading to improvement in the total performance, and enrichment of their work life. (Udpa 2001)

A group of four to 10 volunteers working for the same supervisor or a foremen who meet once a week, for an hour, under the leadership of the supervisor, to identify, analyze and solve their own work-related problems. (Robson 1985)

The common parameters of quality circle that can be derived from these definitions are as follows:

- Small group of employees (4–10)
- Working in the same work area or doing similar type of work

---

[2] http://www.whatishumanresource.com/quality-circles (accessed on 3 May 2014).
[3] www.inc.com/encyclopedia/quality-circles.html (accessed on 5 May 2014).

- Voluntary participation
- Meeting regularly for a short period (maybe about an hour every week)
- Identify, analyse and resolve work-related problems
- Cooperate with management in implementing the solutions
- A mechanism for participative problem solving and management
- Contributes to improvement in the total performance
- Develops mutual respect
- Enriches the work life

The analysis provides a meaningful framework. It states objectives in terms of enrichment of the work life, improvement in the total performance, and identification, analysis and resolution of work-related problems. The second set of components focuses on the process-related components of quality circle, namely meeting regularly and voluntarily. The third set of components focuses on the structure—small group of employees belonging to the same work area. In some way, the descriptions contain structure, process and product of quality circles.

If I were to make an effort, deriving from the efforts of my preceding authors, I shall define quality circle as an 'endeavour in solving organizational problems and innovate through collective and participative creativity'.

There are certain distinguishing features that can be derived from this and other definitions of quality circles.

- First, quality circle is not part of the design of bureaucratic administration. The very fact that it is voluntary makes it different from the bureaucratic structure of the organization.
- Second, it does not necessarily restrict itself to the concerns of quality. It addresses larger issues under the banner of 'work-related problems'.
- Third, it provides an opportunity to participate in organizational decision making in generating an implementable solution. This enhances the self-concept and role perception of the employees enriching their quality of work life.
- Fourth, it obliterates the belief that problem solving and creating solutions is the prerogative of the supervisors and senior managers. Such creativity is distributed among all the employees. Quality circle optimizes human creativity.

Finally, all these attributes create ownership among the employees of the organization.

Udpa (2001), founder executive director of the Quality Circle Forum of India, summarizes tangible and intangible impact of quality circles as given in Table 2.1.

Table 2.1:
Tangible and Intangible Impacts of Quality Circle

Tangible gains	Intangible gains
• Better quality	• Enriched quality of work life
• Productivity improvement	• Attitudinal change
• Higher safety	• Harmony, mutual trust
• Greater cost-effectiveness	• Better communication
• Better housekeeping	• Effective teamwork
• Increased profitability	• Better human relations
• Waste reduction	• Participative culture
• Reduced absenteeism and grievances	• Human resource development
	• Promotion of job knowledge
	• Greater sense of belonging

Source: Udpa (2001).

Quality Circles: Experiences in Education

By all available evidence, quality circle, though began as a post-world war reconstruction of the devastated economy and productivity of Japan, took shape in the 1970s with the formation of JUSE. Its entry into education dates back to the 1980s as indicated by several references on quality circle available from educational researchers (Cohen 1983, Hirshfield 1983, Ladwig 1983, Moretz 1983, Murray 1983). In fact, community colleges adapted the quality circle approach under pressure of quality improvement within budgetary constraints. Several pieces of evidence exist of successful application of quality circle approaches in educational institutions, ranging from nursery schools to secondary schools and colleges. City Montessori School, Lucknow (in India), made a breakthrough experiment in application of the quality circle approach. It pioneered the SQC movement throughout the world. The first international convention on SQC was organized in City Montessori School, Lucknow, in 1997. Since then, such conventions have been organized in Mauritius, Kentucky, Dhaka and Sri Lanka. Kathmandu University's School offers an interesting example of application of quality circle at the school level. The first national convention on SQC was organized in St. Xavier's School, Kathmandu. Deepa Sharma (2006) experimented with quality circle in two schools, one college and six university departments. Her major objective was to test the feasibility of quality control as a tool for quality improvement in education.

As mentioned earlier, community colleges experimented with quality circle under budgetary constraints. *ERIC Digest* (1984) provides stories of quality circle applications in Central Piedmont Community College (North Carolina), Middlesex County College (New Jersey) and a Lakeshore Technical Institute (LTI, Wisconsin). The quality circle in Central Piedmont Community College 'focused on searching why the goals are not met. It used brainstorming to develop the rest of goals, rank ordered those goals on decision grid and drew cause and effect diagrams'. A participant identified a need to develop a better telephone system.

ERIC Digest (1984) records further the case of Middlesex County College that adapted quality circle to improve cost efficiency and project management on a peer tutoring programme. It established one circle comprising peer tutors from business-oriented disciplines and another from engineering-oriented disciplines. To enhance cost efficiency, the first circle recommended 'a stronger emphasis on tutee note-taking, time management, attendance and other factors that are central to a student's self-reliance', whereas the second circle emphasized on improving 'campus awareness of the peer tutoring center through utilization of faculty announcements, student clubs, faculty advisors, and other means' (Cohen 1983).

Origin of quality circle in LTI was the desire of staff at various levels to get involved in decision making and improve work efficiency. LTI also adopted two quality circles—management and non-management circles. The management circle comprised administrators, supervisors, coordinators and education specialists, and the non-management circle comprised faculty and support staff. The 'management circles developed an idea/suggestion memo system, intramural sporting events for LTI staff, guidelines for recognizing staff service and a "who's who/what's what" recognition programme.

The non-management quality circles recommended the development of a computerized information system to assist faculty in record keeping, work processing, and grading' (Ladwig 1983).

In the Technical Teachers Training Institute, Bhopal (Madhya Pradesh, India), the quality circle approach was adopted, rather adapted, in a different manner. In various work areas like research, educational media, management and so on, there were interdisciplinary groups called task forces. The choice of the task force was voluntary, according to the interest and concern of the faculty members, irrespective of their educational background and the departments to which they belong, namely civil, mechanical, electrical engineering and so on. Though not every week, task forces met at a regular interval, usually once a month. Fully backed by the top leadership of the institution, task forces took policy decisions, deed troubleshooting and collectively found solutions for quality improvement in the concerned area (Mukhopadhyay 2007).

Eric Digest referred earlier also refers to application of quality circle in classroom instruction by Hirshfield (1983) and Murray (1983). In Hirshfield's experiment, eight members of the quality circle altered the course structure and contents of East Asian history. It also changed the instructional strategy. After two years of the experiment, Hirshfield concluded that quality circle enhances skills of academic decision making among students, in addition to their increased familiarity with the course and contents. Murray's (1983) quality circle comprised 12 students in an American history survey. It reviewed the type and frequency of written assignments, the content of lectures and the testing methods. Students decided to reduce the time for lectures, increase time for interaction and more rigorous assignments. According to Murray, students moved towards 'a firmer, more scholarly approach'.

Working Parameters of Quality Circles

There are certain working parameters of quality circles that separate it out as a formal mechanism compared to discussions on problem solving, often casual, or done in formal staff meetings. The working parameters deal with structures of quality circles, resource requirements, basic processes, a set of agenda and so on.

Quality circles comprise, as mentioned earlier, a small group of members. Within the members, there is a steering committee, a coordinator, facilitator, leader and deputy leader, members and non-members. Whereas the leader provides leadership in the process management and creates impact of the quality circle, coordinator is the key person in anchoring the quality circle.

Quality circle is essentially a low-cost approach to quality management by optimizing human resources, particularly the intellectual resources. Nonetheless, it requires commitment of certain basic resources. The first and foremost is the commitment of time—about one hour a week—of the leader, coordinator, deputy leader, facilitators and all other members of the quality circle. On the hindsight of the time is the cost of the time that the institution spends by sparing the staff to participate in quality circles. The second is the financial resources that are required to set up the circle and make it functional, which may actually mean expenses on electricity, refreshments and other expenditures associated with quality circle meetings. This should include the cost of consultants, if required, to start off the quality circles. The third resource requirement pertains to resources required to implement the decisions and suggestions recommended by quality circles. Non-implementation of the decision due to lack of resources will not only discourage the members of the quality circle, but also make the quality circle dysfunctional.

It is important to understand the basic objective of quality circle. The basic objective of quality circle is to generate creative solutions to existing problems based on a detailed analysis and cause-and-effect relationships of the problems. Hence, it requires intellectual investment of critical and creative thinking. The following steps are recommended for developing a functional mechanism of quality circles:

1. Develop a list of problems collectively, either through brainstorming or through collecting and collating a list of problems created by individuals. It is a good idea to insist on 15 or 20 problems to be solved. This forces the individuals to think critically about different dimensions of the institution.
2. Classify problems into categories that require no external material resource, require some resource that can be mobilized internally and those require external funding.

3. Prioritize problems in all the three categories of material resource requirement.
4. Select problems that can be actually solved (it is important to taste success on low-ambition problems rather than fail on ambitious problems).
5. Identify data and information required to get to the bottom of the problem and decide on the mechanism of gathering the data.
6. Collect, collate and analyse the data, wherever necessary by using tables, bar charts, histograms, pie diagrams, scatter diagrams, control charts, Pareto chart, fishbone diagram and so on.
7. Adopt cause-and-effect relationships for each of the selected problems.
8. Generate alternative solutions of the problem based on the data.
9. Assess advantages and adverse consequences of each of the solutions and then choose a solution.
10. Create the mechanism of implementing the solution.
11. Propose solutions and the process of implementation, along with the problem analysis, data and the mechanism of arriving at the solution to the management for management support.
12. Wherever necessary, reconsider the solution and process of implementation on the basis of views and suggestions of the management.
13. Mentor the process of implementation and monitor the results of the solution.

How to Begin?

To begin the quality circles, the prime requirement is an organizational decision to set up quality circles for problem solving and continuous quality improvement. This also implies that individual initiatives or initiatives by a group of like-minded people working in a particular area may not effectively function as quality circle. For, it may not derive the support and approval of the management without which it may not be possible to implement the recommendations of the quality circles. Hence, the first and foremost requirement for educational institutions is to take up with the management, faculty and the staff the desirability of establishing quality circles. Practitioners of quality circles strongly recommend that people in the institution must be oriented to the philosophy, structures and processes of quality circle before deciding on the introduction of quality circles. This is because of the misconceptions about the quality circles among the members of the organization. A special warning is given in case of academic institutions, especially higher education institutions. Academicians in higher education institutions are rather individualistic and relate quality to their own individual sense of excellence as compared to collective excellence.

The second important requirement is the training of the quality circle leaders and deputy leaders, facilitators and coordinators. In fact, the analysis of failures of quality circles is often ascribed to lack of or poor training of quality circle managers.

Before starting quality circles in the institution, it is important to study their impact on other sectors and other educational institutions. Quality circle promotes participative culture and empowers decision making among the staff, improves human relations—leading to more effective teamwork and enhancement of job interest—improves problem-solving capabilities including orientation to prevention of problem, leadership development among staff (transformational leadership) and cost effectiveness. Particular attention needs to be drawn to the empowerment of staff to participate, take decisions and develop ownership towards the organization (Blanchard and Bowles 1997).

A few important steps, then, for introducing quality circle in educational institutions are as follows:

1. Circulate a short well-written paper on quality circle among the staff. The paper should comprise descriptions and definitions of quality circle, working mechanism of quality circle, experiences in other institutions and its benefits and risks. A brief history of its origin may enrich the paper.
2. Identify an experienced quality circle consultant or head of another institution who has successfully introduced quality circle.
3. Conduct an orientation programme on quality circle for the staff facilitated by the consultant.
4. Provide focused training on quality circle to the coordinators, leaders and deputy leaders.
5. Indicate active interest in the functioning of the quality circles by participating in the circles as non-members.

These steps are in addition to the steps mentioned earlier about the functioning of quality circles.

Preventing Failures

Instead of waiting for the quality circle to fail, the quality circle planners must consider in advance where the quality circle may fail and create a protective mechanism. Quality circle may fail due to a variety of reasons:

- It may not receive the minimum required resources.
- It may be difficult for the members of the institution to participate in quality circles; the management may not see it as something important for the institute, but introduce as a ritual.
- Institutions may start quality circles without understanding their total implications.
- Lack of training in quality circles is often cited as the most important reason for failure.
- Lack of patience to pursue quality circle activities over a period of time—the average number of successful quality circle meetings are 10 and that for failed quality circles is five (Sharma 2006).
- Quality circles in higher education institutions face added problems. 'Highly educated circle members tend to become over philosophical about the purpose of the circle and may hamper circle progress' (Moretz 1983).
- Unlike the industrial and business organizations, the academic institutional calendar is not uniform throughout the year. Admission and lean teaching seasons, peak teaching season, and end-of-term rush for examination and so on may affect quality circle movement in institutions of higher education.

Conclusion

Origin of quality circle in Japan was to reconstruct quality of its products after the Second World War to face the competitive market. The focus was on quality improvement through optimization of collective intellectual contribution of members of the organization. The experiments carried out by Deming, Juran and Ishikawa generated enough evidence to prove that Frederik Taylor's control-oriented scientific management techniques are not safe for the modern organization in enhancing quality production; on the contrary, it indicated that key to the success of sustainable quality lies in participative management involving people in the organization.

This basic principle of 'human-intensive approach to quality' has been transferred to education. It should fit in the educational institutions rather easily since educational institutions are human-intensive organizations. The emphasis here is on using quality circles for improvement of quality at low material costs and creating a highly human-intensive alternative to quality management.

Quality circle is 'knowledge' driven. Higher education institutions are knowledge enterprises—creating, preserving and promoting knowledge. The industrial and business organizations have a few knowledge workers for many manual workers. The reverse is the case in institutions of higher education; there are more knowledge workers for a few manual workers. Strategically steered, quality circles should find easier access in higher education institutions and competent implementation subject to the caution of individualistic and philosophical detachment of any such creative techniques by the academicians.

3

Total Quality Management

Introduction

Total quality management, usually called by its acronym TQM, consists of three words. Process is *management*; subject of management is *quality* and the qualifying word (adjective) of quality management is *total*. It means, or should mean, management of quality in all major and minor aspects of an institution. If TQM attempts to be inclusive, it ought to involve all characters of an institute's storyboard. Hence, it has to be inclusive of all human beings—from top to bottom in the hierarchy and from east to west in the lateral positioning of people. In simple terms, TQM would expect to involve from head of the institution to gardeners and security guards.[1] TQM refers to the collective efforts of all the members of an institution to develop sustainable quality for a fruitful quality journey rather than a destination, since quality is dynamic and shifts from one position to another with time.

There is no clear definition of the term 'total quality management' as yet, nor is the origin of the title known very clearly. According to one school of thought, TQM is inspired by Feignbaum's book *Total Quality Control* (1983) and Ishikawa's *What Is Total Quality Control?*

---

[1] Professor Moonis Raza, a distinguished scholar, then director of NIEPA, would call the gardener, cartographer and the programme director (a professor) and discuss the beautification and aesthetics of the classroom (programme venue) before every programme. And, the decoration and fragrance of flowers in the venue will change every time.

(1985). Deming's *Out of the Crisis* (1986) is another reference point for defining and understanding this term better.

From another perspective, TQM is seen as a natural evolution from the different facets of efforts of quality improvement and management, which includes quality inspection, quality control and quality assurance. TQM, as can be seen from the dates of important publications, became popular in the mid-1980s and continued to dominate the debate on quality management till the late 1990s when ISO 9000, Six Sigma and Lean came into the picture prominently.

Although TQM is commonly used in the production sector, Deming claimed that the principles of TQM are equally applicable to the government, education and health sectors. Sallis (1996)[2] was one of the pioneers in examining TQM in education. This was followed by my own work (Mukhopadhyay 2001).[3] Frazier's book titled *Roadmap for Quality Transformation in Education* (1997) does not use the term TQM in its title. However, it also exerts significant influence on the interpretation/perception of the authors of TQM in education.

My formulations of TQM in education have evolved over several phases of reflective experiments and experiences. At the first instance, being inspired by the concept and practice of TQM, I tried some sporadic experiments to examine 'what happens', primarily through *Kaizens*.[4] Based on my positive experiences from these experiments, I developed a comprehensive approach to application of TQM in education. During this process, I drew my inspiration from both Western functionalism and Indian metaphysical thoughts on quality.

During the third phase, I experimented with relatively large-scale training and implementation of TQM for a development research. One of my experiments was on a group of 42 primary schools in a village cluster around Udang (Howrah District of West Bengal, India) (Mukhopadhyay 2013a). Another important step/initiative was

---

[2] Sallis book has gone into the third edition. Obviously, this book has a large readership.

[3] Sage edition (2nd ed., 2005) of my book has gone into 12th reprint and rendered into several Indian languages, namely, Hindi, Bengali, Gujarati, Marathi and Tamil. These are some of the indications of the reception of the book by the readers.

[4] Kaizen is a Japanese term that means improvement or change for the best, continuous change. In TQM, it has come to be understood as a strategic entry point for improvement or change for better in an organization. Kaizen is used for the incremental but experimental approach to adoption of innovation and management of change.

the training of principals of all District Institutes of Education and Training (DIETs; about 500 members) on TQM, based on the first edition of my book titled *Total Quality Management in Education* (Mukhopadhyay 2001) sponsored by the Ministry of Human Resource Development, Government of India.

In this chapter, I shall deal with TQM as a methodology of quality management in higher education institutions under four broad heads:

1. Functional meaning of TQM as a technique.
2. Fifteen cardinal principles in applying TQM in education.
3. Organizational micro-analysis that provides the basic architecture.
4. Strategic planning as the approach to implementation of TQM.

In view of great significance of both organizational micro-analysis and strategic planning, full chapters have been devoted to organizational micro-analysis and strategic planning. In this chapter, we may make a few statements in the passing.

TQM: Functional Meaning

The term 'total quality management' comprises three important words. Each word of this phrase has its own significance and context. The central theme of TQM is quality. The word 'total' is an adjective that clarifies the concept of quality using a practical approach. The word 'management' signifies the methodology to achieve quality.

Let us now try to understand the term 'quality'. As a matter of fact, a unanimously acceptable definition of quality is yet to be coined. The definition differs from one author to another. However, there are certain prominent and common facets that provide us with vital references to describe quality.

First, quality is always relative and never absolute. This implies that what is acceptable as quality for one may not be acceptable as quality for another. To that extent, quality is personal and perceptual. This is equally true for organizations. What is quality for one organization is not the same for another. Extending this argument of perception to the context of educational institutions, what is quality for Harvard may not be acceptable as quality for Columbia or Oxford. Similarly, the quality benchmark that is acceptable to a college of the reputation of Presidency College of Kolkata or Chennai may not be acceptable for an equally reputed college like St. Stephens of Delhi.

The second most important and acceptable parameter is: quality is both process and product. While a product carries the manifest quality, the process provides intrinsic support to the manifested quality of the product. In fact, the process ensures the quality of the product. In the context of education/educational institutions, quality takes into consideration not only the students' performance (both quantitative and qualitative) in the university examination, but also their value systems and other personal qualities. An IT company while recruiting IT professionals recruited all candidates from Ramakrishna Mission College, Belur (West Bengal), because they successfully defended their value system inculcated in the college (Mukhopadhyay 2012a). Also, it includes other critical processes such as instruction, curriculum planning, evaluation and all other academic activities.

A group of quality management scientists have defined quality as 'fitness to the purpose'. For example, if a ballpoint pen writes efficiently and smoothly, it is called quality. Nonetheless, there are others who engage themselves into lifting up the definition of quality from just the current level of functionality to the level of 'earning customer satisfaction' by including additional parameters like durability, cost, aesthetics and so on. In the context of education, this may signify an institution that is able to produce graduates who are employable or capable of finding employment. Indian Institutes of Technology (IITs) and Indian Institutes of Management (IIMs) are typical examples from India.

The fourth way of defining quality has been in terms of 'value for money', which is again a functional definition. This is increasingly becoming an issue in Indian higher education as more and more self-financing private institutions are coming up every year. Students and their parents obviously give a serious thought to the 'value for money' that they spend on education in a particular institution. Another example is the capitation fee that is paid for getting admission into professional institutions with the hope of gaining long-term benefits, which could imply benefits due to human capital formation and enhancement of lifetime earnings.

Whereas a majority of these definitions are derived from the functionalist approach, people with metaphysical orientation provide a different dimension to the definition of quality, like concept of perfection, exceptionalism and so on. More importantly, the metaphysical definition of quality signifies continuous or transformative quality improvement. Thus, there is no limit to the prospect of improving quality. I have made brief references to the concept of quality from the Western and Indian tradition in Chapter 2 and also in my book, Total Quality Management in Education (Mukhopadhyay, 2005a).

In the context of higher education, the concept of quality must be holistic. Academic performance or even performances in non-academic areas of the students are not enough indication of quality of an educational institution. In reality, education encompasses the total experience of all its stakeholders. Accordingly, a quality educational institution is the one that provides a rich living experience not only to the students but also to the teachers, administrators, administrative staff and even to the parents and the community who are associated with the institution. We should be able to further elaborate and illustrate this viewpoint as we move on to explaining the concept of 'total'.

One effective way of understanding 'total' is through reductionism, that is, by reducing 'total' into micro-components and their intra-structural linkages and relationships. In the context of TQM for a college or a university, 'total' will imply managing quality in all dimensions of working of an institution, namely academic management, human resource management, infrastructure management, finance management, student services management, administrative management, network and interface management and leadership for quality/change management and institution building. Each one of these eight areas is a conglomerate of several sub-components. For example, use of reductionism on academic management yields curriculum planning and management, instructional or teaching–learning process management, management of quality of learning material in print and digital formats, student assessment of curricular learning, co-scholastic and co-curricular activities and so on. Each component can be further reduced into sub-components and then to sub-sub-components. TQM warrants quality assurance in management of each small component. This amounts to micromanagement with quality. Managing quality of each component that is integrally related to each other in an educational institution is the thesis of Chapter 3. The approach to management of quality through micromanagement can be captured with a few principles. Let us call them cardinal principles in line with the predecessors in the field like Deming, Juan and Crosby.

Cardinal Principles of TQM in Education

As mentioned earlier, Deming, Juran and Crosby provided a set of cardinal principles based on their own experiments and research in implementing TQM in the industrial and production sectors. My research and experiment with quality management and leadership for institution building, exclusively in the domain of education, have led to the formulation of a set of principles that facilitate implementation of TQM in (Indian) institutions. These are discussed here.

1. Nurture a Vibrant Familial Ambience in the Institution

Adoption of innovation is one of the most important instruments of implementing TQM. Adoption of innovation or innovativeness of an institution has been found to be directly related to the organizational climate of an educational institution. The Western research is consistent in its findings that an open climate (classification provided by Halpin and Croft 1963) is conducive to adoption of innovation. My own research on a variety of educational institutions indicates that a familial but vibrant ambience of an educational institution is most proactive to management of change and quality in Indian educational institutions (Mukhopadhyay 1981, 2012a).

Familial climate refers to family-type relationships among the members of an educational institution. The point of emphasis here is the family-type atmosphere, but not of the orthodox style, a family that is vibrant, where every member has the opportunity to express their concern and differ with the elders (read as people in position of authority) of the family.

The other implied meaning of 'family' is that the members may differ in their opinions, but they stand by each other in times of need. There is a strong interdependence among the members of the family. This is also consistent with contemporary research on human thinking that illustrates cultural influence on human thinking (Nisbett 2003). Nurturant-task leadership creates that climate where seniors nurture juniors while exacting on developmental tasks the way it happens in a usual Indian family (Habibullah and Sinha 1980). According to this principle, an institution needs to create an ambiance where it looks like a family—everyone is connected to each other with emotional resonance, rather than by hierarchy.

2. Ensure Proactive Participation of All Partners in the Institution

In a majority of the educational institutions, decisions filter down from top to bottom based almost on the cause-and-effect relationship between wisdom, age and official position. Since innovative ideas and execution mechanisms are creative processes, these are unrelated to the position of authority, age and experience.

John Kotter's now famous *Our Iceberg Is Melting* brings out this fact brilliantly (Kotter 2005) when the junior penguin showed the way—impending disaster. Further, since TQM implies quality in every major and minor departments of the institution, everybody becomes a natural stakeholder in the business of quality management. Anybody left out in the journey of quality and the 'celebration of achievements' risks being sub-optimized of creative energies, which results in counterproductive efforts.

As mentioned earlier, total quality is the effect of integration and synergy of efforts of all concerned at the departmental levels and in every activity of the institution. Hence, for effective TQM, the involvement of all the members of the institution is a necessary condition to create suitable/appropriate opportunities for everyone to contribute.

An example may illustrate this point. The National Institute of Educational Planning and Administration (NIEPA), where I worked for many years, used to organize national and international conferences. Usually, these were organized by faculty members with the assistance of a few administrative personnel. I experimented by handing over food management to two of my junior lady colleagues from administration. Not only were they thrilled about this opportunity, but it also changed the effectiveness of the conference since they brought in their skills and creativity to contribute to enhance participant satisfaction.

3. Create Mechanisms for Expression of Mutual Concerns among the Partners in the Institution

Participative process in quality management is the hallmark of TQM. Participative process is not and should not be driven only by the person at the top or a group of people who are more vocal or stay closer to the power centre of the organization. For meaningful participation, it is necessary to have a provision for expression of alternative approaches or even counter viewpoints. There must be space, such as creative forums, quality circles, task groups and other organizational mechanisms to discuss such alternative views, concerns and assumptions so that every one finds an unbiased and open platform to express their ideas regarding quality management matters of the organization.

A good case is to highlight the team-building process, which goes through four stages: storming, norming, forming and performing (according to Truckman and Jensen 1977). For effective TQM, there should be scope for storming as well. A vibrant and meaningful participatory process must provide ample opportunities for expression of concerns, divergent thinking, defining as well as creating solutions.

Not only tolerance to differences, but also expression of concerns, divergent thinking and so on needs to be nurtured carefully for efficient quality management. This will eventually require creating forums for participation of all stakeholders, to the extent of even consulting students, teachers and parents on a regular basis. Further, such consultations should be recorded in order to be able to review and create a synergy of solutions. Also, this helps documenting organizational history.

4. Create Awareness That In-campus Experience Is a Holistic Living Experience

Campus experience, except in residential institutions, is primarily equated with the engagements in classrooms, laboratories, computer labs and other occasional visits to hobby or play centres by few. This leaves limited impact on the minds of the young graduates. Very often, the quality of an institution is equated with the quality of classroom transactions. No wonder, a large majority of students do not develop adequate life skills and employability skills. One of the cardinal principles of TQM in higher education is designing campus experience as a holistic living experience. Usually, education is considered as 'preparation for life'. The origin of such a contention comes from the human capital formation approach of education. It should be seen differently. Instead of preparation for life, education needs to be seen as life itself. If the prime youth is gone in preparation what will be left to live!

It is rather common to believe that graduation leads to better job opportunities and better lifetime earnings. This needs to be seriously questioned. If we agree with the thesis that human life is lived in four planes, namely physical, emotional, intellectual and spiritual, the argument that education is life itself gets strengthened. The participation of the prime youth in colleges and universities cannot be undermined only as a step towards future. Instead, it is the total experience that matters for today and tomorrow.

Thus, TQM of higher education institutions demands planning for a holistic living experience of every student as well as teacher and non-teaching staff together with the stakeholders of the educational institution.

5. Develop Collective Future Vision and Long-term and Short-term Perspective Plans

Any effort or activity for quality management without a vision is like a celebration without a purpose, or a journey without a direction. As mentioned earlier, TQM is a journey and not a destination. The institution must have a defined direction and move towards that. Vision provides that direction to the institution. For a meaningful journey in quality, all activities must be derived out of the vision and oriented towards the achievement of that vision.

Vision is abstract. It is a declaration or proclamation of the envisaged state of the institution in the future. Everybody is not endowed to foresee the vision of the future. Yet, in the right spirit of TQM, everybody must be involved in postulating a vision for the institution. There are well-established techniques for creating vision statements. Higher education institutions seriously intending to introduce and/or enforce quality management will do well to consult management experts who are adept in creating participative visioning for the institution. Participative visioning is necessary so that all stakeholders identify with the vision and own it. As a natural corollary, vision statements should be unbundled into missions, aims and objectives, along with goals and targets.

For achieving missions, aims and objectives as well as goals and targets, higher education institutions must develop short-term and long-term perspective plans, which will facilitate translating the vision into reality.

6. Develop Indicators of Quality and Benchmarks (Minimum Acceptable Levels) for Each Major and Minor Activity in the Institution

Quality is essentially subjective because it varies depending upon the user or consumer of a product or a process. 'What is quality for one may not be acceptable as quality by the other'. This becomes evident and easily observable in case of lifestyle products.

In the case of institutions, there is a need to find a mechanism for quantifying quality, although it looks like an oxymoron. Institutions need to first define the indicators of quality for each area, sub-area as well as their micro-components, and also verify and validate them collectively so that there is a collective acceptance for quality indicators.

As a second step, it is mandatory to set benchmarks for each indicator of quality. Benchmarking is used to measure performance in selected areas, often in comparison to similar operations in other organizations. It is quite possible that there are multiple sets of quality indicators for each area, sub-area and micro-components.

7. Define Quality Parameter and Insist on Quality in Every Sphere and Activity

As mentioned earlier, TQM insists on quality in every sphere/realm/ department of the institute and in every activity. It abhors quality in selected areas. It accepts Kaizen as an entry point to total quality.

Very often, not all aspects of a college or university get the required attention. For example, on an average, in undergraduate colleges, staffrooms compare better with a railway platform where teachers come and wait for the next period without any facility for academic work or even basic seating comforts. In comparison, facilities, ambience and comforts provided in the principals' office are far too different. On the basis of organizational microanalysis, the quality parameter should be defined for every component. Thus, TQM, by its very nature, demands attention in every aspect of the institution.

8. Review and Redefine Goals and Targets for Continuous Improvement

As mentioned repeatedly, quality is a journey; a journey without an end. In this journey, there is no last milestone. New milestones are set once we reach the known and pre-set targets. It is by setting new milestones that the institute moves forward to optimize its total potential. Besides, it is also the secret to 'stay at the top'. As other competing institutions move up in the ladder, one needs to move further up to retain the top position. Hence, an institution striving for quality management cannot have the same set of goals and targets for all time to come. The scientific technique is to periodically review the goals and targets as much as the distance covered. Based on such reviews, institutions should set up a fresh set of goals and targets. In a way, in TQM, the concept is about moving the target constantly to a higher milestone/level, rather than making it static.

9. Develop Data and Information Systems for Each Activity and Function

TQM generates not only enthusiasm but also some hardcore techniques to achieve goals and targets. Compare this with quality as essentially a perceptual phenomenon. For implementing TQM in higher education institutions, this must change.

Much of institutional management is still perceptual without adequate data and information to support. For example, when a teacher is labelled as either good or bad, there is hardly any data to substantiate. It is pure perception, if not hearsay.

Similarly, an oft lamentation, we hear, is 'the standard of education is falling'. Without recorded data and statistics, this is much more of nostalgia than a fact. If we compare students' performance for the last 10 years in the university examinations for example, we may be able to find a common trend—the performance of students is either steadily going up or going down or staying at the same level. A statement about standard is valid only when it is backed by credible/authentic data and information.

TQM demands developing database and information systems on each activity so that decisions are well established on a reliable database backed by a careful thought process. Hence, it is advisable to define the parameters of quality agenda in each area and collect relevant information and data.

10. Introduce Cost Analysis and Develop Cost Consciousness

The reason why our policymakers postponed quality behind equity is because quality is considered expensive. This is an unfounded concept because of huge spillover of quality into equity and access. However, it needs to be proved by true cost analysis of quality. For example, education is a human-intensive system. Whatever is invested in non-human components is managed by human beings. There are several studies that indicate gross underutilization of resources in educational institutions. Hence, cost analysis of investment on human beings is quite necessary.

Further, institutes must develop cost consciousness like the way it is done at homes. For example, a teacher is hired for 40 hours a week. His/her teaching load can be anywhere between 8 to 18 hours a week depending on whether the incumbent is an assistant professor or a professor. If we extrapolate the salary of a teacher in higher education institution with work, it is possible to calculate the 'cost of teaching per hour' and 'cost of service per hour' (Mukhopadhyay 2005a).

The cost of teaching per hour is more than double the cost of service per hour. This is because the remaining time is allocated for preparation, research, writing and extension. A large majority of teachers continue to dictate notes from old notes, which indicates lack of preparation. Not all teachers research, publish and extend their expert knowledge to others. In such situations, there is a clear imbalance in the cost of quality.

11. Create Mechanisms for Interdepartmental and Inter-subject Group Dialogue and Planning by Breaking Barriers

Before the University Grants Commission (UGC) Regulation making in-campus presence for certain hours daily was introduced as mandatory, a common practice was that teachers used to come only during class (teaching) hours and for attending staff meetings, whenever that was convened. There was very little interaction among the staff members in the same department, leave alone across the departments.

There are universities and colleges where one department performs excellently well, whereas others perform at an average or even below average level. *Gung Ho! Turn On the People in Any Organization* by Blanchard and Bowles (1997) provides a beautiful example. Since TQM is everybody's business, it is necessary to develop proper forums and mechanisms for interdepartmental dialogues and discussions.

This is becoming all the more necessary now due to the emergence of interdisciplinary approach to education. Creating a matrix structure is one of the tested solutions. For example, the Technical Teachers Training Institute in Bhopal had task forces for curriculum, evaluation, research and so on where people from different departments of engineering and humanities participated/contributed.

Thus, in order to ensure TQM, it is important that the barriers between the departments are broken and that they interact with each other so that there are ample opportunities to contribute to enhancing the quality of the institution.

12. Generate a Staff Development Blueprint for Each Staff Member and Execute It with Care

Quality in higher education institutions depends almost exclusively on the staff. From the point of view of institutional economics, the salary cost alone is more than 80 per cent. Hence, quality management without staff development is a utopia. Furthermore, a single approach to staff development will not serve the purpose.

Competence, commitment and confidence are the three main criteria for teacher effectiveness. Confidence comes from competence and commitment. Using these two parameters, the teachers in an institution can be classified into four broad categories. There are teachers who are:

- competent and willing (committed) to teach and engage themselves in other academic activities in the institution;
- competent, but not willing to give their best;
- willing (committed), but not competent;
- neither willing, nor competent.

Conventionally, staff development programmes treat all these four categories in the same style.

1. Those who are competent and willing require greater exposure to the world of knowledge, ideas and support (e.g., seminars and conferences).
2. Those who are competent, but unwilling, need training in behaviour modification.
3. Those who are willing, but not competent, require skill or competency development exercises.
4. Those who are neither willing nor competent require initial training on behaviour modification; then on skill development.

Thus, for developing quality, capacity-building programmes for higher education need to be carefully designed to support the varying training needs of different categories of teachers and non-teaching staff. Although there are provisions for the training of academic staff, howsoever ineffective they are, there is very little opportunity for the non-academic staff to undergo training and develop their capacities. Since TQM emphasizes on the inclusion of all the members and stakeholders in the organization, it is necessary to develop capacity-building programmes for all the staff in the institution.

13. Mentor Leadership

Research on leadership for institution building (Mukhopadhyay 2012a) clearly indicates that delegation is the key to quality management and institution building. Compare this with the other experiences that a large majority of heads of institutions do not delegate as they wish to hold on to all the powers. Participative management has been mentioned as one of the cardinal principles of TQM. This participation means sharing not only of responsibilities but also of rights, especially to decide and innovate. The *Leaderful Practice* (Raelin 2004) provides a potent alternative.

One important step is to nurture and mentor leadership among the staff, so that the process of quality management does not become dependent on any particular individual. Blanchard and Bowles' *Gung Ho!* (1997) referred to earlier documents how one department was performing very well while the rest of the industry was actually sick. It is because of leadership. The Centre of Advanced Study in the M.S. University of Baroda excelled during the leadership tenure of Professor M.B. Buch who mentored young professionals to lead clearly defined areas with the confirmation of his help and support (Mukhopadhyay 2012a).

Thus, the key to sharing rights and responsibilities through delegation for quality management is through mentoring leadership. The old paradigm that depended on a 'leader' has now made way to create more 'leaders' in the organization. It is time for collective leadership for quality improvement. Mentoring leadership is the key to effective collective leadership.

14. Innovate and Encourage Innovations; Document and Discuss Outcomes

Innovation is the key to change. TQM is a process of continuous change by improving quality from one level to another. Hence, the journey of quality will be impossible without innovating and encouraging innovation on a continuing basis. There are two broad components in the principle. One is innovating. The second is documenting and disseminating. There are, again, two underlying messages in the first part of this cardinal principle. These are innovation by the leader of the institution and the encouragement of other members to innovate. This ensures developing a culture of innovation in the institution.

Though few, there are institutions where heads of the institutions, namely, directors and vice-chancellors, undertake research projects themselves and teach classes. They also encourage every teacher to undertake research projects. Thus, they create an ambiance of a research institution.

The second part of the cardinal principle is about documenting and sharing of experiences of innovations. There are innumerable instances of teachers and heads of institutions making significant innovations and bringing about constructive transformations in the educational institutions. However, such innovations and changes go unrecorded and undocumented for others to learn from. It is important that such innovations (both successes and failures) are documented and discussed for better learning.

There is a school of thought that advocates setting up 'Innovation Universities'. This is a dangerous proposition. There cannot be a university that does not innovate. Higher education institutions being knowledge enterprises, innovation and research is everybody's business in higher education. Furthermore, 'no innovation, no quality'. Since quality higher education is the national agenda, every higher education institution ought to innovate, document and disseminate experiences, often called best practices.

15. Celebrate Organizational Successes and Failures

Finally, for TQM, organizational successes as well as failures must be celebrated. Organizations celebrate successes. Unfortunately, in most cases, failures are usually mourned, thus depriving the organization of a significant opportunity to learn from the failure.

The most inspiring experience regarding celebration of failure is the activities of the Failure Analysis Board/Committee of the Indian Space Research Organization (ISRO). Every failure is 'celebrated' by immediate and extensive analysis of the causes of failures and reconstructing the strategies from there on. Indeed, it is all about celebrating through learning. Only those organizations that celebrate failures with equal seriousness as they celebrate success can reach their peak.

These TQM principles provide a broad guideline about dos and don'ts about implementing TQM. For actual implementation, each institution has to develop a strategic plan. Although emphasis is on 'total', for all practical purposes a higher education institution may have to use Kaizens and adopt the incremental approach or piecemeal social engineering design. Hence, every institution must develop a strategic plan for quality management. The ways to go about preparing strategic plan is the subject of discussion of Chapter 7 of this book.

Conclusion

Quality is an endless journey. Even within a limited framework of relativity as well as comparability between institutions, quality cannot be static or stagnant. By the time an institution reaches a particular benchmark, other institutions might have moved farther away in its own quality journey.

Also, since dynamic changes are happening all around the world in the knowledge systems, employment market and in the overall environment, the search for quality has to continue incessantly. TQM brings that dynamic thrust to quality management, making it an ongoing and progressive journey.

A major emphasis of TQM in education is optimization of human resources and their talents. Further, it is not just financial or material resource intensive. Instead, it is human talent optimization intensive. Since there is no dearth of human talent in educational institutions, quality management is possible provided there is serious engagement and commitment of all the concerned stakeholders of the institution to participate in quality management.

4

Quality: Micromanagement*

Introduction

A higher education institution is a holistic entity. Hence, quality management demands a holistic approach. An institution cannot be considered to be a 'quality institution' if it is good in just one aspect and not so good or totally lacking in certain other areas. The reason is quite simple and obvious. All aspects, departments and activities of an institution are interlinked and interdependent. It is like a human body. But, the issue is whether we see the system as a whole and go from whole to parts or deal with the minutest components adopting reductionism and move from parts to the whole? Thus, the choice is between the systems approach and reductionist approach.

I experimented with TQM based on my book *Total Quality Management in Education* in few schools and colleges. During this research, I learnt that words like 'vision', 'mission' and so on are far too abstract for a large majority of the teachers in the average educational institutions. In response to my question, during one of my field visits to a school, to one of the teachers, 'how do you see your institution five years from now?'. The teacher said without any emotion, 'Five years from now! Who knows? I cannot think even about my next class'. This was quite a startling revelation to me.

---

* I formulated micromanagement as an approach to quality management based upon my research on TQM in education; and first published an earlier version in my book *Total Quality Management in Education* (2005).

My understanding was further reinforced during many of our workshops that we conducted for college principals. My colleague Jaya (Professor Jaya Indiresan) plays a game. She asks the principals, 'if you were declared as the HRD minister or education minister in your state and you have no dearth of funds or resources, what would you do?' It was a simple, yet a thought-provoking game of imagination. In short, it was a classic game of visioning.

During more than 50 programmes that we conducted, which cumulatively comprised more than 1,500 principals, we missed this 'imagination' or the 'capability of visioning'. The ideas that they came up with only amounted to 'small repairs' or 'operational changes' here and there. No one had a vision for 'transforming' the institution.

Vision is a function of the creative mind, whereas most people are comfortable with concrete operations rather than extended abstraction and creativity. Hence, most people are comfortable when a holistic creative (and hence abstract) idea is broken down into small and concrete operations; a majority of the people in educational institutions can understand and operate upon a concrete short-term activity or a project. Thus, for quality management, we need to identify small, but specific, operations with the backdrop of the systems approach and systems thinking.

Hence, for effective quality management, it is essential to develop holistic thinking about the institution. The need for 'looking at an institution as a complete organism' comes from the perspective of systems thinking. To implement quality management in the real sense, we would also need to take the anatomical view by getting into minutest details that constitute the subsystems of an educational institution.

I have called this technique organizational microanalysis. Thus, what we need is amalgamation of an analytico-synthetic approach to understand and transform our educational institutions for the better.

Systems Approach

A system is made up of certain components that are interconnected in such a way that each component functions in collaboration with the other components to create synergy. Hence, for any system and its components, the interconnections and their collaborative working are equally important; these are inseparable. Accordingly, system thinking has been defined as an analytical approach that focuses on the way in which the components interrelate to each other in the system as well as how these systems work within the larger context, namely environment (Rouse 2005). Reductionist thinking is the other way round.

Systems thinking stands in stark *contrast* to the analytic or mechanistic thinking that all phenomena *can be understood* by reducing them to their ultimate elements, according to the *Business Dictionary*.[1]

Thus, while the systems thinking approach deals with a holistic view of all the components and their interconnections and roles, reductionism analyses each component separately and then reconstructs the system again by putting all of them back together and interconnecting the components.

The origin and development of the systems approach can be traced back to cybernetics, biological sciences and industrial management. Romiszowaski (1994) contended that 'the term "systems approach" emerged from the general systems theory and cybernetics as a creative and heuristic approach to the understanding and improvement of probabilistic systems'. It was recognized that the complexity involved in social systems could not be controlled or maneuvered easily as it can be done in simple mechanical processes. Hence, a systems approach is characterized by careful analysis of interrelationships and interdependence of the constituent units and subsystems and 'the interpretation of these interactions in terms of predicting what may happen to the other parts of the system if certain changes are made in a particular part' (O'Neil 1979).

From the perspective of managing change, a system may be defined as being an organized assembly of components, which are related in such a way that the behaviour of any individual component will influence the overall status of the system. 'All systems,

---

[1] www.businessdictionary.com/definition/systems-thinking-ST.html (accessed on 12 May 2014).

"physical" or "soft", must have a predetermined objective that the interrelated components strive to achieve' (Paton and McCalman 2000).

Page and Thomas (1977) defined the systems approach to education in the *International Dictionary of Education* as

> Conscious use of systems analysis and systems design techniques in an endeavour to identify and solve complex problems in learning and instructional systems. The components of this approach include the establishment of the system's boundary, the identification of all actual or possible inputs and outputs to the system and the examination of their interaction.

Thus, we observe that the systems approach has conventionally been defined in terms of input–process–output with a feedback loop to examine how these three components relate to and complement each other. Further, the system defined by input–process–output has a boundary statement and is set in a context termed as 'environment'. If we take the example of a college as a system, it may differ in its problems and the coordinates of input–process–output depending upon the environment, for example, rural or urban and other such definable environmental factors.

Another important aspect to be taken into consideration is the interrelationship among the components—input, process and output. It is rather common to hear the claim for more input, especially finance, for delivering quality. In the semantics of research methods, especially experimental designs, output is the criterion or dependent variable, process is the intervening variable and input is the independent variable.

The systems approach proposes the following hypotheses in the form of mathematical formulations.

> Hypothesis 1: Process remaining constant, output varies with the input.
> Hypothesis 2: Input remaining constant, output varies with the process.

Also, it is equally possible to propose that

> Hypothesis 3: Output is the function of both the input and process; hence, it is dependent on the variations and changes in both the input and the process.

Soft Systems Methodology

An emerging discourse and debate is between systems approach or systems management and soft systems methodology (SSM).

Peter Checkland, Professor of Systems, Lancaster University, is credited with propounding this brand new concept.

> Soft Systems Methodology (SSM) is a systemic approach for tackling real-world problematic situations. Soft Systems Methodology is the result of the continuing action research that Peter Checkland, Brian Wilson and many others have conducted over the last 30 years to provide a framework for users to deal with the kind of messy problem situations that lack a formal problem definition.[2]

There seems to be some confusion arising out of its very name prefixed by 'soft' that SSM deals only with soft problems. In the real world, problems are neither soft nor hard. A problem is just a problem. 'The very notion of a problem is contingent upon human beings perceiving it as such, e.g. one man's terrorist is another man's freedom fighter'. SSM deals with the notion of systems differently, compared to the known systems management, mentioned above. Hard systems are definitive, whereas soft systems are largely a mental construct.

Soft systems is a notion of a system—a mental construct guided by the world view of the people involved in conceptualizing the system. Some scholars have tried to differentiate 'hard systems' from the soft by differentiating between ontological and epistemological entities. SSM is an approach to solve problems through mentally constructing systems. According to Wilson and Morren (1990), it is a cyclic process of learning about the situation on hand and about the methodology used (Karim 2009).

Several authors including Checkland (1985), Ison (2008) and Karim (2009) have contrasted hard systems thinking with soft systems thinking. The core comparisons and differentiations can be summarized in the following statements:

- Hard systems thinking (HST) is goal oriented, whereas SSM is learning oriented.

---

[2] http://www.skybrary.aero/index.php/Toolkit:Systems_Thinking_for_Safety/Soft_Systems_Methodology_and_Rich_Pictures (accessed on 30 March 2014).

- HST assumes that systems can be engineered, whereas SSM contends that the world is problematic and can be explored using systems models.
- For HST, problems are complex (unitary), whereas for SSM, these are complex (pluralist); the difference lies between agreement and disagreement, 'between those defined as involved and/or affected, respectively'.
- HST defines/assumes systems models to be models of the world (ontological), whereas SSM contends that systems models are intellectual configurations (epistemological).
- HST highlights problems and solutions; SSM highlights issues and accommodations.

Checkland (2000) proposed a seven-stage process for SSM, as follows:

1. Entering the problem situation.
2. Expressing the problem situation.
3. Formulating the root definitions of relevant systems.
4. Building conceptual models of human activity systems.
5. Comparing the models with the real world.
6. Defining changes that are desirable and feasible.
7. Taking action to improve the real-world situation.

From our understanding of the HST and SSM approaches, we should now look at an educational institution as a system.

Educational Institution as a System

An educational institution as a system has inputs, such as students, infrastructure, financial resources and instructional resources. The processes are admission, instruction, evaluation and so on. The outputs are the learning outcomes, generic graduate skills and employability skills, hobbies and excellence in co-scholastic domains and so on.

The systems discourse in education takes a special meaning because the output at one stage can very well be an input in another stage. Thus, it becomes a cyclic process. For example, if we consider management and administration as processes, they generate teachers' job satisfaction as the output. Further, teachers' job satisfaction becomes an input for generating an improved instructional system and student performance as output.

Another major challenge in applying the systems approach in education is the difficulty in quantifying and measuring input and output. Let us look at what constitutes input, output and the process in an educational institution (Figure 4.1).

Figure 4.1:
Input–Process–Output: Systems in Educational Institutions

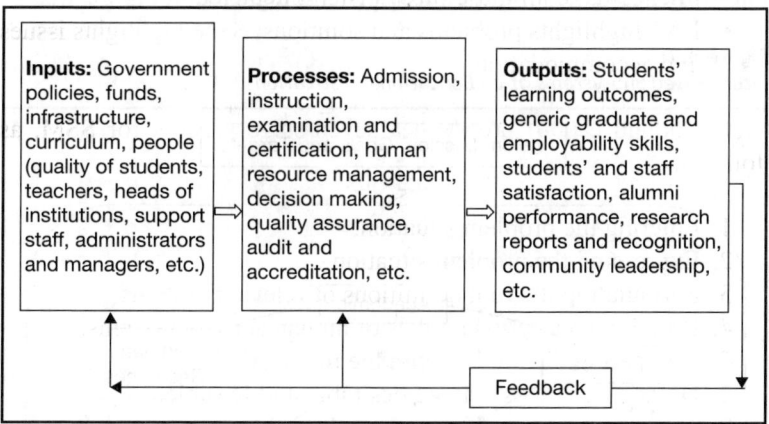

| Inputs: Government policies, funds, infrastructure, curriculum, people (quality of students, teachers, heads of institutions, support staff, administrators and managers, etc.) | Processes: Admission, instruction, examination and certification, human resource management, decision making, quality assurance, audit and accreditation, etc. | Outputs: Students' learning outcomes, generic graduate and employability skills, students' and staff satisfaction, alumni performance, research reports and recognition, community leadership, etc. |

Source: Author.

Another way of looking at the systems approach is through the lens of subsystems. A system obviously comprises several subsystems. The basic approach to systems thinking is identifying the subsystems and understanding their interrelationships and interdependence. In fact, it is the interlinking and interdependence of the subsystems that configure a system. Hence, a subsystem can never be equal to the system.

The subsystems concept as applied to educational institutions can be defined and described in several ways. The various subsystems are infrastructure, instructional systems, linkages and interfaces, management and administration and so on. Another way of categorizing educational subsystems is faculties, departments, administration, examination, construction and maintenance and so on. A common theme that cuts through all these subcomponents like the thread in a garland is 'management of quality'. TQM involves ensuring quality in each of these functions and moving beyond.

Furthermore, the subsystems vary from one to another in their very nature. For example, finance and infrastructure are somewhat concrete and measurable, whereas vision, mission and goals are abstract. Similarly, academic activities, student services and managing people at work are examples of few organizational processes. Further, their interdependence is obvious. For example, infrastructure and finance are mutually interdependent, as much as academic activities are dependent upon infrastructure and finance. Besides, vision, mission, goals and targets guide all aspects of the institution. The interrelationship of all these subsystems is depicted in Figure 4.2.

Figure 4.2:
Interrelated Subsystems of an Educational Institution

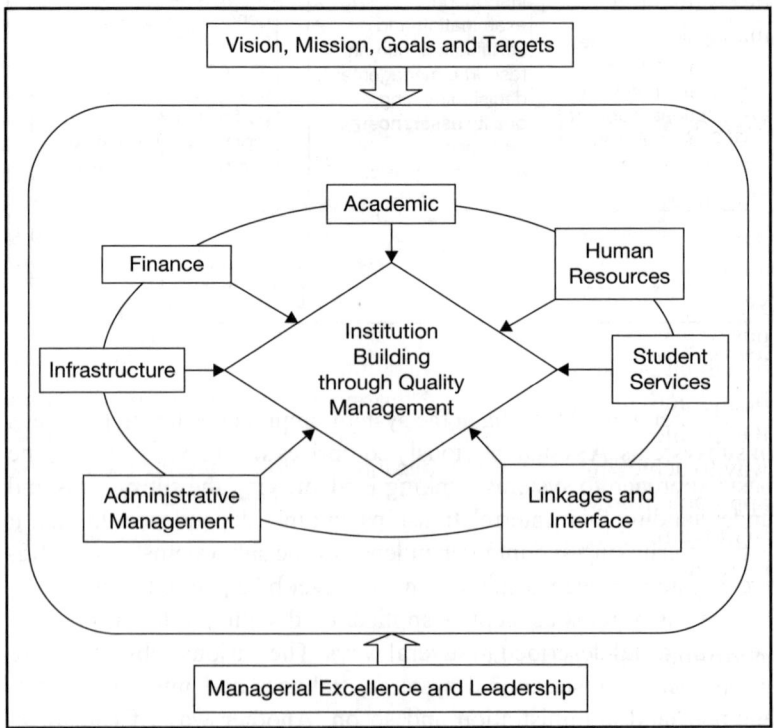

Source: Author.

Institution Building

Institution building is the central theme of quality management. Institution building involves developing the 'process capabilities' of the institution for sustainable development and making it free from being dependent on any particular individual 'around the man/ woman' approach (Chowdhry 1977). In other words, it deals with developing the self-renewing capability of the institution in such a way that it continues to evolve and transform itself over a period of time. Figure 4.2 indicates the interactive pattern of various aspects of institutional management for institution building. The process of institution building with inputs from all the departments and activities is inspired and guided by the vision and mission and energized by managerial excellence, especially leadership.

Vision, Mission, Goals and Targets

Vision provides inspiration and the direction in which the institution has to strive in order to achieve its goals and targets. In fact, vision is a futuristic statement, highlighting what an institution will be in a few years to come. However, vision statements are often vague, ambiguous or generic that can fit into any institution. Missions are the means by which the vision of an organization is unbundled by setting time-bound activities to achieve the vision. In other words, missions are the enablers of vision. Goals and targets are the milestones on the way to achieving each of the missions. By following the reductionist approach from vision to mission to goals and targets, we are also able to move from the abstract to the concrete. Goals and targets are more concrete statements when compared to either mission or vision.

Academic Management

Academic management forms the core of the functioning of an institution. It comprises planning and management of admission, curriculum, instruction, examination, co-scholastic and co-curricular activities.

Human Resource Management

An educational institution is a human-intensive system. Hence, human resource management can hardly be overemphasized. Human resource management comprises personnel planning, recruitment and induction, professional development, maintenance of personnel records, staff appraisal, management of staff unions, conducting staff meetings, staff welfare, job allocation and management, incentives and disciplining and so on.

Finance Management

There are several aspects of financial management in an educational institution. These include budgeting, resource mobilization, resource development and optimization, resource utilization, expenditure control, cost analysis and cost–benefit analysis, accounting and auditing and so on.

Infrastructure Management

Infrastructure management comprises construction and extension of buildings, utilization and maintenance of infrastructure, library, laboratory, audiovisual aids, hostel, sanitation, sports and games facilities, vocational education facilities, information and communication technology (ICT) facilities and so on. Proper planning and resource optimization can contribute to better quality of education.

Network and Interface

Institutions no more live in isolation. Instead, these are located in a larger environment where the institutions and the environment mutually influence each other. Further, with the new emphasis on 'client orientation' in quality management, the need for linkages and interfaces with 'clients' or beneficiaries has assumed additional significance. The linkages and interfaces are directly or indirectly related to the educational institution and can be examined in relation to parents, alumni, immediate neighbourhood and community, higher authorities, non-educational authorities like the public works department, transport, health and so on, educational institutions at the local, regional, national and international levels, employers, scholars at a distance and so on.

Student Services

Students are the main beneficiaries of an institution. Hence, student services are the key to improving the quality of life in institutions. Management of student services can be examined with respect to the creation and management of student (and parent) information systems, guidance and counselling facilities, student amenities, incentives and other facilities (like scholarships) as well as student involvement and participation in decision making.

Administrative Management

Educational institutions are formal organizations that are governed by certain rules and regulations, which are common across institutions under one dispensation, say, a university, state government, or a DAV College managing committee. Quality management requires not only familiarity and understanding of rules and regulations, but also dynamic interpretation of various administrative procedures like purchase, departmental promotion, writing off procedures, performance appraisal, grievance handling, vigilance procedures, inventory control and management, costing and cost optimization and so on.

Managerial Excellence and Leadership

Managerial excellence permeates through all aspects of institutional management and is based on the personal qualities of the head of the institution—a principal or a vice-chancellor—a person in the leadership position. This component includes understanding of self and others—group dynamics, teams and cliques, communication (oral and written), leadership, participative management and team building, decision making, management of motivation, time and change management and so on.

Since quality management (and institution building) is expected to bring about a total effect on quality management in each of the above components, systems management implies management of each component (subsystem) woven into a holistic pattern for overall impact on the institution.

Each area mentioned above comprises several activities or components. For quality management, it would be good to break down each area/activity into its most minute details and adopt the technique of micromanagement through 'organizational microanalysis' (Mukhopadhyay 2005a).

Organizational Microanalysis

Organizational microanalysis, as described earlier, is a reductionist approach to quality management, which is achieved by breaking down each and every component of the system to its most minute details, thereby ensuring attainment of highest quality in each component. As Karim (2009) wrote:

> One way to understand systems thinking is to contrast it with the reductionist approach to tackling complexity. Reductionist thinking has been remarkably successful, particularly in developing successful theories and models of the inanimate world when combined with scientific procedures. The essential aspect of the reductionist approach is that complexity is simplified by dividing a problem into sub-problems or lesser components. The process of sub-division is continued until the resulting bits are simple enough to be analysed and understood. The operation of the original complex entity is then reconstructed from the operation of the components. (Chapman 2002).

Furthermore, this reductionism is equally applicable to both input and processes. For, if the input stays constant, output varies directly with the processes involved. The important assumption here is that if quality management is implemented on all the subcomponents, it will create a holistic effect on the overall quality of the educational institution. To give a concrete example in this context, if a college or university is able to manage its classrooms, laboratories, libraries, staffrooms, corridors, washrooms and all other such major and minor components well—safe, clean and aesthetically—the institution will have quality infrastructure.

In order to implement organizational microanalysis, there has to be a serious effort. Let us examine academic management, to illustrate the point. It constitutes five major components, which are admission, curricular planning and management, management of instruction, management of student assessment and planning and management of co-curricular activities (Figure 4.3).

Figure 4.3:
Interrelated Dimensions of Academic Management

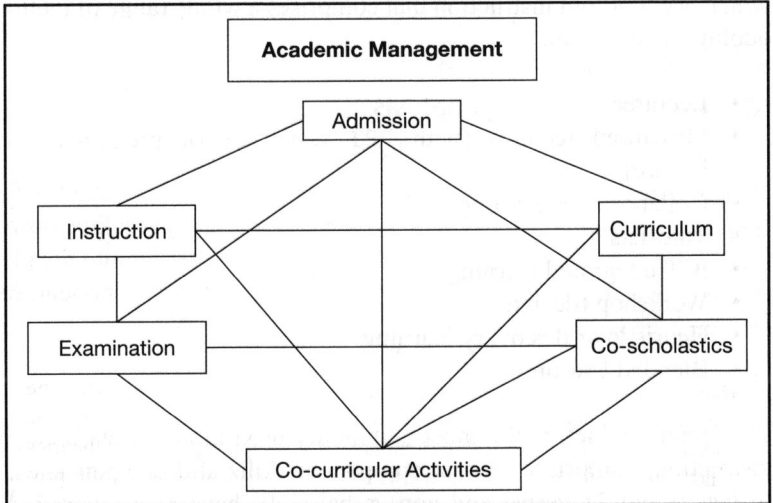

Source: Author.

Figure 4.3 depicts interrelated components and highlights interdependence among the components. For example, instruction is dependent on curriculum, examination, admission as well as co-curricular activities. The quality of instruction is guided and informed by the quality of students in an institution, nature of the curriculum, expected learning outcome and so on.

Each component of academic management further comprises several subcomponents. This should be further analysed into multi-stage micro-components. Let us take the case of the teaching–learning process or instruction as an example. It includes the following:

- Classroom instruction
- Collaborative or group learning
- Assignments
- Seminars
- Project work
- Laboratory practical
- Field visits
- Peer group consultation
- Internet surfing
- And others

Let us go one step further and analyse just one aspect of the above, which is classroom instruction that comprises a whole range of methodologies and so on:

- Lectures
- Structured lectures (with PPT slides and/or pre-structured lecture)
- Collaborative learning
- Tutorials
- ICT-integrated learning
- Workshop (design)
- Heuristic or discovery learning
- Blended learning

The lecture, which is the most commonly used mode of classroom instruction, comprises several component skills and competencies. In fact, about 21 verbal and non-verbal skills have been identified through research on microteaching. The most commonly used verbal skills are as follows:

- Introduction
- Explanation
- Illustration with examples
- Using chalkboard/whiteboard/projection/smart board
- Asking questions
- Reinforcing student response
- Summarization

The 5E constructivist model comprises the following:

- Engage
- Explore
- Explain
- Elaborate
- Evaluate

In lectures, verbal communication is complemented with non-verbal communication that primarily comprises movements in the classroom, hand gestures, facial expressions and other forms of body management.

This stage-wise analysis of different components and their sub-components and micro-components is the organizational microanalysis. In the example described earlier, we analysed the following.

- Academic management into five micro-components.
- Of the five, we analysed instruction or teaching–learning process into nine components.
- Of the nine components, we further split classroom instruction into nine micro-components.
- Of the nine, we chose lectures to break down into seven micro-components.

This is an example of a four-stage organizational microanalysis. Despite such elaborate analysis, the total number of micro-components is not exhaustive, and many more components can be added to the list.

There is yet another dimension to this microanalysis. The argument is to ensure quality in each component. However, quality is a generic concept. For effective quality management, this generic statement has to be converted into specific. In other words, quality has to be spelt out in terms of indicators and benchmarks. Due to the differences in the nature of the micro-components, one cannot use the same set of quality indicators and benchmarks. To take an example, let us review the 19 quality indicators of a lecture.[3] We had created a Classroom Teaching Competence Scale to measure classroom teaching competence (read as 'quality of lecture').

---

[3] These indicators are adapted from the author's Classroom Teaching Competence Scale that was developed in a research project and published in *Total Quality Management in Education* (Mukhopadhyay 2005a).

We defined 19 indicators, listed below:

1. Clarity of aims of the lecture session to both the teacher and the students.
2. Appropriateness of the stated and unstated aims and level of students.
3. Appropriateness of lecture (techniques) for the theme of the lecture and to the students as well.
4. Effectiveness of introduction (beginning the lecture), in terms of drawing attention of the students.
5. Contents presented in smaller bits to ensure that the students learn step by step.
6. Learning of concepts and principles ensured through relevant and concrete examples.
7. Sequencing of contents—smaller bits and examples—was logical.
8. Appropriateness of questions asked by the teacher.
9. Active participation of the students in the class—raising doubts, asking questions, making observations and so on.
10. Positive reinforcement by the teacher to student participation.
11. Effectiveness of communication during the lecture.
12. Effectiveness of using whiteboard/chalkboard.
13. Use of electronic (digital/online audiovisual) aids, for example, PPT slides, videos, Internet-based material and so on.
14. Sustainability of students' interest.
15. Appropriateness of the assessment of student learning with respect to the stated aims of the lecture.
16. Linking up main points (summarization) before concluding the lecture.
17. References and further reading/learning assignments for the students.
18. Evidence of preparation for the lecture by the teacher—written or otherwise.
19. Confidence in communication and classroom management.

These 19 indicators are rated on a five-point scale based on 'Ground Rules for Classroom Observation', which sets the benchmark.

Let us now take the example of infrastructure that is little more concrete (Table 4.1).

Table 4.1:
Quality Indicators of Infrastructure

	Items	Adequacy	Functionality	Aesthetics	Comfort	Utilization	Remarks
1.	Classrooms						
2.	Laboratories						
3.	Library/libraries						
4.	Corridors						
5.	Students common rooms						
6.	Washrooms						
7.	Principal/VC Office						
8.	Dean's Office						
9.	Reception						
10.	Staffroom(s)						
11.	Facilities for lady staff members						
12.	Office rooms						

(Continued)

Table 4.1:
(Continued)

	Items	Adequacy	Functionality	Aesthetics	Comfort	Utilization	Remarks
13.	Canteen						
14.	Lawns and gardens						
15.	Computer labs						
16.	Furnishings						
17.	Staff quarters						
18.	Gym						
19.	Sports and games facilities and materials						
20.	Students' union room						
21.	Hostel						
22.	Please add…						

Source: Author.

Table 4.1 breaks down 'infrastructure' into 22 items. This list is not exhaustive as any one of the items listed may have many more micro-components. For example, classroom includes space per student, furniture, lighting and ventilation, writing boards, projection instrument, screen or white wall and so on. We have mentioned five indicators of quality, namely adequacy, functionality, aesthetics, comfort and utilization. It is possible to add more criteria. In each of the cells, we have to enter the benchmarks to complete the microanalysis exercise.

Similar microanalysis needs to be carried out for other areas as well. Success in quality can be assured only with quality management of each of these micro-components of an organization. It should be evident by now that the various dimensions (subsystems and subcomponents) of an educational institution are inseparable. A change in quality in any one area triggers changes in multiple areas. Hence, it is essential that the entire institution's focus is on enhancing the quality. Thus, ensuring quality of every subcomponent will not only have summative but also productive effects on the overall quality of the institution.

Conclusion

This chapter has dealt with systems approach, soft systems management and organizational microanalysis. Although organizational microanalysis adopts reductionism, it derives its contents from the systems approach. It also argues that by reintegrating each micro-component, it should be possible to reconstruct the entire system. A further argument is: systems reconstructed with improved quality components should result in an improved system. This seems to be a contentious argument, though.

There is a third, and often unseen, element in a system. These are the connections interlinking the interdependent individual subcomponents of a system. The relevant question here is whether improving the quality of subcomponents would automatically improve the quality of interdependences. The answer cannot be a confident 'yes'. It may or may not be.

Knowledge management provides a close and relevant metaphor to this contention. Organizational knowledge, which is unmanaged, is often less than the sum total of the knowledge of individuals in the organization. However, with proper knowledge management, organizational knowledge can be the product of knowledge of the individuals. Hence, the challenge here is to strengthen the interaction of the subcomponents in the system through participatory processes, strategic planning, continuous mentoring and monitoring quality.

Another important debate is about whether educational institutions are 'soft systems' or 'hard systems'. Are problems 'messy' or concrete? Is the 'reality' of a college or a university just a mental construct of the people in the institutions, or is it real? The literature on management of change and institution building (Latchem and Hanna 2001, Mukhopadhyay 2012a) clearly establishes that the 'realities' in educational institutions are constructed by people. The case studies documented in *Leadership for Institution Building in Education* (Mukhopadhyay 2012a) clearly establishes how the world view of principals and vice chancellors saw through the reality and actually reconstructed and created a new reality, thereby transforming a sluggish institution into a well-performing institution.

It is possible to conclude that SSM may be a better alternative. Further, for quality management, higher education institutions need to adopt the seven-step learning paradigm advocated by Checkland (1998).

The main argument in favour of the application of a systems approach to management of quality in educational institutions is that it can ensure that the institution is seen as a dynamic living organism and not as a static conglomeration of various tasks, people and infrastructure. The fragmented view is manifested in various ways, such as teachers being placed in-charge of examinations or the library or student activities considering their respective areas as the most important and thus insisting on priority. However, the head of an institution cannot afford to possess such a fragmented view.

Similarly, principals who are good teachers and enjoy teaching tend to devote most of their energies into teaching at the cost of other critical areas of institutional management. There are others who enjoy the 'authority' associated with the position and concentrate on rules and regulations and financial management. As a result, the academic management or management of linkages and interfaces with the outside world gets neglected (for example). Only later do they realize the lopsided developments in the institution, where hands do not cooperate with the legs, and the collective body (staff) refuses to work with the head (the principal).

Institution building, the central agenda of quality management in education, is a wholesome game. Hence, a holistic view has to be taken. Further, it is important to percolate systems thinking down to the staff in order to facilitate an understanding of the mutuality of roles, functions and interdependence of subsystems.

5

Strategic Planning

Introduction

Quality management is function of enthusiasm, initiative (innovation) and technique. Quality management surfaces like dolphins as and when there is a crisis or a sudden thrust due to change of policies or change in guard of the institution, external challenges or threats, for example, coping with the challenge of globalization. Since quality is an endless journey, it is not easy to sustain enthusiasm for new initiatives over a long period of time. Sustainability is critically important for quality management. It is this deficiency of sustainability that brings in ups and downs in an institution. The 'technique' of quality management is the key to sustainability.

Strategic planning and management provides a sound approach or technique for quality management. This chapter brings in a few alternative models of strategic planning and proposes a working model, especially suited for Indian higher education institutions.

Strategic Planning

The word 'strategy' is derived from Greek *stratēgia*, 'art of troop leader; office of general, command, generalship'; 'the art of planning and directing overall military operations and movements in a war or battle'.[1] Thus, at least to begin with, the word 'strategy' had a military overtone. However, what is common between war and quality management? Or, how relevant is this metaphor? We tried to decipher the analogy.

In war, the strategies are focussed on the following:

- A single point agenda—win and only win. There is no plan to fail. War strategies do not glamorize the concept of 'learning from failure'.
- Win at the least cost to human life, equipment and money.
- Win within the shortest possible duration.
- Strike at the most vulnerable point of the opponent with the greatest strength.
- Carefully choose the timing of the strike.
- Skilfully deploy army, navy and air force to create synergy on the war front.

There are many other components of war strategy. But, how are they relevant in the context of education and quality management? By extrapolation, we may interpret the following:

- Quality management as an attack on poor quality.
- Protecting an innovative effort like quality management (or any other meaningful innovation) from failing.
- Achieving quality at the least cost (dealing with the issue of cost of quality).
- Improving quality within the shortest possible time. This also means reducing the incubation period and take-off time.
- Finding a safe entry point using the Kaizen (an important intervention strategy) to identify an area where success can be ensured for future efforts.
- Timing and sequencing quality interventions to get the best results (cost-effectiveness).
- Ensuring deployment of the best human resources and encouraging teamwork to ensure continuous improvement.

Therefore, strategic planning and management implies putting various techniques in place to manage quality, backed by initiative

---

[1] www.oxforddictionaries.com/definition/english/strategy

and enthusiasm. Since quality is a journey, strategic planning demands charting out/designing a long-term plan by spelling out appropriate medium- and short-term plans that lead to achieving long-term goals, missions and vision of the educational institution.

Strategic Plan Models

There are several strategic plan models that have been presented by various authors. In this section, we will examine the strategic plan models formulated by Malcolm Baldridge,[2] Murgatroyd and Morgan (1993), Kaufman (1992), Sallis (2002), Approach–Deploy–Results–Improvement (ADRI) Quality Cycle Approach and Mukhopadhyay (2005a).

Malcolm Baldridge offered a continuous improvement (CI) model for quality improvement on a continuing basis. The Baldridge model[3] for performance excellence identified 11 core values (Walpole and Noeth 2002). These are:

1. Visionary leadership
2. Learning-centred education
3. Organizational and personal learning
4. Valuing faculty, staff and partners
5. Agility
6. Focus on the future
7. Managing for innovation
8. Management by fact
9. Public responsibility and citizenship
10. Focus on results and creating value
11. Systems perspective.

The ACT Policy Report (2002) reduced 11 criteria to 7, namely

1. Leadership
2. Strategic planning
3. Student, stakeholder and market focus

---

[2] www.baldrige.com/tag/strategic-planning/
[3] www.baldrige.com/tag/strategic-planning/

4. Information and analysis
5. Faculty and staff focus
6. Core process management
7. Organizational performance results.

The Baldridge model provides a simple tool for assessment of status of continuous improvement through status of each of the seven components. The model also allocates scores on different status under each of the seven components. There are differential emphases or weightages on different components. The highest emphasis is on customer satisfaction and the minimum on the status of strategic plan and mission statement.

Murgatroyd and Morgan (1993) proposed a new way of looking and classifying an educational institution based on two parameters: access and service. Access implies who or who cannot take part in education in a particular institution, or universal versus restricted access. Service implies some kind of a specialization or specialized services that differentiate one institution from another. In this model, access has been dichotomized into open and niche access, and service into basic and enhanced. Thus, if access and service are plotted on a matrix, we obtain four types of institutions (Figure 5.1).

Figure 5.1:
Four Generic Types of Educational Institutions

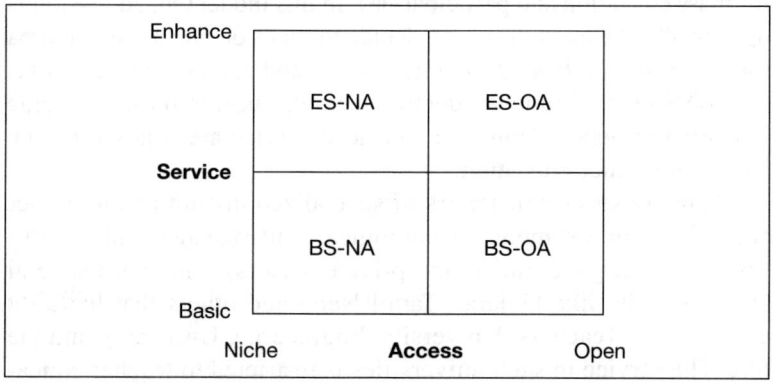

Source: Author. (Based on Murgatroyd and Morgan's classification)
Notes: 1. BS-OA: Basic Service—Open Access
      2. ES-OA: Enhanced Service—Open Access
      3. BS-NA: Basic Service—Niche Access
      4. ES-NA: Enhanced Service—Niche Access

T-I: BS-OA: Basic Service—Open Access

Let us call this as Type I. A very large majority of publicly funded Indian higher education institutions belong to this category. By rule, they admit all candidates who fulfil admission (eligibility) criteria irrespective of caste, creed, religion, gender and so on. According to the available statistics, these institutions cater to the educational needs of nearly 90 per cent of Indian higher education students. Hence, any strategic plan model for this category will be applicable to most Indian institutions. Although the admission remains open, the strategic planning for quality would emphasize quality improvement of basic services. Basic services include curricular and co-curricular activities for the students, besides satisfaction and recognition of the teachers and other staff.

In another paper, I have argued that the enhancement of the services in open-access institutions of higher education is of far greater significance than the fancy and fantasy of how many universities figure in the top 100 or 200 lists (Mukhopadhyay 2014). Thus, the Level I institutions form the majority of Indian higher education.

T-II: ES-OA: Enhanced Service—Open Access

Type II institutions still focus on open access (read as opportunity for mass education and participation). In this model too, admission is open to all. The institution may decide to focus on one particular area for specialization (e.g., academics, sports and games, cultural activities, NSS etc.). Within academic areas, the institution may decide to excel in science. Thus, the enhanced service area chosen by the college is science education.

There are several instances of specialized institutions in higher education, for example, technological and management institutions (in both government and private sectors). There are several states in India like Gujarat, Tamil Nadu and others that have set up dedicated Teachers' University, Engineering University and the like. The service in such universities is restricted to teacher education or engineering education, but with open access. These kinds of institutions need a different strategic plan to achieve high quality.

A debatable question is about institutions like IITs, IIMs and top-end colleges like Presidency, St. Stephen's, LSR, St. Xavier's, Kala

Bhavan (*Viswa Bharati*), Loyola and others. Are these open-access or niche-access institutions? The admission is open to all, but there are a limited number of seats. Because of their reputation, there is a huge demand for admissions in these institutions. Therefore, technically, the access to admission becomes restricted by merit.

T-III: BS-NA: Basic Service—Niche Access

Type III institutions are niche-access institutions where admission is restricted based on certain preset eligibility criteria, but they provide basic services. All denominational institutions come under this category because access is restricted to the people from the defined denomination. All mono-gender institutions like girls' colleges, women's universities and men's colleges belong to this category. The strategic plan for such institutions needs to be conceptualized differently for improving the quality of basic services while retaining their niche-access characteristic. For example, how do we plan the improvement of services for a girls' college that empowers girls and also develops confidence in them to fight against gender stereotyping and discrimination.

T-IV: ES-NA: Enhanced Service—Niche Access

The Type IV institutions differ from T-III with respect to enhanced services, while the criteria of niche access remain the same. The difference is based on the emphasis of the enhanced services. However, there are major variations in the characteristics of these 'niche' institutions. For example, two women's colleges can differ widely in the quality of the basic services that they offer—one providing higher quality of general education than the other, or certain specialized services (read as 'specialization'), such as commerce, IT education and so on.

These four generic models provide a sound reference point for identifying and classifying higher education institutions into meaningful categories and present the institution with an opportunity to examine the focus of quality within the larger framework of the service mix. Some of the questions addressed could be whether to continue in the basic service category or consider offering enhanced services; or whether to introduce a series of enhanced services in sequence over a pre-planned time frame. The model also offers these institutions the option to shift from one category to another and accordingly choose their strategic plans.

Kaufman (1992) offered a four-stage model for strategic planning. These are:

1. Scoping
2. Data collection
3. Planning
4. Implementing and evaluating

Scoping

The quality initiative of an educational institution can have a small or a large agenda. It may imply quality improvement in a relatively smaller domain of a college or a university, impacting a department, a group of subjects or a group of students in a particular subject. In such cases, the scope is limited only to certain micro-operations. All the cases of quality improvement in classroom transaction or staff selection, for example, the case of NIEPA (Mukhopadhyay 2012a), are examples of micro-scoping.

When any quality initiative is intended to have an impact on the whole college or the university, it becomes a case of macro-scoping. The case of Chowgule College (Mukhopadhyay 2012a) highlights macro-scoping. Whenever an institution steps out of its defined boundaries to include transforming a community or a society, it is also a case of mega-scoping. Hence, the first stage of strategic planning is to define the scope of quality initiative.

Data Collection

The second stage of strategic planning deals with collecting data and information on a variety of issues, which intrinsically determine the baseline on which the quality initiative is to be mounted.

Authentic data and information are needed for defining the following:

- Ideal Vision: An articulated statement displayed in public or known to all the members of the organization (staff and students).
- Beliefs and Values: The beliefs and values of the members of the institution, which highlights whether 'we can do it' or 'this is not possible' and citing a variety of reasons and alibis for the same.
- Current Missions: The immediate tasks, goals, objectives and targets.
- Ideal and Current Results: The current level of performance on the 'ideal' criteria as laid down by the institution. In the metaphor of cricket, we can refer to this as the current run rate versus required run rate.
- Needs: An action plan to achieve the required run rate or ideal results.

Instead of collecting data sporadically, it is advisable to continuously gather data according to a schedule over a period of time to understand the trend. In many cases, we have experienced significant changes or improvements without any necessarily planned intervention. For example, increase in enrolment during the last several years, the gender parity index in the colleges or the universities, or even the results may have changed without any change in infrastructure, academic staff or additional financing. Only consistently collected data can provide such revelations about the latest trend.

Thus, for the purpose of decision making based on the current facts and as a prerequisite to strategic planning, it is essential to develop an inventory of items about various aspects of the institution wherever data are necessary. The next step is to determine the nature and source of data and the frequency of data updation. All such areas with defined interrelationships create the 'Educational Management Information System'.

Planning

Planning comprises five important activities.

1. The first and foremost is the identification of matches and mismatches. While there are certain areas and activities that can complement (match) each another, others can contradict

(mismatch) one another. It is important to identify these inter-relationships clearly.
2. The second stage is reconciliation.
3. The third stage is to collectively develop short-term and long-term missions, which would help in guiding future initiatives.
4. The fourth stage is to carry out a SWOT analysis and identify strengths, weaknesses, opportunities and threats. On the basis of the SWOT analysis and mission statements (both short-term and long-term), the strategic move is to decide institutional policies and rules for decision making. Further, the focus should be on rules and practices in decision making rather than on the actual decisions per se.
5. The final stage is to develop strategic action plans by identifying and planning activities that could become enablers for each of the stated missions, and 'projectizing' each activity (by splitting into sub-modules) for time-bound completion with predefined criteria for evaluation of success.

Implementing and Evaluating

This is the final stage, comprising the following:

- Putting the plan into action
- Carrying out formative evaluation
- Carrying out summative evaluation
- Continuing or revising (as and when required)

Kaufman's (1992) four-stage mechanism of strategic planning with all its subcomponents provides a working model for strategic planning.

Sallis (2002) approached the issue quite differently. He identified six events as planning sequence for TQM. These are mission and vision, values and goals, customer learner requirements, routes to success, quality performance, investing in people and evaluating the process. For each of the seven issues, he raised some useful guiding questions. For example, the most fundamental question is 'what's the purpose of the institute?' What do students expect from an institution and how does an institution ascertain those needs; what are the critical success factors and what are the plans to achieve success;

what are the quality benchmarks, delivery mechanisms and cost of quality of pre-specified benchmark; how to make best use of staff and enhance their capacities; what are some of the indicators of success and whether there are mechanisms to take charge of something goes wrong.

Thus, according to Sallis, important issues in strategic planning for quality management are learners' requirements, routes to success (action plans), quality benchmarks, human resource management and monitoring and evaluation.

ADRI Quality Cycle

Curtin University (2013) offered another strategic plan model. This comprises the ADRI cycle. Each component has been further elaborated with indicators and benchmarks.

- Approach: Looks at the intents and goals of improvement; strategies, structures and process and their justification; benchmarking of performance indicators against best practices, and mechanisms of monitoring progress in performance.
- Deployment: This dimension concentrates on how effectively the approach is being put to practice.
- Results: Assessment of results or effects of deployment of approaches and strategies.
- Improvement: A major concern is to assess whether the institution is conscious and actively engaged in the understanding of its improvement.

A modified version is practised in University of Tasmania, Australia (UTAS) (Broatach 2007). In this version, objective is taken out of approach and used as standalone. It is represented as (O) ADRI.

Swinburne University (2012) has set up a semi-permanent mechanism known as 'strategic planning and quality (SPQ) unit' for continuous quality management. A few of the responsibilities of the SPQ unit are to deliver better integrated planning mechanisms, stakeholders' feedback and statistical and quality management services.

Further, the unit is also responsible for managing the implementation of the university's planning framework, providing comprehensive strategic reporting for the key internal and external stakeholders, developing and implementing procedures to gather and report feedback from a wide range of stakeholders, supporting all units within the university in audit, reviewing and benchmarking processes, as well as coordinating the annual Vice-Chancellor's Awards process.[4]

As it is evident from the above descriptions, there are overlaps on different issues and structures among the various strategic planning models. The four models (Murgatroyd and Morgan, Kaufman, Sallis and ADRI Cycle) that have been presented above offer certain orientations to the concept of strategic planning for quality management in educational institutions. However, it is possible to integrate these models and create a synergy (Mukhopadhyay 2005a).

Each category of institution (e.g., OA-BS or ES-NA, as described by Murgatroyd and Morgan) needs to define its scope and methods of data collection, planning, implementing and evaluating (Kaufman), as much as it must define its missions and vision, customer focus, routes to success, quality performance and methods of investing in people (Sallis). Similarly, each type of institution must define its approach to quality management, deployment of resources and infrastructure as well as policy parameters, in addition to evaluation of results/outcomes with reference to key performance areas, internal self-assessment, student satisfaction survey and actual improvement (ADRI).

Ideally, a new strategic planning model should be derived by taking the best, but compatible components from all these models, and quality circle. Since the largest single proportion of Indian higher education institutions belong to the OA-BS typology, special efforts are needed to create strategic plans for quality management in this category of institutions.

Proposed Strategic Plan Model (Mukhopadhyay)

On the basis of my learning from various models and our experience of quality management in certain Indian educational institutions,

---

[4] Available at http://www.swinburne.edu.au/corporate/spq/ (accessed on 7 May 2014).

I propose a model with seven interlinked and interdependent components that is more culture specific (Figure 5.2).[5] These are:

1. Beliefs, vision, missions and goals
2. Learners' needs assessment and client education
3. Quality audit
4. Quality policy and intervention plan
5. Cost of quality
6. Planning for implementation
7. Evaluation and feedback

Figure 5.2:
Strategic Plan Model for Quality Management

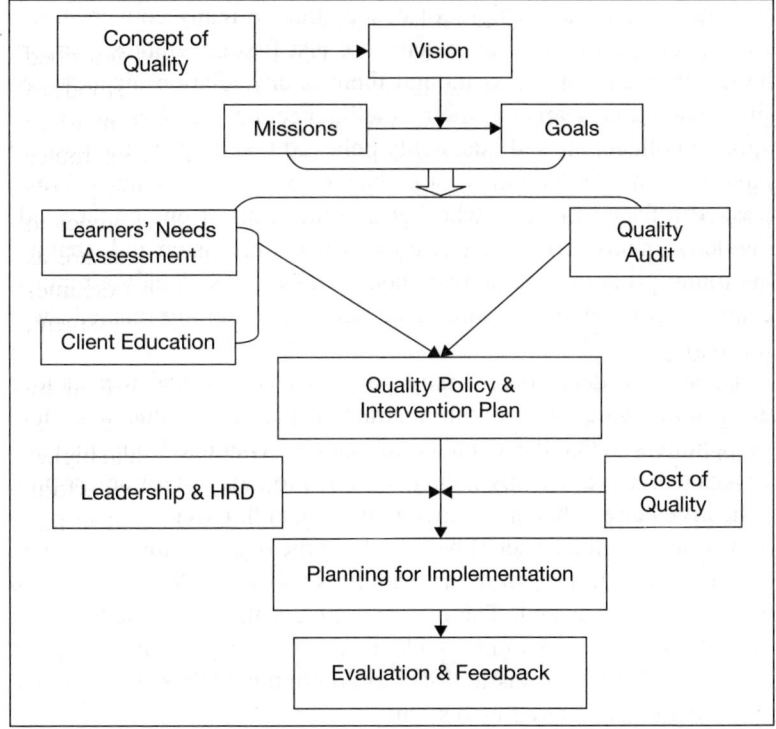

Source: Author.

---

[5] The figure has been adapted from author's earlier model published in Mukhopadhyay (2005a).

Beliefs, Vision, Missions and Goals

Our beliefs guide our actions. Although there are no formal mechanisms in educational organizations for articulating beliefs, there is ample evidence about what we believe in our utterances.

When you visit a college or a university and interact with teaching and non-teaching staff, the people in senior management, students and student leaders, you can more or less decipher their inherent beliefs from their thought processes that reflect 'possibility thinking' (Schuller 2006) versus 'impossibility thinking'. This determines whether an innovative practice or a quality initiative can be successfully implemented in the institution or not.

I have come across signs of desperation in many conversations, such as a 'majority of our students are just first generation learners; hence, they cannot...', as though there is any relationship between first-generation learners, their intelligence or learning skills. In another college, the staff staunchly believed that they are the best till I asked them: 'Are you the best in the world or in the country?' When I asked a friend of mine who became the head of one of the leading departments in a university about what is his vision and what are his future programmes, he responded coolly, 'It is already a reputed centre, there is nothing more to be done'. He literally relaxed there for three years!

Beliefs are deep-rooted; they guide our action, and they colour the vision. Hence, one possible strategic plan is to understand and share beliefs so that the actual beliefs can be separated from what one wishes to believe, thereby laying down the foundation for developing collective beliefs that are founded on rational thinking.

Vision is built on a set of beliefs about the organization, its people, environment, culture, structure, facilities and so on. Vision is of two types: near and distant. The distant vision is the dream or imagination. According to Swami Vivekananda, imagination plays a great role in one's life. An institution should continuously strive to reach that imagined and envisaged status.

Such a vision is not limited by time and quality. Even 'best' is relative and there is a continuous shift in what is defined as the 'best'; for, the 'good' ones are always moving towards the 'better' and the 'better' towards the 'best'. Even if being the best can be time bound, staying there is a timeless endeavour.

Vision can just be a philosophical description that 'inspires people for generations to come', or a pragmatic statement that is developed through rigorous participative exercise involving all the stakeholders. To cite an example, I conducted development workshops using the Appreciative Inquiry Model in several higher education institutions. After two days of this intensive workshop involving all the 75 teachers and the principal, St. Joseph's College for Women, an autonomous college in Visakhapatnam, set up their vision to reach A+ National Assessment and Accreditation Council (NAAC) rating within two years and become a deemed university within 10 years. This aspiration looks more concrete, defined and goal-oriented compared to visions like 'world-class institution' or 'creating leaders in all walks of human endeavour'.

Missions are nothing but vision unbundled. Missions are directional statements that define the purpose of an institution. Unfortunately, most institutions do not have a documented articulation of mission statements. Through reductionism, we can arrive at goals that are missions unbundled. Goals are like mileposts. Each goal should contribute to the achievement of the missions. Goals determine the activities, programmes and processes that are followed in the institution. Also, goals determine the method by which a programme needs to be offered.

Learners' Needs Assessment and Client Education

There are two different strands with respect to learners' needs assessment. These are 'needs' versus 'wants'. Further, higher education students are ready for employment, and they live almost an adult life at home. Hence, the needs and wants paradigm also has 'self' versus 'others' issue—what does a student need and what does she/he want versus what do members of the family and friends think about the needs and wants of the graduate student (Figure 5.3).

Figure 5.3:
Learner Needs–Wants Matrix

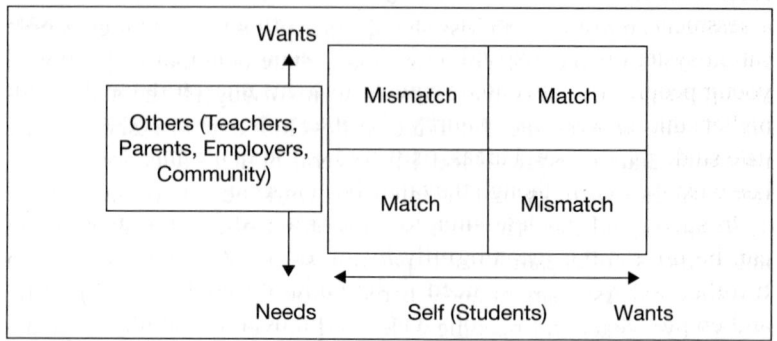

Source: Author.

While needs are 'hygienic', wants are 'motivating'. Needs are necessary conditions, whereas wants are sufficient conditions. There is yet another issue—unknown or unrecognized versus recognized needs and wants. For example, passing the graduate examination is a known need for most students, and performing well in the examination may be known needs for some, especially good students. What goes unknown or unrecognized to a majority of students is that qualification is no guarantee to gaining employment. In fact, the university certificates act only as an 'admit card' for competitive examinations, say, civil services examination, teacher recruitment through National Eligibility Test (NET) or State Eligibility Test (SET), Central Teacher Eligibility Test (CTET) or Teacher Aptitude Test (TAT), banking recruitment through BSRB or recruitment to the Indian Army through the Army Recruitment Board and so on. What is also unknown and unrecognized is the delinking of jobs from qualifications.

Another dominant issue in contemporary Indian education is the issue of employability. The authorities of a majority of colleges and universities are still oblivious of the significance of specifying and developing employability skills and 'generic graduate skills' among their students. The same is the case with the students. 'Transition to work' kinds of programmes have not been introduced in the Indian universities as yet.

The next critical dimension is the self versus others issue. The needs and wants perceptions of self (students) and others (employers, parents, peers, teachers and community) may or may not match. But others, especially employers, are an important constituency. Hence, a usual market survey that gathers details about 'graduate students' needs assessment' is not appropriate, especially when the Indian higher education system is fast expanding and embracing a huge mass of 'new' young people who have just ventured into this unexplored territory of higher education. A large majority of the students, especially undergraduate students from rural areas, may not be able to meaningfully articulate what they need, though they may be able to say what they want.

In such a not-so-clear situation, the needs and wants assessment can be done more meaningfully by introducing 'client education'. In other words, students need to be educated about employability and employability skills, jobs and entrepreneurial opportunities and diversities, local and global markets in local areas and exclusive local markets, emerging skill scenarios and their demand and so on. In this manner, students should be oriented and made aware of what exists currently and what is likely to emerge in the future and then make an informed decision (about what they 'need' versus what they 'want').[6]

Thus, the second important step in strategic planning is to provide 'client education' or orient higher education students about the emerging job market, skill requirement and so on and then clearly assess the learners' 'needs' in addition to what they 'want' to learn.

Quality Audit

Quality audit is the starting point for any quality journey. The purpose of quality audit is to clearly and objectively ascertain 'where does the institution stand currently on the quality continuum?' Should we call it

---

[6] An incident may illustrate this point. I was evaluating an adult education programme in one of the districts in West Bengal. In one of the centres, as part of a literacy test, a lady was reading out to me from her book in Bengali. I noticed the pattern of her 'halting' and her errors in reading. I told her to use spectacles, but she brushed my suggestion aside with near ridicule and said, 'I chop vegetables without even looking at the *banti* (the cutter used in Bengali homes). I have no problem with my eyes'. I cajoled her to put on my spectacles as my younger sister. Now, she obliged, and then read absolutely fluently. Without spectacles, she was missing the dots that make 'ba' as 'ra' or a slash that change 'ya' to 'sha', in Bengali script and so on. Only now did she realize that she needs to check with an eye specialist and probably needs an assistive spectacles.

'Baseline Survey of Quality'? Since it is not possible to classify a complex multidimensional organization like a college or a university based on one single point on the quality scale, the quality audit should also ideally serve the purpose of what a SWOT analysis would do, namely identify the areas of strengths, weaknesses, opportunities and threats.

We carried out the SWOT analysis exercise with several hundred principals of colleges during our management workshops (a sample SWOT sheet is given in Table 5.1). While strengths and weaknesses are easily recognizable, principals often find it rather difficult to identify opportunities and threats. This may be because opportunities and threats are often hidden and not apparent.

Table 5.1:
SWOT Analysis of an Educational Institution

Strengths	*Weaknesses*
• Good building facilities	• Poor academic results
• Strong dramatics and sports activities	• Poor staff quality
• Strong social action activities	• Inadequate sports and games facilities
• Enthusiastic management	• Lack of recognition for social action programmes
Opportunities	*Threats*
• Multiple use of building	• Teachers union activities and low staff morale
• Excellence in dramatics and sports activities	• Exodus of talented students for better sports facilities
• Enthusiastic and supportive local community and alumni	• Loss of image from being a high-profile socially sensitive institution to being termed as a conventional institution
• Fund mobilization for innovative activities	• Withdrawal of community support

Source: Author.

A SWOT analysis is a participative process of organizational diagnosis. There are several ways in which this is actually carried out. A SWOT analysis can be done through a participative focused group approach or based on an institutional profile developed through some kind of organizational assessment instrument (Mukhopadhyay's Institutional Assesssment System [MIAS] in Mukhopadhyay 2005a is one such example). There are many such instruments. I have found better results through a three-step process of SWOT.

1. Administer an institutional assessment instrument
2. Tabulate the data to draw a profile
3. Present the profile to the staff to discuss and develop consensus.

Another very useful practice is to adopt a four-dimensional (4D) model of Appreciative Inquiry following the Discover, Dream, Design and Deliver cycle. It is one of the recognized ways of strategizing change management. While SWOT analysis is possible, quality audit through NAAC's instruments, I guess, is a better choice. These evaluation instruments are well developed, and NAAC has rightly been encouraging setting up of an internal quality assurance cell (IQAC) and quality audit.

Thus, the third important step in strategic planning is to carry out a quality audit through a collective process.

Quality Policy and Intervention Plan

Following the quality audit is the task of deciding the quality policy. The starting point of this stage depends upon two fundamental questions: 'What is the current status and position of the institution and where does it want to go?' To answer this, the most fundamental questions include the following:

- Is the institution still in the formative period—a budding one and still to brand itself?
- Is the institution in its rapid growth period, say, three- to five-year-old?
- Has the institution reached the steady state? Is it one of the average ones?
- Has the institution earned reputation—Is it already a reputed one?
- Is the institution in a crisis, facing threat to its reputation or existence?

The quality policy will obviously differ according to the present state of the institution. For example, the quality policy for an institution in crisis will be to come out of the crisis so that normalcy is restored and the stage is set for development. The quality policy for a stable running institution will be to improve its quality and standard further. The quality policy for a reputed institution will be to retain its top position or 'stay there' (as we say in TQM), and scale up its standards to distinguish itself as a 'great' institution.

Furthermore, the quality policy for the top 10 institutions like Harvard, Oxford, Caltech and others will be to sustain their top positions and strive for further excellence. The quality policy for a NAAC's 'B' grade college or a university will be to reach the standard of 'A' or 'A+' grade. Thus, the journey has to go on by setting higher targets with the passage of time. The intervention plan is guided by the quality policy and quality agenda—near and the distant ones. Let me refer back to our workshop at St. Joseph's College that set its near and distant goals (read as 'grounded quality policy') to

a. achieve A+ grade in NAAC assessment (at that time, it was in the 'B' grade category),
b. rank in the top 10 autonomous colleges in India and
c. become a deemed university.

The staff worked in smaller groups and identified the following areas of development to achieve the quality policies and goals:

- High-quality professional course in journalism and mass communication
- ICT-enabled learning
- E-learning/online learning hub
- Total interdepartmental flexibility through choice-based credit system (CBCS)
- Effective placement network
- Networking and collaboration/tie-ups for projects with other agencies
- PG centre for excellence in home science
- Enhancing student enrolment
- Starting a research centre

This incidence illustrates how college teachers spelt out their intervention plan. The next step was to convert each of the nine items into a time-bound project. Similarly, colleges and universities are recommended to devise their intervention plan to implement the quality policy. Another innocuous intervention plan is the use of Kaizen, a Japanese term that is used to describe a small intervention that can contribute to improving quality in a particular area. Let us take an example to illustrate the same (Box 5.1).

Box 5.1:
A Kaizen in Staff Development

It is a story that dates 30 years back. Technology has changed but the relevance of the case remains valid.

The principal of a college in Mumbai arranged a few audio-cassette recorders and some blank cassettes. His articulated intention was to develop a collection of audio lessons in the library for students to access if they missed a class or needed remedial learning. He asked the teachers (whosoever was willing) to take a cassette recorder and blank cassettes to the class and record their lectures. The teachers were also asked to take the recorded cassette and the recorder home and listen to the recorded lecture. Only if the teacher was satisfied with the quality of the lecture and recording, the cassette could be submitted/delivered to the librarian. If the teacher was not satisfied, he/she could erase the contents and re-record the next class. The teachers were not expected to get feedback from any other person, including the principal; however, the teachers were free to consult anyone they liked.

What happened was quite surprising and interesting. During the first four months, no audio cassette was submitted in the library, though the teachers regularly borrowed the cassette recorders and blank cassettes. Every teacher received self-feedback while listening to their recorded lectures. In fact, many teachers voluntarily started sharing their recorded lectures with their peers and took feedback. In the end, besides developing a rich repository of good quality audio lectures, the standard of classroom instruction in the college improved substantially.

Source: Author.

This is an interesting example to illustrate how a simple intervention can result in long-term improvement. On the one hand, the library was getting enriched with a new form of instructional material, which could help in reinforcement of learning to those who needed to listen to the same lecture or missed a particular class. On the other hand, it gradually helped in improving the quality of classroom instruction.

An important strategy is to raise relevant questions vis-à-vis quality management in the institution. The answers to such questions should help in drafting the list of intervention areas and activities. To translate strategic planning with involvement of all, you can use an institutional planning form (Table 5.2).

Table 5.2:
Institutional Planning Form

Target Year	Goals	Activities	Responsibilities	Monitor Quality	Resources
2021					
2020					
2019					
2018					
2017					
2016					

Source: Author.

This form has been used to develop a perspective plan for several educational institutions. This is usually done by a group of teachers in a committee, and the draft of this perspective plan is presented to the entire faculty. On the basis of further discussions and consensus, the perspective plan is finalized.

I experimented with another implementable strategy in several institutions. The principals were asked to identify three improvements that could be made to the current state of the institution without requesting for additional resources. Subsequently, they had to take certain decisions and tabulate them. An example for such a short-term intervention plan is given in Table 5.3.

Among many interesting results of such experiments, the story of a DIET in Punjab is worth highlighting in this context.[7] While

---

[7] The story has been told in Chapter 10.

Table 5.3:
Planning Format for a Short-term Intervention (a Kaizen)

	Activities		
Decisions	*1*	*2*	*3*
Responsibility			
Time frame			
Possible problems			
Possible solution to each problem			
Criteria for success			
Desirable resources			
Remarks			

Source: Author.

conducting a workshop on TQM with principals of DIETs in Punjab, one of the principals complained about the pathetic condition of the campus—a big campus—buildings are dirty and untidy, open space is full of bushes and jungle. There was no staff or financial provision for maintenance. The principal broached the issue during the workshop. I asked the principal to speak with teachers and students whether they would like a beautiful campus; if yes, how can it be developed without any additional resources. He submitted the case of transformation during one of the video conferences.

Under the guidance and active involvement of teachers, groups of students were formed who took charge of small sections/areas of the campus. Within six months the campus became sparkling clean and stood beautiful with a bounty of flowers and plants. This was just one of the three ideas proposed by the principal that had an enormous impact. Similar exercises can be conducted within the institution by calling all the teachers to identify two or three possible improvements that could be made to the present state of the institution.

Each idea for activity can be strategically planned in the format given in Table 5.3. Some activities can be done individually, some implemented in groups and some others executed by the institution as a whole. This will satisfy the important criteria of continuous quality improvement with participation from all members of the institution.

Cost of Quality

There is a common belief that quality is expensive and can be achieved only when there is a large flow of resources (human, infrastructure, finance and so on). In reality, this is a myth (Burke and Mckenzie 2009; Crosby 1979).

Many a time, the element that goes unrecognized in the discourse on cost of quality is the cost of wastage and stagnation due to poor quality. Having invested a huge amount of money that may not be comparable to the per student expenditure in the top 100 universities in the world, poor quality education leaves more than 80 per cent of graduates unemployable (Aspiring Minds 2013) and 47 per cent engineering graduates unemployable. The cost of such unemployable graduates and its impact on (poor) economic growth far outweighs the cost of quality.

A critical aspect of quality management is cost consciousness, wherein the efficiency of every small investment may be assessed in terms of its contribution to quality improvement and management. Let me cite an example. During my recent visit to one of the reputed colleges, I was shown a brand new computer laboratory. On the first look, it was a huge and impressive facility. However, on critical observation, I found that the gallery style class had rows and rows of desktops placed at a level that would most probably hide the face of the student.

I asked a few questions to the principal:

- Why did you buy desktops and not laptops or even Netbooks?
- Why did you mount them on bench-like furniture and made students to sit on uncomfortable wooden stools?
- Would it be more cost effective if this room was carpeted and students were allowed to squat with their pre-charged laptops on their laps (since fully charged laptops work for almost three hours, whereas each lecture session was conducted only for 45 minutes to 1 hour)?
- What other options would be less expensive and more comfortable to facilitate learning?

Without any hesitation, the principal accepted that he had neither seen nor thought of such a design, nor could he imagine this arrangement. However, he did acknowledge that such a design will reduce the cost of the set-up, especially the cost of furniture and provide better ambience for learning. From this viewpoint, it is evident that effective utilization of resources is more important than the quantity or sophistication of the resources.

If we take the case of human resources, the salary alone costs more than 80 per cent of the annual budget of a college. Unless human resources are optimized, wherein all the teachers take all the scheduled classes and update themselves by reading and researching (they are already paid for [preparedness cost]), any amount of investment will be infructuous. From a strategic planning perspective, there are certain associated issues. UGC has mandated that teachers must stay in the college for certain number of hours every day. In most colleges, teachers do not have a dignified place to sit and work, and the only provision is a few wooden or folding steel chairs (bought under L1 quotation), often inadequate to sit all the teachers around a long table full of chalk dust and a few newspapers strewn around. I have seen the college where I started my college teaching in 1969; I have seen it in 2013 in the college where I was a student. Even if a teacher wants to utilize his/her time, she/he does not have the ambiance for academic work.

Another fundamental element is the optimal use of infrastructure: library, laboratory, audiovisual aids, sports and games facilities, gymnasium and so on. It is important to identify all the available resources. While some are obvious, others are latent and often go unnoticed. The strategic plan for quality must identify and document and exploit all the available resources.

Thus, cost consciousness and cost management are two important components of the cost of quality issue. Very often, we are not cost conscious. For example, what is the hourly teaching cost of a college teacher vis-à-vis the hourly cost of his/her service? A full-time professor usually has a teaching load of 8 hours per week. In 42 weeks, he/she teaches 336 periods (hours). At the rate of, say, ₹ 0.1 million per month, the annual salary of a full professor is ₹ 1.2 million. Thus, the cost per class hour comes to ₹ 3,571.00. However, if we extrapolate the expected hours of service at the rate of 40 hours a week, the cost of service becomes ₹ 715.00. There is a five-time jump from the cost of service to the cost of a class. The reason for this is that a professor is also expected to read, research, write, publish (profess) and extend[8] his expertise with others, especially the community. If all the time is used for the defined purposes, the quality of education will surely improve.

There are several studies including those conducted by the National Commission on Teachers (1983) indicating that not many teachers prepare before class. There are innumerable cases of the lack of research and research publications to help cross the career advancement scheme (CAS) barriers. In addition, investment in staff development is far too limited. Academic staff colleges (ASCs) are an apt example for this contention. First, they lack scientific organizational design. Without adequate senior and suitably qualified staff, ASCs have been left to fend for themselves as an 'event management outfit'. The policymakers have made elaborate provisions for airlines and Indian railways to benefit, but not as much for the purpose of staff development. An 'expert' is paid ₹ 20,000 for airfare, but only ₹ 500 or 1,000 for a technical training session! There are countless cases of ASC directors apologizing to the guest speakers for this demeaning provision.

Academic staff is the most critical factor for success, and we are not deriving enough from this resource. Most institutions offer conventional programmes that contribute to maintenance learning, but not innovative learning (Botkin, Elmandjra and Malitza 1979). Hence, strategic planning must accommodate a detailed mechanism of human resource development.

Strategic planning for quality must have cost consciousness and Return on Investment (ROI) estimates for every investment made, either as a routine or as an innovative programme.

Planning for Implementation

Fancy statements like 'we are good planners, but bad managers' are made by armchair planners who are miles away from the grassroots realities. No plan is good unless it can be implemented and managed. No plan is good unless it takes into account the level of human

---

[8] This holds good even if we club the time for student evaluation with teaching hours considering that no teaching takes place during examination days.

resources and material and financial resources. Quality management has no space for romanticizing planning. Plans must be executable. Planning for implementation is that component of strategic planning which details out the activities, time frame, resource allocation, monitoring details and benchmarks of success. In other words, planning for implementation looks for answers to a series of questions that are associated with each of the seven stages of planning. To understand this, please refer to the short-term intervention plan sample discussed earlier. To illustrate further about developing suitable questions with respect to planning for implementation, just two sample questions for each of the four criteria, for each of the seven stages, are given in Table 5.4. Each institution intending to improve and manage quality must raise such relevant questions on the basis of its own background and personality.

Evaluation and Feedback

A strategic plan is incomplete without the mention of evaluation and feedback. The first and foremost task in this stage is to define the criteria for evaluation of success. Then, the frequency and mechanism of evaluation and feedback is established. The basic purpose of evaluation and feedback is quality assurance, not quality control. Hence, evaluation does not mean passing judgments about the success or failure of a plan or an activity. The purpose is to assess quantitative and qualitative aspects of implementation of the strategic plan—the distance travelled from the place of origin and the distance remaining to reach the destination (which is the target quality standard). These are directly linked to the milepost concept mentioned earlier.

Thus, evaluation has to be formative. Besides listing achievements, it should point out the weaker aspects of the plan implementation, warning signals about prospective disasters so that the mid-course corrections can be planned and executed. The frequency of evaluation should depend upon the kind of activity planned. It can be carried out on a monthly, quarterly or half-yearly basis for the annual plan, annually for the short-term plan and bi-annually for the long-term plan. It is extremely important that the strategic plan contains the

Table 5.4:
Sample Questions for Developing Planning for Implementation

Seven steps in Strategic Planning	Activities	Indicators of Success	Resources	Monitoring
Beliefs, vision and missions	• What are the activities to be undertaken for developing a shared vision of the institution? • How will the vision be unbundled into missions, goals and activities?	• Do you have a vision and missions statement? • How feasible is it to achieve the stated vision and missions?	• What financial resources are required? • What expert resources are needed?	• How would you monitor the process of development of vision, missions and so on? • How would you ensure the quality of vision, missions and so on and their worthwhileness and achievability?
Learners' needs assessment and client education	• What activities will be undertaken to assess learners' needs? • How would you educate your clients?	• Do you have a document that describes learners' needs? • Do you have a report on client education and its results?	• What financial resources are required to assess learners' needs? • Who will carry out the learners' needs assessment and client education?	• How would you ensure timely accomplishment of learners' needs assessment and client education programmes? • How would you ensure quality and reliability?
Quality audit	• Which tool would you use to assess your institution? • When and to whom would you administer it? • How would you develop a SWOT analysis sheet?	• Do you have an institutional profile? • Do you have a mutually accepted SWOT analysis sheet?	• What financial resources are required? • What kind of expertise is required to carry out institutional assessment and SWOT analysis? Where will you get that expertise from?	• How would you ensure timely accomplishment of these tasks? • How would you ensure quality of assessment, organizational diagnosis and their acceptability among staff?

Quality policy and intervention plan	• When and how would you develop your quality policy? • How would you develop intervention plans and ensure that these contribute to the achievement of the quality policy?	• Do you have a statement of quality policy that highlights the standard to be achieved? • Do you have a set of activities that are identified to achieve the quality policy?	• What financial resources are required to develop the quality policy and intervention plan? • Where would you derive those financial resources from?	• How would you ensure timely development of the quality policy and intervention plan?
Cost of quality	• How would you work out the differential contribution of investment items on quality? • How would you estimate the financial requirements for implementing the planned intervention?	• Do you have a cost analysis of spending on various aspects of the institution vis-a-vis contribution to quality? • Have you worked out the cost estimation for each activity of the planned quality management?	• How much time do you need to assess the differential contribution of investment from quality management? • Who will carry out the cost studies?	• How would you ensure that the intervention plans indeed contribute to and will lead to fructifying the quality policy?
Planning for implementation	• What will be the mechanism for developing a plan for implementation? • How would you identify those factors that can potentially be the roadblocks in implementing the strategic plan?	• Do you have a mutually agreed upon PERT chart for implementing the strategic plan? • Do you have a document identifying these risk	• What financial resources are required to implement the plan? • Who will be responsible for each of the listed activities?	• Does the implementation plan take into account the cost of all the activities? • Has an individual or a group been identified and assigned the responsibilities for each of the listed activities?
Evaluation and feedback	• What tools would you use for evaluation and feedback? • What would be the frequency of evaluation? • How would you ensure that the evaluation is objective and not coloured by self-fulfilling prophecies?	• Do you have a documented plan for evaluating the listed activities? • Do you have a document on how the feedback will be given and how the mid-course corrections will be carried out?	• What resources (financial, human and time) are required to evaluate and give feedback?	• Do you have a schedule for evaluation? • How would you ensure that the evaluation process is neither fault finding nor a self-fulfilling prophecy?

Source: Author.

details of evaluation methods and frequency of evaluation in addition to the people responsible for conducting the evaluation.

A more competent way of conducting evaluation is to develop a 'monitoring and evaluation framework', which clearly spells out wherever possible in quantitative terms, the outputs, outcomes and impacts.[9]

For each of the seven stages of the strategic plan, every institute needs to answer certain questions (Table 5.4). The answers to these questions will provide the basis and substance for the strategic planning.

Conclusion

A strategic plan is the way to transform a quality agenda into reality. We have reviewed a few standard recommended models and proposed a new model that should fit in an Indian context. What is important is to identify the basic pattern and style of the institution and adapt a suitable strategic plan model. In the process, an institution may develop a plan that is unique and best suited for it. The real indicator of success lies in devising a strategic plan that reflects that uniqueness of the institution and showcases it successfully to the world.

---

[9] In this framework, in staff development (for example), the output is measured in terms of the number of teachers trained. The outcome is the change in the work style of the teacher (trainee), and the impact is measured in terms of the changes that are observed in the system (quality).

SECTION II

In-campus Quality Management

6

Curriculum in Higher Education

Introduction

The quality of higher education has often been equated with the quality of curriculum. Notwithstanding the question of validity of such an equation, it indicates the central role played by the curriculum as being the primary determinant to assess the quality of education in higher education. Such a perception is dominant in higher education largely because the structure of knowledge or the 'discipline' is the prime concern in higher education. The reasons are not far to seek. Since research in higher education is concerned with knowledge creation, the structure of knowledge naturally occupies the prime space in higher education mindset. Consequently, the list of contents identified for different levels of courses in higher education is considered as the prime indicator for the quality of higher education.

Despite such strong faith and belief on the content as being the sole indicator and determinant of the quality of higher education, there is ample scope for a critical debate as to what constitutes the quality of curriculum in higher education. The taste of a pudding actually lies in eating it. On a similar note, the quality of higher education is singularly defined by the product quality, namely the quality of students (their academic and non-academic skills). Curriculum would have played a significant role in the development of knowledge, skills and attitudes. Hence, curriculum (as the list of contents covered in a subject) cannot be attributed to be solely responsible for the quality of graduates. Yet, curriculum plays a very significant role in determining the quality of higher education. In this chapter, we will examine the issues regarding the quality of curriculum in higher education in Indian universities under six major heads (Figure 6.1).

Figure 6.1:
Quality of Curriculum in Higher Education: Concept Map

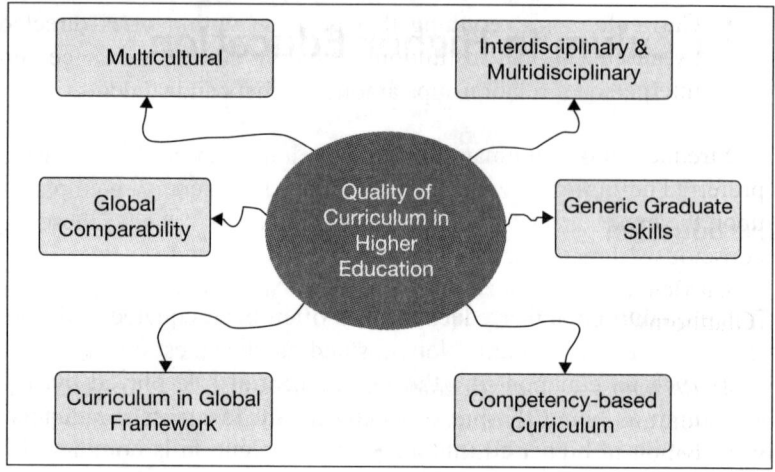

Source: Author.

Curriculum Defined

Before we enter into the debate and discussion on the quality of curriculum, it is important to revisit the concept of curriculum itself.

Curriculum is often equated with syllabuses and contents. This is typically the narrow and conventional description of curriculum. In reality, syllabuses and contents are actually only a subset of a curriculum. Just as a subset can never be equal to the complete set, syllabuses and contents are not equal to curriculum. This leaves us to explore the concept and definition of curriculum. Let us review a few definitions on curriculum from standard literature on educational sciences.

Oliva (1982) illustrates the 'amorphous nature of curriculum' using a range of definitions gleaned from different sources:

- Curriculum is a set of subjects.
- Curriculum is content.
- Curriculum is a set of materials.
- Curriculum is a set of performance objectives.
- Curriculum is experience of guided learning.
- Curriculum is everything that goes on within or is directed by an educational institution, including student guidance and interpersonal relationships among teachers and students.

Streuner and Tuijnman (1994) conclude: 'through the years, preferred definition of curriculum has placed an increasing emphasis upon the experiences of the learners, regardless of whether these are consciously directed or indirect'.

Curriculum has been distinguished into several categories (Glatthorn 2000):

1. *Recommended curriculum*: A document in which a committee, an individual or an institute has formally laid down what is believed to be a useful curriculum for a discipline or for some interdisciplinary topics.
2. *Written or mandatory curriculum*: Giving the curriculum an official status by prescribing the list of targets to be attained/ topics to be covered, examination syllabus and so on.
3. *Taught curriculum*: The topics that the teachers actually teach in the classroom.
4. *Supportive curriculum*: The learning resources, such as textbooks, manuals, timetables, equipments and so on used in classrooms.
5. *Tested curriculum*: Curriculum covered by tests, evaluations and examinations.
6. *Learned curriculum*: This is what students actually learn during the educational programme. These are not measured by tests and examinations. It does not even include what is prescribed. It may have a broader scope.

One important indicator of the quality of curriculum is the extent of match between the recommended curriculum and the learned curriculum.

Foshay (2000) presents an interesting 3D model of curriculum consisting of purpose, substance and practice. Foshay's conceptualization of the purpose of a curriculum opens new ground for thinking about the fundamental purpose of the curriculum itself.

According to him, there are six different purposes of curricula as follows:

- The transcendent self
- The aesthetic self
- The physical self
- The emotional self
- The social self
- The intelligent self

Contrary to conventional conceptualization, Foshay does not see the purpose of curriculum as promoting only the intelligent self or, at best, a combination of intelligent and social self. According to him, a curriculum becomes comprehensive and fulfils the purpose only if it includes emotional, physical and aesthetic self and, most importantly, self that transcends known and normal boundaries of life. This echoes well with the description of the nature of education in ancient Indian literature that says, '*sa vidya ya vimuktaye*' (what liberates is education from Sri Vishnupurana[1]) and my 'educatedness paradigm' described in Chapter 1.

For Foshay, substance includes mathematics, science, history (social studies), language and literature and so on. The components of practice comprise evaluation, cost, governance as well as circumstances, such as when, where, how, why, what and who. He represents this in his 3D model.

---

[1] *tatkarma yanna bandhāaya sā vidyā yā vimuktaye| āyāsāyāparaṁ karma vidya'nyā śilpanaipuṇam*

That is action, which does not promote attachment. That is knowledge, which liberates (one from bondage). All other action is merely (pointless) effort/hardship. All other knowledge is merely another skill/craftsmanship.

The primary goal of higher education is to equip a young person with those fundamental knowledge, skills and values that help her/him in 'transition to work'—a successful and balanced professional, personal and social life (responsible and responsive citizenship). This cannot be achieved by just learning a set of subjects, howsoever modern they are. This transition to work, family life and society requires a large variety of generic life skills and employability skills that can only be developed through a variety of learning experiences, such as collective living, tolerance to differences, relating to others and so on. Hence, higher education curriculum must necessarily ensure a comprehensive, rich, positive in-campus experience, which constitutes training and practice in a formal setting, such as classrooms where curriculum is transacted through a series of structured methods (instruction and examination), as well as in an informal setting, such as peer-group interaction and interaction with teachers and non-academic staff, besides participating, organizing and managing a variety of co-scholastic and co-curricular activities.

In a very definite, yet a subtle way, the total in-campus experience is also influenced by the overall climate and ethos of the institution, which are determined by interpersonal relationships among the staff, staff and the students, the local community and the institution and leadership in the college or the university. In the absence of a structured programme for developing such life skills and competences, students in the colleges and universities pick up life skills largely from these informal, but important, experiences within the campus. For example, organizing and participating in the college/university union activities provides opportunities to develop leadership skills. In fact, a good number of Indian parliamentarians and legislators of different states underwent their initial experiences of politics and political leadership by playing an active role in college/university student unions. This is equally true for other professions like sports and games, music and so on. For our purpose, we will consider *curriculum as the total campus life experience*. Therefore, the quality of curriculum is determined by the quality of life in the campus. This also includes non-scholastic or co-scholastic activities, especially for developing the generic graduate skills.

Generic Graduate Skills

A world of work awaits university graduates. In the world of works, graduates are no more on the receiving end (knowledge); they switch over to the contributing end—contribute to productivity and performance of the organization. Their effectiveness on the job is evaluated by their contribution to the organization and by effectively performing their explicit and implicit roles. What matters is their knowledge, technical and professional skills and social and emotional skills. This transition to work[2] demands certain skills that are not cultivated by traditional transaction of conventional curriculum. It needs something more.

Conventionally, the focus of evaluation in higher education is on the learning outcome of the prescribed subjects by the students as measured by the performance in the examination. The hidden and far-reaching objectives are often different. These far-reaching objectives are to equip an individual with the required skills and competencies to lead a successful and responsible life in the society. Hence, the key purpose of higher education is developing and honing such skills and competencies of an individual that lead to an effective personal and professional life. Such skills are called generic graduate skills; some call these skills as life skills and even employability skills.

In fact, generic graduate skills are getting increasingly recognized as a major indicator of curriculum (holistic in-campus experience). The discourse on curriculum for graduates with respect to the generic graduate skills occupies an important space across the universities all over the world. These discourses have attempted to respond to some questions like the following:

- What are generic skills?
- Why should students have generic skills? What are its benefits?
- What are the current trends in generic skills learning in higher education?
- What are the various ways of developing generic skills?

---

[2] Available at https://ministers.employment.gov.au/abetz/new-transition-work-service (accessed on 12 May 2014).

Generic skills are often used to define a set of intellectual, social and emotional skills that are generic to the performance in learning both academic subjects and the skills required for leading a successful professional and personal life. A few generic skills include thinking skills like critical and analytical reasoning, creative thinking, problem solving, curiosity, intra- and interpersonal skills, effective communication skills (oral and written), teamwork, leadership, identifying, accessing and effectively utilizing knowledge, using technology, values and ethics, persistence, integrity and tolerance to differences and so on (Hager et al. 2002). Other skills are ability to cooperate with others, learning new skills, adapting to a new environment, being resilient, recognizing one's own strengths and weaknesses, managing emotions and so on. There are lot of overlaps between the list of employability skills mentioned in Chapter 3 and the generic skills mentioned here.

A major thrust for generic skills comes from businesses and employment since today's employers expect newly recruited employees to be readily productive to ensure business and work efficiency. In the recent past (also referred in Chapter 3), employability skills were flagged for national economic growth after the economic recession in the early 2000 in Europe and the United States (ECDL Report 2011). Also, the demand for generic skills emerged due to changes in technology and organizational landscape. These technologies are transforming the production and business processes as well as giving rise to new methods of functioning in the organizations to cope up with the developing trends. Generic skills provide the requisite skills and competencies to adapt to these evolving trends.

Due to a paradigm shift in the academic learning expectations from just assimilating existing information to discovering knowledge through exploration by means of problem solving and other academic pursuits, a new set of learning skills that is generic in nature needs to be defined and devised. The immediate and evident benefits of generic skills are enhanced employability for graduates, especially considering that in India, about 80 per cent of non-technical graduates and 47 per cent of engineering graduates are unemployable (Aspiring Minds 2013).

Generic skills education and assessment is relatively common among the Western universities, including the top 100 universities in the world. Many universities have a well-articulated policy on generic graduate skills. For example, the University of Sydney stated on its website:

> Graduate Attributes are central to the design, delivery and assessment of student learning in the Faculty of Arts and Social Sciences. Students are encouraged to acquire attributes in scholarship, global citizenship and lifelong learning.
>
> In the context of their learning in a range of disciplines and subjects, students will develop key generic skills in:
>
> • Research and inquiry
> • Information literacy
> • Personal and intellectual autonomy
> • Ethical, social and professional understanding
> • Communication

The University of Sydney has also formulated and revised its 'Generic Graduate Attributes policy' based on its in-house research while benchmarking similar interventions at other international universities, like Oxford.[3]

Research indicates that there are different kinds of teaching–learning methodologies that contribute directly to the development of generic skills (Moy 1999). These include andragogy (principles of adult learning), holistic or integrated approach to learning, problem-based learning, reflecting or articulating the learning process, meta-cognitive learning, activity-based learning, blended learning, meaningful learning; teacher adopting various roles, such as mentor, coach, facilitator and evaluator while also teaching/manifesting several generic skills to learners. Hence, it has been observed that the need for generic graduate skills has been taken seriously to engage in research and development and to further identify and revise the skill set.

Rigby (2009) provided a very detailed and useful review on generic graduate skills covering a wide range of topics, including definitions of graduate skills and their importance, while describing

---

[3] Teaching and learning, academic support and graduate attributes. The University of Sydney project. Available at http://sydney.edu.au/arts/teaching_learning/academic_support/graduate_attributes.shtml (accessed on 12 May 2014).

the best practices and approaches towards teaching and learning of these graduate skills. In addition, there is a rich source of information on generic graduate skills on the Internet (Crebert 2000). Unfortunately, there is no such policy so far on generic graduate skills in Indian universities and colleges. Nor are there any well-designed programmes to develop, evaluate or certify generic graduate skills. In India, graduates mostly pick up some of these skills through on-campus experiences, more through incidental learning, which include the way the curriculum or the subjects are transacted by the teachers in the classroom and the laboratories, the interpersonal relationships among the teachers or between the students and the teachers, or through organizing and hosting various social events like student union elections, sports and cultural events, conducting examination and so on. And, there are some learning practices outside the boundaries of the university framework.[4]

The most realistic social goal of higher education is to develop and produce front-line manpower for various sectors in all fields of work. By implication, it also means generating leaders equipped with skills and competencies in different walks of social life. Therefore, it is not difficult to understand and appreciate that achieving such a social goal is not necessarily linked to a particular subject. It requires learning of the subject and beyond. A quality curriculum is characterized by defining such generic graduate skills, which are common amongst all graduates in the country irrespective of the university or the college, though some generic skills may be specific for a particular institution.

There have been some deliberate efforts, as mentioned earlier, in defining the generic graduate skills as the expected outcome of graduate programmes in the western world, especially during the recent years. Similar exercises have not been done in Indian higher education, though it does not mean that the graduates of Indian higher education institutions do not develop any generic skills. The difference is that such generic skills are developed only incidentally (or randomly)

---

[4] Many years ago, postgraduate students, usually the better ones, in Calcutta University used to form groups of four or five and learn together—examining the notes from the teacher, visiting libraries and sharing reading, discussing, critically analysing, differing and converging, making fresh and greatly richer notes as preparation for examination. There were rival groups as well, but rivalry for capturing the top honours. The practice may still be there; I said 'many years ago' just to be sure.

and not as part of the curriculum design. In view of the research evidence linking generic skills with employability, higher order cognition and academic excellence, it is possible to argue that Indian higher education institutions should create space and opportunity for developing a well-defined set of generic skills among the graduates to make the curriculum more contemporary, relevant, updated and of high quality.

Competency-based Curriculum

Competency-based education (CBE) is another trend in defining quality curriculum that began during the late 1970s and picked up momentum especially in vocational and technical education as well as in staff training. There are also a number of CBE programmes in the K-12 space. CBE is now trying to create its mark in higher education. The primary objective of CBE is to emphasize upon what the students 'can' do compared to what the students 'know'. In other words, the priority of the curriculum is changing from merely assimilating knowledge to application and skills development, which represent higher order thinking capabilities. Such competencies belong to more than one single cluster or category, namely, subject-related competencies, generic and employability skills-related competencies and so on.

The subject-related skills and competencies may include, for example, the kind of problems that an undergraduate student of physics or geography would be able to solve, the kind of concepts that a student would be able to explain, or the theoretical constructs that a student would be able to verify or prove through experiments and research. In addition, it also includes other factors, such as how competently a student can identify relevant information, source them, filter and classify them and utilize the information to postulate solutions. How ably would a student be able to question and challenge theories and propositions? How would a student demonstrate his/her skill to discover knowledge and invent solutions?

The difference between quality curriculum and conventional curriculum can be measured on the basis of competencies with respect to the level of cognition ranging from the lower to the higher order cognition. Experiences of teachers corroborated by research evidence indicate that a large majority of graduates learn at the lower level of cognition. They cram information and store it in their temporary memory for limited time and purpose (examination). This only results in some kind of fragile learning without any deep understanding and application. Consequently, the learning loss is huge. Some studies also indicate that there is no direct relationship between scoring high marks in examinations and developing higher order cognition like analysis, synthesis, extended abstraction, creativity and so on. Due to various loopholes in the system, loose ends in the examination pattern, students are able to score high marks without deeper learning. Hence, a good quality curriculum should be able to define the level of cognition, particularly higher levels of cognition like application, problem-solving abilities, analytical ability, synthesis and creativity to be achieved through a higher education programme.

Another important domain of CBE is the generic graduate skills. A graduate should be able to demonstrate his/her competencies in critical and creative thinking, problem solving and decision making, analytical thinking, managing self—anger, sadness and frustration, greed—one's emotion, as well as managing interpersonal relationships and so on. By laying down such benchmarks, CBE can help students to move from lower level to higher level competencies.

CBE in higher education is still under debate. For classical theorists, higher education is the sanctum sanctorum of knowledge seeking and knowledge generation where skills and competencies are unacceptable. Another group of theorists argues that CBE is the fertile ground for constructivist ways of learning. The backbone of knowledge and higher knowledge education is cognitivism and behaviourism. In view of the nagging problem of non-employability of the graduates, CBE offers an opportunity to enhance employability of the young graduates.

Multicultural Curriculum

With globalization, the world is gradually emerging as a multicultural society. The civil societies of every nation and state are increasingly becoming multicultural. Whereas some countries are naturally and historically multicultural (e.g., the United States and Canada due to European settlers settling down in these countries over the last few centuries), some others are multicultural within their own geographical boundaries. India is one of the best examples for the latter case. India is a multilingual, multi-religious and multicultural country with multiple streams of social ethos and mores contained in a multiparty polity. The hallmark of Indian multiculturalism is best expressed as 'unity in diversity'.

In the absence of due recognition of multiculturality and its careful nurturing, societies tend to resort to the process of cultural exclusion or submission, wherein diverse minority groups lose their cultural identities to the dominant culture. Evolution of American nationality is an interesting example. The people from various regions of Europe, as they landed in America, learnt to keep aside their European ethnic identity, and worked together to take charge of economic and political power in the new country. Another version of cultural assimilation is the melting-pot theory, whereby minorities are expected to lose their cultural identity and get merged with the majority culture. This has been termed as 'majoritarianism'.

Yet, a third order is best represented by Rabindranath Thakur in his inspiring poem 'Bharat Tirtha':[5]

> My heart, awake in this holy land of India; it is a place of pilgrimage *for nations to mingle in a confluence of humanity*. Nobody knows who urged them yet they came from different lands and merged in a single body—the Aryans, the non-Aryans, the Dravidians, the Chinese, the Scythians, the Huns, the Pathans and the Mughals—all of them like so many separate streams flowing irresistibly to lose at the end of their journeys their individual identities in one vast sea (emphasis added by author).

---

[5] http://cms.boloji.com/index.cfm?md=Blogs&sd=Blog&BlogID=477#sthash.LR9prYjQ. dpuf (accessed on 14 May 2014).

Rabindranath's poetic expression is termed 'melting-pot' theory in the contemporary discourse on multiculturalism. However, Rabindranath celebrated the unity in the cultural diversity.

In the ever-changing scenario of globalization, it will be necessary to carefully nurture the development of multicultural societies. This cannot be done without generating a new framework for multicultural education founded on multicultural curriculum, for education is a culturally embedded process.

There is no agreed definition of multiculturalism and multicultural education among scholars and practitioners. Jay and Jones (2005) defined multicultural education as 'the common term used to describe the type of pluralist education' where 'its advocates are seeking for all children receiving an education, pre-K through college' (p. 3). Kahn (2008) described multicultural education as a 'process, a philosophy, a concept, which is dynamic, multifaceted, and polemic' (p. 531). The National Association for Multicultural Education (NAME, 2001) described multicultural education as a

philosophical concept built on the ideals of freedom, justice, equality, equity, and human dignity as acknowledged in various documents, such as the U.S. Declaration of Independence, constitutions of South Africa and the United States, and the Universal Declaration of Human Rights adopted by the United Nations.

Ameny-Dixon (2010) identified several long-term benefits of the global perspective of multicultural education based on the articles from various authors. Some of these long-term benefits are as follows:

1. Multicultural education increases productivity because a variety of mental resources are available for completing the same tasks and it promotes cognitive and moral growth among all people.
2. Multicultural education increases creative problem-solving skills through the different perspectives applied to same problems to reach solutions.
3. Multicultural education increases positive relationships through achievement of common goals, respect, appreciation,

and commitment to equality among the intellectuals at institutions of higher education.

4. Multicultural education decreases stereotyping and prejudice through direct contact and interactions among diverse individuals.

5. Multicultural education renews vitality of society through the richness of the different cultures of its members and fosters development of a broader and more sophisticated view of the world.

Ameny-Dixon concluded that the four major interactive principles and dimensions of the global perspective of multicultural education that allow the global perspective to be a more useful in promoting core human values than the 'melting-pot' perspective are multicultural competence, equity pedagogy, curriculum reform and teaching for social justice.

Although India has been historically and naturally a multicultural society, it has not been able to generate a multicultural education framework and a multicultural curriculum. This is one society where all the 12 major religious traditions are practised by a large number of people; 22 languages find their place in the Eighth Schedule of the Constitution; there is demand for another 38 languages to be added under the Eighth Schedule. According to The People's Linguistic Survey of India (PLSI), 'Currently as many as 780 different languages are spoken and 86 different scripts are used in the country'.[6] By another estimate, there are more than 2,000 dialects. The social traditions, mores and cultural practices like celebration of birth, marriage, initiation to education and observance of mourning at death and other circumstances vary widely from one linguistic community to another, although they belong to the same religious tradition. For example, Hindu marriage in West Bengal is quite different from Hindu marriage in northern and southern states. The same is true for birthday celebration, initiation to learning in different communities even within the same religious groups.

Generally speaking, Indian education has failed to recognize and respond to the needs of education of a multicultural society. This is painfully evident in the nationally developed textbooks on history,

---

[6] www.peopleslinguisticsurvey.org/

social sciences and other subjects where the regional contributions to the freedom movement as well as the cultural diversity and richness of different regions of the country have often been overlooked. For example, the state boards of secondary education conduct term-end examination in several Indian languages for various linguistic groups resident in the state, but the curriculum is the same, reflecting only the cultural specificities of the linguistic majority.

The multicultural composition of the educational community in higher education is much more prominent. The demographic composition of students in higher education in the metropolitan cities easily reveals this truth. Also, due to increasing interstate migration of students during the last few decades, especially after the opening of numerous professional colleges under private initiatives, many more campuses have become multicultural as compared to a few decades ago. Despite the presence of multicultural groups in higher education, the educational system tends to ignore and continue with just one single curricular agenda, which largely suits the educational requirements of students coming from the background similar to those of the curriculum framers (who are cultural elites). The experiences in the teaching–learning process, evaluation and other associated supportive activities designed in the campus in this form are not responsive to the intellectual (learning) styles and needs of the large number of students coming from the other states and religious groups. In other words, the campus experience suffers from 'majoritarianism'. The seriousness of this issue has to be examined with respect to differential learning styles and even thinking. Contemporary research indicates that thinking is culturally embedded (Nisbett 2003, 2009). Hence, majoritarianism can be a potential threat to learning optimization. The absence of serious research on multicultural education indicates lack of sensitivity to the issue of multicultural curriculum in India.

Sleeter and Grant (2006) proposed five approaches to multicultural education. First, 'Teaching the Exceptional and the Culturally Different' students to equip with the academic skills, concepts and values of American institutions. Second, focus is on 'Human Relations' to live in harmony and promote unity. The third approach is study of 'Single Groups'—comprehensive and in-depth studies. The fourth approach is for inculcating 'Values for Cultural Diversity', including respect for differences. The fifth approach is 'Education that is Multicultural and Social Reconstructionist', which proposes complete redesign of an educational programme.

> A multicultural curriculum has three major components: (1) content, (2) method, and (3) people. 'Content' includes scholarship, theories, concepts, facts, contributions and perspectives of people of different race, ethnicity, gender, language, social class, religion, sexual orientation, abilities and disabilities, political beliefs, etc. that have been historically underrepresented in all educational arenas. 'Methods' include pedagogical strategies, that accommodate diverse teaching learning styles, academic policies, that support the recruitment, mentoring, and retention of a multicultural students, faculty, and staff population, and curricular processes that support exploration, development and implementation of multicultural curriculum. 'People' includes a multicultural student, faculty, and staff population that supports and engages in the development and implementation of multicultural curricular through the methods described. (Kitano 1977)

Another way of looking at the issue of multiculturalism is through the prism of campus diversity. A multicultural curriculum should be able to respond to the issue of cultural diversity. There was a major Campus Diversity Initiative supported by the Ford Foundation in 1994 through Educational Resources Project Centre Trust (ERPCT), New Delhi. It addressed diversity issues by challenging the colleges to be creative and to make diversity the central mission in the educational system. Hearing about this programme, a group of Indian educators, policymakers and concerned persons saw the value and importance of addressing diversity issues in their own context because the issues of social tension and youth dynamics were parallel and, perhaps, even global in their upsurge. During this process, the importance of taking some initiative in India was also felt, and there was open discussion and a frank dialogue on such issues of nationwide concern. Subsequently, a study of eight colleges in different parts of the country was carried out. The study clearly brought out the need for a diversity initiative that would improve communication between different socio-economic groups, address their genuine concerns effectively and build harmony in and around campuses (Nayak 2005).

In addition, there are several instances of the Diversity Education Programme offered by institutes of higher education. The mission of the Diversity Education Programme is 'to develop a safe, respectful and inclusive campus environment'. The mission is achieved through a series of:[7]

- Training workshops, presentations, courses and other educational activities that enhance further understanding of the multicultural nature of our campus community.
- Consultation of administration, faculty, staff and students on federal and state laws and regulations as well as about university policies and procedures regarding diversity, affirmative action and equal employment opportunity, initiatives against crimes and other matters related to fostering a respectful campus climate.
- Referrals to appropriate service departments for university and community members having concerns and/or complaints.

The Indian higher education can pick up a few leaves from the above-listed practices as well as from India's own experience in the campus diversity programme led by Sharada Nayak.

International Comparability

The quality of curriculum is a dynamic entity. Although the curriculum is generally not changed or revised for many years in a number of universities, the growth of knowledge remains unabated. Hence, the curriculum has to be dynamic and resilient to be able to accommodate the new developments. It must reflect the current status of the knowledge in the field. There are several implications in conceptualizing dynamism as an indicator of the quality of curriculum. In its essential and most primary configuration where curriculum is equated with syllabus and contents of study, dynamism implies continuous revision and update of the contents.

---

[7] http://occr.ucdavis.edu/diversity/ (accessed on 15 May 2014).

In this era of globalization of education, there is hardly any choice, but to maintain the global standards of curriculum. One primary component of globalization is the cross-border delivery of education. E-learning, open education resource (OER) and other forms of cross-border delivery are a big challenge due to the academic resilience of the universities. For the semi-developed countries like India and other developing nations, globalization of education must necessarily mean achieving global standards in education where curriculum, instructional systems and student assessment are the main pillars. Only this can bring up the standard of courses for international comparability and competitiveness.

In order to achieve global and competitive standards, what is needed is not only frequent and periodic comparative research on curriculum, but also an ongoing mechanism for curriculum watch, knowledge assessment and adaptation. Such comparative research is now substantially facilitated by Internet and cyberspace communication among scholars across the countries, which enables review of curriculum of a subject at a particular level. By comparing the curriculum prescribed by the leading universities of the world, like the Ivy League Universities in the United States, as well as prestigious British Universities like Oxford, Cambridge and London, among others, it is possible to understand the global standards and then adapt curriculum to suit Indian conditions and to match global standards.

Following the National Policy of Education 1986, the Government of India constituted a Technology Watch Committee that was chaired by (Late) Professor P.V. Indiresan, former director of IIT, Madras. I represented educational technology in the committee. Our main concern in the committee was to review the technological developments all over the world, primarily as an output of research and development (R&D) activities, their applications in industrial and non-industrial sectors and also incorporate such technological developments into the curriculum of our institutions. Although the committee was dismantled as fast as it was constituted, its relevance and significance remain unaltered. In fact, it is probably more relevant today with education getting covered under the World Trade Organization (WTO) and the General Agreement on Trade in Services (GATS). Either at the national level (e.g., UGC), or at the state and institutional levels, such 'curriculum watch' committees in different subjects need to be constituted so that the curriculum prescribed for the students may gradually evolve into a state-of-the-art curriculum. This is also possible at the institutional and individual levels. For instance, some professors in Indian universities do keep themselves updated on the latest trends and developments in their own subjects and incorporate it in their curriculum. This needs to be practiced at a wider scale.

In a more difficult and deeper sense, 'curriculum updatedness' takes a different form. When curriculum is defined as the total experience in the campus, it includes not only the prescribed contents and the subject matter, but also their method of transaction in the classrooms, library research, field works, individual and group assignments as well as experiences in the play fields, auditorium, gymnasium, art gallery and so on that fulfil the demands of multiple intellectual needs and contribute to the development of generic skills. Hence, 'updatedness' in this case implies comprehensive curricular reforms, inclusive of designing and implementing the overall campus experience.

The processes of construction of learning experiences in the campus are changing fast, although the academic community tends to hold strongly on to the conventional structure of experiences by equating the quality of education with the transaction of prescribed contents only through classrooms and laboratory processes. Take, for example, the enormous gap between the students' and teachers' enthusiasm as well as skills and comfort level in using the Internet or even emails. This is equally true for mobiles and smartphones. Instead of exploring the possibilities of using mobile phones as a learning tool for consultative learning across classrooms as well as campuses, the education system has been banning the use of mobile phones in classes!

Even if the teachers or the system managers in higher education fail to accommodate the psychology and preferences of the new generation (which includes their attitude and approach to technology and other aspects of life), students will not find themselves inadequate. They have already been using the latest technology for peer conferencing, solving academic problems and participating in debates (e.g., through news channels, chat services and SMS). Of course, one cannot overlook the fact that they also use technology for other juvenile interests.

Hence, there is a need to take a comprehensive view of campus experience since the graduates of tomorrow will be prepared not just for the national market, but also for the global scenario.

Interdisciplinary and Multi-disciplinary Curriculum[8]

There are two major shifts in the development of knowledge systems, which are important for developing the quality of curriculum in higher education. On the one hand, knowledge is growing at an exponential rate. This is easily visible when we get into the Internet search mode. Almost any entry through any of the search engines offers hundreds or thousands of references. The second important shift is a qualitative shift in knowledge. This implies that the known boundaries of disciplines are melting, giving rise to the emergence of convergence of disciplines, thereby unfolding interdisciplinary learning. Now, established subjects like electronics, biotechnology, microbiology, nanotechnology, regional planning and so on are actually products of conventional disciplines like physics and electrical engineering, biology, technological sciences, mathematics, geography and so on. This, probably, is just the beginning of such kind of fusion of different disciplines bringing integrated knowledge having direct relevance to human society.

Conventional subject disciplines create barriers between specializations. For example, physics and chemistry are not only two clearly distinct disciplines, but even within a particular subject, say, chemistry, there are almost independent subdisciplines, such as physical, inorganic and organic chemistry. Conventionally, there are walls between the

[8] There are few terms used in the studies in curriculum of higher education. These are multidisciplinary, interdisciplinary and transdisciplinary. Multidisciplinary curriculum draws on knowledge from different disciplines but stays within their boundaries. Interdisciplinary curriculum analyses, synthesizes and harmonizes links between disciplines into a coordinated and coherent whole. Transdisciplinary integrates the natural, social and health sciences in a humanities context and transcends their traditional boundaries. http://www.ncbi.nlm.nih.gov/pubmed/17330451 (accessed on 16 May 2014).

subjects; there is a tendency to undermine one discipline by another. I still remember how teachers of mathematics and science looked down upon subjects like history or political science; or how teachers of English literature floated on cloud 9 almost permanently in my first job as a college teacher. Emergence of interdisciplinary subjects is breaking these artificial walls, adding value to the knowledge. This emergence of inter-disciplinary subjects is not only specific to science. It is equally true in the case of social sciences like politics and political science, economics and so on, which significantly derive from other disciplines.

Integrated learning is the new emerging trend. There are many topics taught in higher education that cannot be dealt as an independent subject category. For example, unemployment (or employment) is a common theme in economics. But, the issue needs to draw multiple references from history, economics, political science, psychology and sociology. Similarly, a discourse on energy (energy crisis) in natural sciences can derive from physics, chemistry, geology and biology, among other subjects. Social issues like women empowerment, abortion, dowry and education can be studied better when learnt through the perspectives of history, religion, philosophy, contemporary literature and the like. Such interdisciplinary approach helps students (and also scholars) to 'see all sides of the story'.

There is some interesting research and anecdotal evidence that students of interdisciplinary curriculum manifest (Newell 1990).

- More sensitivity to ethical issues
- Ability to synthesize or integrate
- Enlarge perspectives or horizons
- Expand creative, original or unconventional thinking
- More humility or listening skills
- Sensitivity to bias
- Interdisciplinary in style (understand and appreciate values of other disciplines)

Another related dimension is the multidisciplinarity. Solving many of the problems both at the theoretical and at the practical levels is significantly facilitated by drawing knowledge from different disciplines. A quality curriculum should provide scope for multidisciplinarity so that students of the next generation are well equipped to draw from different branches of knowledge to solve problems and not close their eyes and search for solutions within the conventional structure of knowledge of a particular discipline.

There can be two different objectives for the existing curricular choices in higher education. The choice of prescribing a set of subjects in a particular discipline like science, humanities or social sciences is to equip students with the epistemology of the concerned discipline. The second important goal is to prepare students for transition to work and life, which do not depend exclusively on the knowledge of a subject in a particular discipline. Of these two goals, the first is the enabling one, whereas the second is the ultimate or superordinate goal of higher education. In the contemporary practices of curriculum framework and choices, the enabling goal has been given precedence over the actual target. The reason for huge unemployability of Indian graduates can be attributed significantly to such misplaced curricular choices.

The unidisciplinary approach, wherein a student is offered courses belonging to one particular discipline, for example, physics, chemistry, mathematics, or any one group of subjects, severely restricts the optimization of the potential in the young students. The contemporary curricular choice does not allow offering, say, history with electronics and linguistics. A choice-based credit system[9] is an important innovation adopted in many Indian universities that can respond to the need for multidisciplinary courses to suit the academic needs and choices of students.

> CBCS has several unique features, such as enhanced learning opportunities, ability to match students' scholastic needs and aspirations, inter-institutional transferability of students, part completion of an academic programme in the institution of enrolment and part completion in a specialized (and recognized) institution, improvement of educational quality and excellence,

---

[9] CBCS has been launched by the UGC. Under this scheme, the students in higher education can choose from courses that are categorized into core, elective and foundation courses. Students learn at their own pace, and assessment is done based on the credit system. There are certain non-credit courses that are assessed as satisfactory or non-satisfactory. The main features of the CBCS is that the assessment is done semester wise, each course is assigned a credit, there is provision of credit transfer, students are continuously assessed and assessment is done through 10-point grading system. Based on the guidelines issued by the UGC, many universities have adopted CBCS.

flexibility of working students to complete a programme over an extended time as well as standardization and comparability of educational programme across the country.[10]

Thus, introducing a multidisciplinary curriculum in higher education can actively support such diverse learning needs for optimizing potentials among the young scholars.

Local Curriculum in Global Framework

With the changing dynamics of the economy, the educated labour market has also changed substantially. What Indian graduates used to do after migrating to another country some 20 years ago now do it here without migrating. A few years ago, the labour market was restricted only to the natural citizens within the country. Local expertise, whether sufficient or not, was the only choice. This choice is undergoing a quantum shift. Through outsourcing, the market economy has opened up globally without shifting the natural citizens physically to another country. Thousands of young Indian graduates are working in the call centres in various Indian locations and serving the European and the American clientele. Multinational companies have set up offices in India and are engaging Indians because doing so is cost-effective. The working hours in such companies located in India are decided by the working hours in the client's country. For this, people in India need to build technical skills that are required to cater to the needs of those countries that they are serving virtually. Therefore, Indian higher education is faced with the challenge of building skills and competences that could cut across the economic and cultural boundaries of the countries.

Although the size of such working population will continue to be miniscule compared to the size of the employment market for the Indian graduates within the country, it is necessary for such graduates to understand the global framework of the industry, services or agricultural sectors in which they work.

---

[10] http://gujarat-education.gov.in/

Universities are publicly funded institutions. Hence, they are accountable to the public. University graduates must be able to respond to the local and regional needs in addition to the national needs. Hence, there is a need to reorient our curriculum as well as design and develop learning experiences and outcomes so that it can be locally relevant within a national and global framework.

Conclusion

The curriculum in Indian higher education has so far been viewed as just a list of units and topics belonging to a particular discipline that need to be covered as part of an educational programme offered by a college or a university. The curriculum has till now been designed by keeping in mind only the subject of specialization. This can continue if the curriculum is defined only as a set of subjects and contents. However, this very notion of curriculum has not only been questioned, but also been steadily replaced with the concept of 'total experience', which contributes to the overall development of the generic graduate skills along with specialized subject skills in order to enable smooth transition to work, family life and society. Hence, it is necessary for the Indian curriculum development mechanism to implement a paradigm shift and adopt a more professional and contemporary approach.

Curriculum is a well-researched subject. It finds extensive and intensive significance in the standard encyclopaedias of education. The new trend in curriculum does not only discuss about interdisciplinary and multidisciplinary curriculum, but also demands a multidisciplinary team of experts to design and develop the curriculum. Besides the subjects and content experts, professionally sound curriculum development must also involve instructional designers, educational technologists, educational media specialists, librarians, sociologists and social psychologists to collectively design the higher education programme for the youth, where the choices of subjects just becomes a medium for attaining the larger goal.

7

Cogitagogy: Quality Teaching–Learning

Introduction

Curriculum, teaching–learning and student assessment are the three pillars of academic quality. For bringing about a holistic development in a young graduate, these three aspects need to be seen in conjunction with each other. In the previous chapter, we deliberated upon what makes a quality curriculum. Curriculum is only as good as it is transacted and lays down the learning pathways for the students to move ahead.

The objective or purpose of the teaching–learning process is to optimize the learning experience and discovering the knowledge planned and designed in the curriculum. If curriculum is considered as the input, teaching–learning is the process, and learning outcome as measured by student assessment is the product. Many of the generic graduate and employability skills can be developed by appropriate use of instructional designs and their proper implementation.

21st-century Learners

At a time when knowledge is rapidly becoming obsolete due to aggressive transitions and technological developments, we should envisage how 'a smart learner' should evolve or even look like! This should help us to construct a suitable teaching–learning paradigm that could facilitate promoting quality education. Contemporary research literature often describes students as '21st-century learners' largely because of their access to technology. In fact, this principally 'sets them apart' from other generations in the way they process information and choose to actively participate in the educational experience.[1] The attributes of 21st-century learners as depicted by Eaton (2011), and posted on the website of Educational Technology and Mobile Learning.[2] According to Educational Technology and Mobile Learning, they are respectful, focused, problem-solving user of common sense, can work with others, caring, risk taking, willing to work and are responsible, motivated and confident.

Designing effective teaching–learning processes in higher education should be guided by the kind of learners (graduates) who we want to shape in our colleges and universities based on the attributes of 21st-century learners. There is little doubt that 21st-century learners are different from their predecessors. Their ease of access and exposure to technology and other forms of contemporary media are attributed to bringing about a major change in their brain wiring and learning mechanisms.

Yet, in another study, the author lists 21st-century skills to be information and communication technology (ICT) literacy, ability to think and solve problems, interpersonal and self-directional skills, global awareness as well as financial, economic, business and civic literacy. Most importantly, students are increasingly learning about 'how to *keep learning* continually throughout their lives' (Partnership for 21st Century Skills 2002).

Pant (2012) proposes the following three attributes:

1. The speed with which a person can learn something completely new, with or without the help of a guide or a teacher. This implies a level

---

[1] http://www.educatorstechnology.com
[2] http://www.educatorstechnology.com

of meta-cognition that helps in his being able to differentiate between what he can learn by himself and where he needs to be guided or taught.

2. The speed with which he can give up undesirable habits and develop desirable habits, such as time management, overcoming procrastination, eye for detail, accuracy in spelling and numbers, deferred gratification and other cognitive virtues.

3. The agility and flexibility to adopt newer world views and mindsets oriented towards growth and welcoming change while thriving in chaos and uncertainty, rather than a conservative and status quo ante mindset.

According to these lists, a 21st-century learner is a combination of knowledge, academic and generic skills and attitudes. The important point that should not be missed is the emphasis on learning skills rather than accumulating knowledge. Sugata Mitra's (2006) experiment, the 'Hole in the Wall' on the self-organizing learning system is yet another example of how 21st-century learners behave in learning situations.

We cannot overlook the fact that there is a social angle to the teaching–learning process. What kind of a nation or a society do we want to create should be factored in defining the learners' attributes as well.

India has declared her ambition to become a knowledge superpower (Planning Commission 2001) as mentioned in Chapter 1. The Planning Commission document clarifies the nature of 'India as knowledge superpower' with the following attributes:

1. It uses knowledge through all its constituents and endeavours to empower and enrich its people.
2. It uses knowledge as a powerful tool to drive societal transformation.
3. It is a learning society committed to innovation.
4. It has the capacity to generate, absorb, disseminate and protect knowledge and also use it to create economic wealth and social good for all its constituents.
5. It enlightens people to take an integrated view of life as a fusion of mind, body and spirit.

There are four ways by which a society responds to knowledge power. These are knowledge consumption, knowledge archival, knowledge retrieval and knowledge processing and creation. These four patterns are not exclusive, which means that societies cannot be exclusively classified as based on one or the other pattern.

In most cases, societies combine two or more attributes. However, every society indicates a dominant trend. Most developing countries are primarily knowledge consumers—while some choose knowledge archiving, others concentrate on knowledge retrieval and processing. Only few countries are knowledge creators—they invent new processes, products and new ways of solving problems (as indicated by various invention awards, patents, Field Medals, Nobel Prizes and so on).

Knowledge creators are the genuine knowledge superpowers; they lead the world and wrest the global leadership through knowledge wars. For India to establish its global leadership and supremacy and become knowledge superpower, the country must orient herself towards becoming a knowledge creator, creating new processes and products, inventing new solutions and so on. Knowledge creation is a function of thinking, especially critical and creative thinking (inclusive of heuristic and intuitive thinking), instead of just being a storehouse of massive overload of information.

Let us now revisit the discourse on attributes of 21st-century learners and examine these aspects in the context of India's ambition in asserting its global role and presence. We also need to account for the dramatic changes in the environment that is influencing the learning styles in the 'incidental' and 'non-formal' learning formats.

I would like to specifically draw your attention to the developments in the field of ICT, especially, hand-held devices like mobile phones, iPads, and the Internet and social networking media. The speed and accuracy with which people are able to communicate through multiple channels like emails, WhatsApp, Facebook, Twitter, blogs and so on are amazing. These mediums are both entertaining and educative. The penetration of mobile phones is tremendous, touching life of almost all the young persons in the country. ICT is helping them in social networking and learning. This is now termed as 'social connectivism'.

We must define certain criteria that would help us to measure the learning efficiency, which is considered as the core of the teaching–learning process. Whom should we call as a qualified learner? Since we have already presented a list of generic graduate skills in the previous chapter, let us list those attributes that are specific to the learning processes. Twenty-first century learners are the ones who:

- Learn on a continuing basis to cope with the dynamic content using multiple learning media.
- Discover knowledge that is hidden in multiple learning resources and invent solutions.
- Experiment with new ways of learning.
- Extensively and effectively use technology, for example, the Internet and social networking for learning.
- Have a well-thought-out learning agenda.
- Rapidly update them about the latest information with accuracy.
- Process information for synthesis and drawing conclusions with speed and precision.
- Readily challenge and verify knowledge, postulates, hypotheses and theories.
- Master the process of problem solving—diagnose and define problems in all its parameters, identify alternative solutions, weigh pros and cons of every alternative solution, consult the right person and arrive at the most rational solution.
- Examine his/her own thinking processes and outcomes and develop higher-order thinking skills (meta-cognition).

The challenge of the present teaching–learning process is to develop higher-order thinking skills among the graduates. A dire need of higher education is to nurture and foster a thinking mind through analysis-based learning designs.

In more precise terms, the current education system is challenged to develop capabilities among students to:

- discover their hidden talents/potential,
- discover knowledge and
- invent solutions.

Given this backdrop, let us now analyse what is happening in the present and what should happen to improve the effectiveness of the teaching–learning process in the years to come.

Old Story

Imparting instructions in higher education has been primarily equated with classroom lectures. The lectures are classified as good, average and not so good. Then, there is the classical method of 'dictating notes' from well-preserved aged, soiled into yellowish pages with age inherited from the grand and great-grand teachers. There are occasional additions of experiments to the laboratory practical sessions for science courses every few years. Not to mention that the monotonous monologues (lectures) have been repeated a million times over the years, decades and even centuries!

No wonder that the search for innovative solutions to promote the quality of higher education has often turned out to be more about 'improving the quality of classroom lectures'. This practice is backed by the existing assumptions about human nature (students), their learning process/techniques and the role of teachers who, like 'watermen' in the summer, fill the tanks of the 'room coolers' (students' brain)! Then, behaviourists made meaningful contributions that finally led to the creation of structured or programmed lectures, which were relatively more scientific and effective than the conventional lecture sessions. There are studies that prove that the performance of students increases with structured lecture sessions as compared to unstructured lectures. Nonetheless, lecturing that is conventional or structured is the 'old story' in the teaching–learning process. In this method, students are passive listeners, and may or may not be even passive learners! This old story fails to pass the tests of recent developments in the understanding of the human brain and its learning mechanism.

With good or not-so-good lectures, good or not-so-good dictation of old notes, learning is all about memorizing facts, figures, concepts, principles, explanations, illustrations and examples. As indicated by brain-based learning, many of these items that are stored in our memory are discarded as soon as their purpose (examination) is over. The actual retention is negligible (after adjusting 80 per cent learning loss)! Thus, 21st-century learners need and deserve an alternative science of learning.

New Story

In the old story, the teaching methods and strategies are treated as 'constant' while learning (outcome) is considered as the 'variant'. Hence, there is a wide variation in the performance of students. In sharp contrast, contemporary research and experiments in the field of the teaching–learning process have generated evidences that the variations in the learning outcomes or performance can be significantly reduced (Benjamin Bloom's Mastery Learning Theory) provided the teaching method can be reconstructed as a variable to match the learning needs and styles of students. Thus, the new story is all about the thought process that 'if students can't learn the way teachers teach, why teachers can't teach the way by which students can learn?'

The college and university students come in with huge amount of information (knowledge!) besides having acquired well-established learning styles (habits!) and experience. More importantly, they carry a world view of their own that they have developed during their growing years. Hence, their brains are not clean slates where anything can be scribbled. Wherever instructional processes (teaching) are designed in such a way that it helps students to discover knowledge in the context of their own world view, students perform at a much higher level. They construct knowledge. This is the new story.

Thus, in the new story, the focus shifts to 'learning' and teaching becomes just a supportive action. The teacher's role changes to that of a designer who creates suitable learning designs and offers the scope and space for a diverse group of learners to benefit from.

Deriving largely from the design science, such learning designs offer opportunities for diverse thinking and learning to suit varying styles, requirements and world view of the learner. This new story is backed by constructivist paradigm, gift of new psychology, brain research and democratic convictions, in addition to andragogy (the science of adult learning).

Hindsight to the Story

There is also hindsight to the story. Instructional processes cannot be independent of the curriculum and the content.

Just as in the teaching–learning process, there are old and new stories in the context of curriculum and content development. While the curriculum based on global knowledge assessment adapted locally is the new story, the old story is based on a few teachers of the subject (labelled as experts) drafting a curriculum.

A holistic view of the teaching–learning process in higher education should offer an interactive framework between the curriculum/content and the instructional processes. This combination of curriculum and instructional process offers different subsets. (Figure 7.1).

Figure 7.1:
Old and New Story Matrix for Curriculum and Instruction

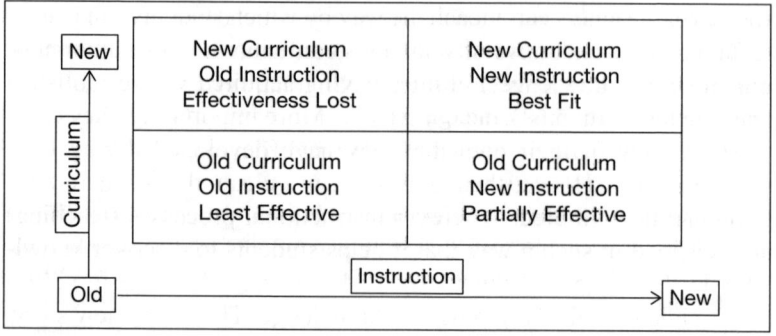

Source: Author.

The most preferred or 'best fit' combination is the new curriculum with new instructional designs and practices, which is the practice in the world's leading institutions of higher education like Harvard, Caltech, Columbia, Princeton, MIT and so on. Within India, this paradigm is prevalent in Indian Institute of Science (IISc), IITs, IIMs, National Institute of Design (NID), National Institute of Fashion Technology (NIFT), and in some departments of certain universities. Examples are rare, if at all, of old curriculum with new instruction. Exceptions may be a few teachers wherein they follow the old curriculum of the state or the affiliating universities, but incorporate new-generation instructional processes at their own initiative. The fourth and the most common combination are the old curriculum and old instruction. This unfortunately prevails in a majority of the colleges and universities in India!

Alternative Sciences of Human Learning

There are several alternative sciences of learning on the horizon, such as andragogy, technogogy, heutagogy, brain-based learning, constructivism and multichannel learning.

Andragogy is primarily the science of learning by adult learners propounded by Malcolm Knowles. Knowles et al. (2005) described andragogy as the 'art and science of teaching adults to learn'. It is often interpreted as the process of engaging adult learners with the structure of learning experience.

Technogogy is defined as the convergence of technology, pedagogy and content in the transformative use of technology to foster learning (Idrus 2008): 'Technogogy is the convergence of technology, pedagogy and learner-based content where the three components have a three-dimensional relationship resulting in a specific learning object design'.

Heutagogy is a term coined by Hase and Kenyon (2000):

> Heutagogy is the study of self-determined learning. It is also an attempt to challenge some ideas about teaching and learning that still prevail in teacher-centred learning in addition to emphasizing the need for 'knowledge sharing' rather than 'knowledge hoarding' (as Bill Ford (1997) eloquently puts it). In this respect, Heutagogy envisages a future in which 'knowing how to learn' will become a fundamental skill, given the pace of innovations and the changing structures of communities and workplaces.

Heutagogy's argument of learning to learn is 'learning to know'—one of the four pillars of learning (UNESCO 1996). In some ways, it also derives from the concepts and practices of meta-cognition.

Contemporary brain research has given new insights into the mechanism of human learning. Human brain is made of approximately 100 billion nerve cells called neurons. Information passes from one neuron to another through an electrochemical process making connections. These connections are flexible, overlapping and webbed. Excited neurons form patterns. The more frequent the use, the stronger is the pattern. The stronger the pattern, more frequent is the reorganization (Jensen 2007).

Learning is nothing but the function of this brain patterning. The science of brain-based learning that has emerged out of brain research has been captured in 12 self-explaining principles (Abou-Elgheit 2012).

According to Talking Page,[3] these are:

1. The brain is a parallel processor.
2. Learning engages entire physiology.
3. The search for meaning is innate.
4. The search for meaning occurs through patterning.
5. Emotions are critical to learning.
6. Every brain simultaneously perceives and creates parts and whole.
7. Learning involves both focused attention and peripheral perception.
8. Learning always involves conscious and unconscious processes.
9. We have at least two types of memory—a spatial memory system and a set of systems for rote learning.
10. The brain understands and remembers the best when facts and skills are embedded in its natural spatial memory.
11. Learning is enhanced by challenges and inhibited by threats.
12. Each brain is unique.

The three instructional techniques associated with brain-based learning[4] are as follows:

1. Orchestrated immersion: Creating a learning environment that fully immerses students in an educational experience based on the principles of immersive visualization.
2. Relaxed alertness: Creating a relaxed environment by removing threat perceptions, yet remain alert by maintaining a highly challenging environment (principle 10 above).
3. Active processing: Allowing the learner to consolidate and internalize information by actively processing it.

---

[3] http://www.talkingpage.org/artic011.html (accessed on 22 April 2014).
[4] http://www.funderstanding.com/theory/brain-based-learning/brain-based-learning/ (accessed on 22 April 2014).

Constructivism

It is a branch of the philosophy of science that explains how human beings construct knowledge from 'real-life' experiences of interacting with people, objects, events and environment. In another way, our world view—the way we interpret the world around us—is ascribed to constructivist philosophy.

Accordingly, constructivism is a learning strategy that draws on students' existing knowledge, beliefs and skills. With a constructivist approach, students synthesize new understanding from prior learning and new information. The constructivist learning has given rise to an instructional paradigm called the 5E paradigm,[5] which comprises five aspects—Engage, Explore, Explain, Elaborate and Evaluate.

The 'Engage' aspect connects the past and the present learning experiences. It anticipates activities and focuses on the aspect of students' thinking on the learning outcomes of current activities. During this phase, students are expected to become actively engaged in the concept, process or skill to be learnt.

'Explore' provides 'students with a common base of experiences. During this phase, students actively explore their environment or manipulate materials', which help them to identify and develop various concepts, processes and skills.

'Explain' helps students to explain the concepts that they have been exploring. They are given ample 'opportunities to verbalize their conceptual understanding or demonstrate new skills or behaviours. This phase also provides opportunities for teachers to introduce formal terms and definitions in addition to explaining new concepts, processes, skills or behaviours'.

'Elaborate' extends students' 'conceptual understanding and allows them to practise skills and behaviours in real life. Through new experiences, learners develop deeper and broader understanding of major concepts, obtain more information about areas of interest and refine their skills'.

'Evaluate' 'encourages learners to assess their understanding and abilities and lets teachers evaluate students' understanding of key concepts and skills development'.

---

[5] http://enhancinged.wgbh.org/research/eeeee.html (accessed on 25 April 2014).

Multichannel Learning Systems

Although conventional belief is that students learn from classroom lecture sessions followed by reading textbooks and class notes, the reality is significantly different. Students use a host of other self-learning media and tools, such as the following:

- Non-text books (e.g., guides)
- Mutual consultation among themselves and other cooperative learning methods
- Private coaching (substitute for tutorials and individualized instruction)
- Television programmes (educational and non-educational)
- Audio and video programmes and digital contents (online and offline)
- Internet-based resources (in cybercafes)
- Projects and other problem-solving approaches

The new lexicon for these learning media and tools is multichannel learning. Thus, students actually learn, or rather construct their learning in a multichannel learning environment (MCLE). Currently, these learning channels are unorganized. Just as these channels reinforce, complement and supplement each other, they also interfere with each other because of weak design. Thus, they affect the quality of learning. MCLE is already a reality. However, it is an incidental configuration. Hence, it has to be converted into a multichannel learning system (MCLS) to reap its true potential.

An MCLS is an organized and a deliberately designed mechanism that has a planned configuration to synchronize the power of various media to achieve optimal learning. The major objective of this system is to reinforce one another in achieving predefined learning goals and also provide alternative learning paths to the learners according to his/her learning styles and medium of preference (Anzalone 1995, Mukhopadhyay 1995). Though new, it derives significantly from the already established principles and practices of learning. Thus, MCLS is a pre-planned and organized mode in which:

- the channels mutually reinforce each other to optimize learning;

- the channels can be used as stand-alone sources to suit the learning styles and interests of a learner; and
- the learners can configure their road map using various channels.

Cogitagogy[6]

Cogitagogy is the science of learning through thinking. According to the *Oxford English Dictionary*, the word 'cogitate' means 'to think deeply about something; to meditate or reflect'. The *Merriam-Webster Dictionary* defines cogitate as 'to think carefully and seriously about something'.

In the paradigm of science of human learning, our focus is to develop the thinking skill while learning—learning to think and thinking to learn (Figure 7.2). Our contention is that the thinking skill should take care of learning. In other words, if a student can think, the rest of the learning process (contents) should fall into place.

Figure 7.2:
Thinking to Learn–Learning to Think

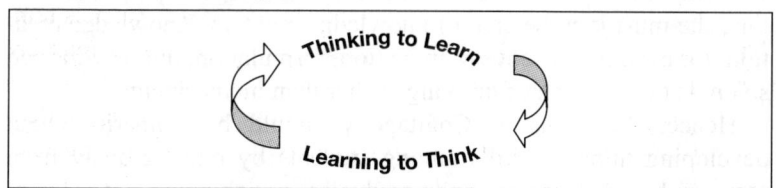

Source: Author.

Cogitagogy should help students to discover knowledge and invent solutions, and thereby continuously rediscover and optimize their potential. Hence, I will call this new science as 'Cogitagogy'—science of learning through cogitation. Cogitagogy derives its inspiration from two sources. One is metaphysical and another pragmatism, rather functionalism.

---

[6] Unlike heutagogy, andragogy and so on cogitagogy is not a known name in the field of human learning. I coined this word to represent my thesis of thinking-based learning or 'Learning to Think, Thinking to Learn' cycle.

The metaphysical inspiration is best represented by Indian scriptural theses that are well articulated by Swami Vivekananda:

> If I had to get my education all over again and I had any voice in the matter, I would learn to master my mind first and then get the facts if I wanted them. It takes people a long time to learn because they can't concentrate their mind at will.

The emphasis on the control of mind focuses on thinking and thinking deeply, and cooling it down.

> Knowledge is inherent in man. No knowledge comes from outside; it is all inside. When we say man 'knows', in strict psychological language, it should mean what he discovers or unveils. What a man 'learns' is what he actually discovers by taking off the cover of his own soul, which is a mine of infinite knowledge.

Here, the focus is on discovering knowledge that is resident within every human being. The title of Delor's Report, 'Learning: The Treasure Within' (UNESCO 1996), also reflects the idea of discovering this treasure within individuals.

The functional or pragmatic inspiration comes from an obligation to fulfil India's dream of becoming a knowledge superpower. For this, she must join the club of knowledge creators. Knowledge creation, for example, discovery, invention, formulation, innovations and so on, is the function of thinking, rather than memorizing.

Hence, the focus of Cogitagogy should be primarily about developing thinking skills among students by moving away from memory-based learning and gradually transitioning into learning based on thinking. The importance of 'thinking' as opposed to 'memorizing information' has to be understood afresh.

The concept of 'reinventing wheels' is often discouraged by labelling it as foolishness largely because we miss to read the product (wheel) and the process (invent) separately. It is very important for students to think constantly.

Even if there was no need for reinventing wheel, reinventing the process is extremely important. Reinventing is the mother of inventing. No scientist, technologist, poet or painter has ever done just one experiment, one product, one poem or one painting day after day or week after week. As they keep exploring, they think deeply, which develops creative thinking and ultimately leads to creating masterpieces. When knowledge becomes obsolete, it is thinking that will provide young people the arms for survival and excellence.

Thinking

'Thinking is essentially a conscious cognitive process'.[7] It is neither haphazard nor emotive; rather, it is deliberate and organized and helps people to create their own world view.[8] Thus, it gives a meaning to the world around us. Brooding and daydreaming do not qualify as thinking since they are not planned or organized.

Two people perceive and describe the same event, person or environment in different ways. This is because we interpret differently according to our own style and process of thinking. During the process, some people turn out to be diehard optimists (positive thinkers) while others become perennially cynical and incorrigibly hopeless (negative thinkers). Thus, cogitation is qualified thinking, which is thinking at higher and deeper levels.

Thinking is not of one type. In fact, several different adjectives are used to qualify thinking. The examples include abstract thinking, analytical thinking, constructive thinking, convergent thinking, creative thinking, critical thinking, divergent thinking, heuristic thinking, integrative thinking, intuitive thinking, lateral thinking, logical thinking, positive thinking, reflective thinking, strategic thinking, systems thinking and vertical thinking.

A large number of scholars have contributed to the understanding of human thinking (Gagne, Merrill, Bloom, Anderson and Krathwohl, Biggs and Collis, Paul Torrance, Edward de Bono, and many others). We shall refer to those contributions that have come in the form of taxonomies of educational objectives or instruction and classify thinking based on a certain hierarchy.

Based on the behaviourist school, Gagne proposed an instructional taxonomy of nine events, namely

1. Gain attention
2. Describe the goal

---

[7] www.psychologytoday.com
[8] http://www.venusproject.net

3. Stimulate recall of prior knowledge
4. Present the material to be learned
5. Provide guidance for learning
6. Elicit performance 'practice'
7. Provide informative feedback
8. Assess performance test, if the lesson has been learned
9. Enhance retention and transfer

Benjamin Bloom developed the taxonomy of educational objectives in 1956. Bloom's taxonomy has had the most powerful influence on our thinking related to the science of human learning. He divided learning into three domains, namely, cognitive, affective and psychomotor. Bloom's cognitive taxonomy classified thinking at six levels, namely, knowledge (low end), comprehension, application, analysis, synthesis and evaluation (high end) (Figure 7.3).

Figure 7.3:
Bloom's Taxonomy of Educational Objectives

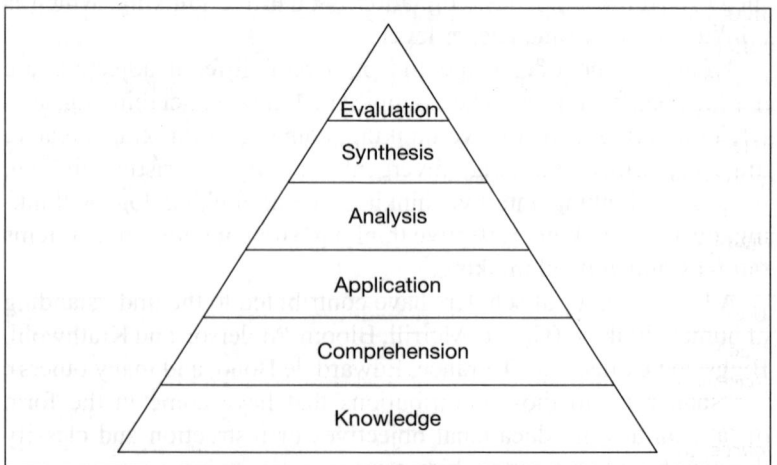

Source: http://juliaec.wordpress.com/2011/03/23/blooms-taxonomy-encouraging-higher-cognitive-thinking-in-primary-school-classrooms/ (accessed on 5 November 2014).

In 2001, Anderson et al. revised Bloom's taxonomy and proposed a modified version with a new matrix structure comprising of two dimensions—knowledge and cognitive processes (Figure 7.4). They made a four-layer classification of knowledge consisting of facts, concepts, procedures and meta-cognition and plotted it

Figure 7.4:
Anderson and Krathwohl's Revised Bloom's Taxonomy

Knowledge Dimensions ↓	Cognitive Process Dimensions					
	Remember	*Understand*	*Apply*	*Analyse*	*Evaluate*	*Create*
Facts						
Concepts						
Procedures						
Meta-cognition						

Source: Krathwohl (2002).

on the *Y* axis of the matrix. On the cognitive processes, they added creativity as the highest level of thinking.[9] The different levels of cognition were placed in the *X* axis.

The component display theory is an instructional model that was developed by David Merrill in 1983. The most important point of this theory is that it is designed for developing instructions for different concepts. Merrill used a two-dimensional matrix (Figure 7.5). On the *X* axis, the type of contents listed were facts, concepts, procedures and principles. On the *Y* axis, the three levels of performance were listed—remembering, finding and using (see similarity with Bloom's revised taxonomy on one axis).

Figure 7.5:
Merrill's Component Display Theory

Use				
Find				
Remember				
	Fact	Concept	Procedure	Principle

Source: Merrill (1983).

Biggs and Collis (1982) introduced the concept of structure of observed learning outcomes (SOLO) taxonomy. The focus here is on the learning outcomes and thus on the learners. In short, SOLO taxonomy describes the learners' understanding of concepts through five stages, namely, prestructural, unistructural, multistructural,

---

[9] http://laurant.edublogs.org

relational and extended abstraction. Plotted on an incompetence–competence continuum, prestructural is at the incompetence end and extended abstraction is at the other end of the continuum (competence). According to this taxonomy, prestructural is characterized by missing points or fail to catch a point; in the unistructural level, one relevant aspect is understood that can be verified by ability to identify something, name and follow simple procedures. At the multistructural level, a learner understands several independent aspects as verifiable by his/her ability to combine, describe, enumerate, list and so on. At the relational level, a learner integrates his/her understanding of several independent items into a structure as verifiable by skills of analysis, application, comparison and contrasting, criticizing and so on. At the extended abstract level, the learner generalizes and creates new domain. This can be verified by abilities to create, generalize, generate, hypothesize, theorize and so on.[10]

Paul Torrance's (1962) contribution is on creative thinking. According to him, divergent thinking is characterized through a combination of four components:

1. Fluency of ideas
2. Flexibility of the kinds of ideas
3. Originality of the ideas generated
4. Elaboration of other ideas

The concept of lateral thinking is the contribution of Edward de Bono (1970). Lateral thinking deals with changing concepts, perception and reasoning about a problem in ways that would not ordinarily be possible with traditional forms of logic. De Bono stated as follows:

- Creativity is a skill and not just a matter of individual talent. Therefore, it can be learned. Also, it is not merely a matter of inspiration.
- Creativity is more than just being different. A creative idea is not just different for the sake of being different. Creative ideas must necessarily have some inherent value of their own or add more value to the original idea.

---

[10] https://www.google.co.in/?gfe_rd=cr&ei=wwZlU6zVK8bM8gfBuIBg#q=SOLO%20Taxonomy (accessed on 25 April 2014).

- Thinking outside the box—this means escaping from or breaking out of the box to change concepts, perceptions, constraints and rules. It involves developing an idea that would not have been expected in our usual behaviour and our usual thinking.

We created an eclectic model of taxonomy of human thinking (Mukhopadhyay et al. 2014) deriving from Bloom's, Anderson and Krathwohl's, Merrill's, Biggs and Collis' taxonomies in addition to Paul Torrance and Edward de Bono's theories of creative thinking and intuitive thinking from the Indian scriptural literature, we propose a more comprehensive taxonomy. Unlike a staircase model, our preference is for tree/plant as the metaphor; the plant slowly unfolds. I call it a 'Thinking Tree' (Figure 7.6).

Figure 7.6:
The Thinking Tree

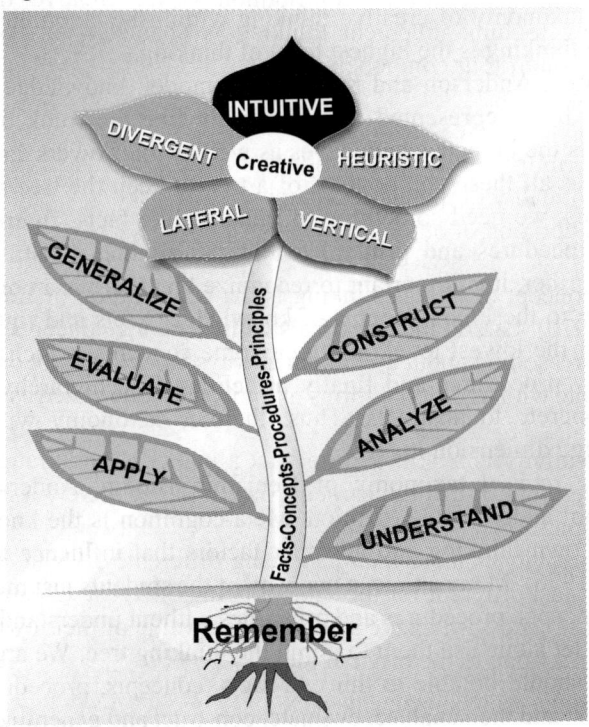

Source: Author (2012b).

Roots appear first (remember). A small stem (facts) with just one or two early petal-like leaves evolve next (understand and application). As the plant grows, stem grows taller (concepts, procedures, principles) and new leaves appear (analysis, evaluation, construction, generalization). Finally, the plant flowers and bears fruits (creativity).

Thinking is classified into two levels—lower-order thinking and higher-order thinking. Lower-order thinking is the foundation on which stands the edifice of higher-order thinking. Therefore, lower-order thinking is a necessary condition for higher-order thinking to grow. The primary consideration here is that there is a logical sequence in the development of thinking from one stage to another, except possibly in the case of intuitive thinking, which is considered to be the basis of revealed knowledge.

The new features of this taxonomy are construction and generalization together with creative thinking at five different levels. Thus, there is taxonomy of creative thinking within the taxonomy where intuitive thinking is the highest form of thinking.

Adapting Anderson and Krathwohl's model, knowledge dimension has been represented metaphorically like the trunk of a tree that holds the branches and leaves as well as the flowers and fruits. It nurtures all these components of a tree to keep the tree alive. In real terms, we need something to think of like facts, figures, concepts, procedures and principles. For us, all that constitutes the trunk. Further, it is important to recognize that there is an order and sequence to these components of knowledge. Facts and figures are placed at the lowest level, and then come concepts, which are followed by procedures and finally principles. The hierarchy moves from concrete to abstracts. Thus, there is taxonomy within the knowledge dimension itself.

In the revised taxonomy of Benjamin Bloom, Anderson and Krathwohl added meta-cognition. Meta-cognition is the knowledge of one's own thinking and all other factors that influence thinking (Flavell 1976). Many a time, a majority of the students just memorize facts, concepts, procedures and principles without understanding any of them, let alone use them to climb the thinking tree. We argue that students should be able to think of facts, concepts, procedures and principles, and then analyse, evaluate, construct and generalize them. It is this thinking that helps subsume new knowledge into the existing knowledge mass (Ausubel 1962, 1963). Thus, students should be able to explain, compare and contrast different facts and concepts, and also evaluate them, and then construct and create new procedures and principles. In short, our essential agenda is to create a mechanism of thinking among the students around this trunk of the tree that is hidden in the curriculum, syllabus and textbooks.

Thinking in Behavioural Terms

As discussed earlier, thinking is a covert behaviour. We do not know what our students are thinking when they are apparently listening to our presentation. We gauge other's thinking, through certain forms of overt behaviour. Professional literature provides 'action verbs' as overt behaviour indicators against each level of covert behaviour (thinking) (Table 7.1).

Table 7.1:
Action Verbs for Different Levels of Thinking

Level of Thinking (Covert)	*Action Verbs: Behaviour (Overt)*
Remember	Define, state, list, recite, recall, recognize and so on.
Understand	Explain, describe, illustrate, classify, select and so on.
Apply	Demonstrate, compute and draw conclusions, make an assessment, solve problems
Analyse	Break down a problem into smaller parts, identify relevant facts, interpret the meaning of the facts, compare, contrast, and connect different facts and prospects
Evaluate	Critique, judge, defend, argue, decide, attach values and so on.
Construct	Discover, combine, summarize, organize, hypothesize, relate, formulate and so on.
Generalise	Identify relevant information and data, classify, decipher trends, generalize events and processes and propose principles. Students should be able to predict, state principles and hypothesize.
Create	Invent, design, compose, draw, create a new solution, develop a new product and so on.

Source: Author (selected from larger repertoire of action verbs referred in the text to relate to the Levels of Thinking (Covert)).

A more detailed list of action verbs on Bloom's taxonomy can be accessed at http://www.clemson.edu/assessment/assessmentprac-tices/referencematerials/documents/Blooms%20Taxonomy%20 Action%20Verbs.pdf

Operating only at the lowest level of cognition, namely memory, is gross underutilization of brain potential. There is enough evidence that by developing a well-thought-out instructional design system, it is possible to boost the level of student learning to higher-order cognition and thereby ensure sustainable learning. Hence, the first important parameter for designing a new story of the teaching–learning process is to ensure achievement of higher-order cognition so that a student is able to explore, experiment, 'create solutions' and, most importantly, evolve as an autonomous learner with the skill of 'learning to learn'.

The primary ideas conveyed across all taxonomies are the following:

- Human cognition is a multilevel process and is hierarchic in nature.
- There are several levels between information and creativity.
- Highest level of cognition is extended abstraction (Biggs and Collis 1982) and creativity (Bloom's revised taxonomy) depending upon the school of thought.

Learning Designs in Cogitagogy

For creating competent learning designs, it is necessary to lay down the boundary conditions. One of the primary concerns of teachers is 'covering the curriculum'. This means teaching every chapter/topic of the prescribed syllabus in the class within the given time frame. Teachers differ in their style of handling the curriculum. While some of them prepare in advance for every lecture and engage deeply with the students, others deliver good or bad monologues. Some others just dictate self-made or inherited notes in class. This means that they do nothing more than just 'speaking out the course contents'. Though students are able to learn only at lower levels due to this kind of conventional methodology, it has been followed for quite a long time. Further, it lays the foundation for higher-order thinking.

- Thus, the first challenge in Cogitagogy is to lay down a strong foundation in a shorter duration of time and thereby overcome the constraints of time; also, create space for other instructional or learning activities that can create opportunities for students to actively participate and think at higher levels.
- The second challenge is to identify key *learning tactics* that can engage students in learning tasks to develop higher-order thinking while imparting the course prescribed by the university.
- The third challenge is to select and combine the right tactics to create a greater impact in learning for achieving higher-order thinking.

We did some interesting research involving more than 1,200 teachers over four years to find possible solutions to these challenges. The response to the first challenge is to use digital content in order to build a strong foundation and create greater impact in a shorter time frame. Normally, the course content that we teach in three to four periods through conventional lectures can be covered in about 15 minutes of digital content. The reason is that preparation of digital content goes through a rigorous process of preparation, production and post-production processes. It is based on a detailed content research and analysis, media research, academic note, script writing, story boarding, location identification, identifying content experts and so on as the pre-production preparation; shooting, lighting, sound recording and so on are the production-stage activities, and post production includes editing, sound mixing, animating, and finishing and packaging and so on. This rigorous process ensures complete coverage of each and every major and minor component of the contents sequenced in a logical manner and presented by an expert to maintain high standard. Many kinds of illustrations are possible in digital media that is not possible in face-to-face classroom transactions.

I have personally been involved in a large number of digital content generation. Consortium for Educational Communication (CEC) possesses a huge repository of such digital educational programmes in higher education, produced by the Audio-visual Resource Centres (AVRCs) and Educational Media Resource Centres (EMRCs). Even if all of them are not of good quality or even related directly to the curriculum and syllabus, a small proportion of this 'digital content inventory' is relevant and of high quality, it is useful to increase the quality and effectiveness of imparting higher education. The National Programme on Technology Enhanced Learning–National Mission on Education through ICT (NPTEL [NME-ICT]) is a project on digital content. It has contents comprising live recording of classroom lectures by eminent professors of IITs.

Media studies indicate that live video lectures, even by best of the teachers, are not able to hold the attention of the students. Also, these lectures do not save on time as they are conventional lectures consuming full time for achieving lower-order cognition. However, these lectures serve a very important purpose. It makes up for the huge staff deficit in the engineering institutions all over the country, and over several decades.

There are lot of digital content in the OER domain as well, especially in YouTube, TED and other such portals. The first and foremost challenge in this direction is to identify, access, evaluate and create an archive of the relevant digital content so that these are readily available to the teacher. We have done some experiments in training teachers to develop their own digital contents that represent their own unique styles. Such digital content does not have adequate media sophistication, but it becomes fully relevant non-threatening to the teacher.

The fundamental advantage of quality digital content is that it takes approximately one-third of the time taken to cover the prescribed syllabus as compared to the conventional mode. Also, it builds a strong foundation of knowledge and understanding with better impact and clarity. Further, it automatically reduces the inter-teacher variability on quality. By involving the best of teachers in creating the digital content, it is possible to extend the reach of such outstanding teachers to all the students in our country. In fact, this was precisely the idea behind NME-ICT.

By covering the syllabus in one-third of the time, two-thirds of the time is available for direct engagement of students in other appropriate learning activities/tactics that help to develop higher-order thinking skills. The Cogitagogy design is based on the scientific principle that thinking is activated through active learning processes, like projects achieve this goal in a much better manner than passive learning process, such as listening to a lecture. This is also true in every other sphere of life. For example, we think a lot more when we actually drive ourselves than listen to a lesson about how to drive. Similarly, we learn better when we cook ourselves rather than just watch a cookery show on TV. In other words, in order to develop higher-order thinking skills, students must find space to actively engage themselves in a variety of learning tasks like collaborative learning, survey and research, case studies, gaming and so on.

The second challenge in Cogitagogy is to identify appropriate learning activities and tactics. We have created an inventory of as many as 68 learning tactics that are classified into five broad categories. These are:

1. Active reception: Listening to lectures, audio, video, observing, reading, digital content (non-interactive) and so on.
2. Collaborative learning: Group discussions, team learning, projects, group assignments, phone conferencing, teaching and mentoring and so on.
3. Exploratory learning: Research, surveys, experiments, projects, brainstorming, buzzing, problem solving and so on.
4. Experiential learning: Games, simulations, role play, case studies and so on.
5. ICT-enabled learning: Interactive digital content, blogs, open education resources, chats and video conferences, phone conferences and so on.

Each category of learning tactics supports thinking at different levels. Generally speaking, active reception group of tactics support knowledge and understanding (lower-order cognition). Collaborative learning supports a wide range of thinking from understanding to analysis and synthesis. Learning tactics, in the exploratory and experiential learning categories, support only higher-order thinking; hence, most often, these are not stand-alone tactics. ICT-enabled learning tactics can again support a wide range of levels of cognition, from knowledge to construction and generalization. However, the effectiveness of the Cogitagogy design depends upon the choice of tactics and also the diligence in weaving it into a suitable pattern. A safe and effective choice is collaborative learning—without any additional cost, it enhances learning while building several graduate and employability skills like analytical and creative thinking, working in teams, sharing responsibilities and so on.

There are six guiding lights that may help us to choose the tactics for a particular theme/topic. These are:

1. *Nature of subject and contents*: All tactics are not applicable to either all subjects or all topics of the same subject. The nature of the topic/theme must be carefully taken into account while selecting the tactics. For example, experiments go well with science subjects whereas survey fits better in the context of certain social sciences. Similarly, library research can be a suitable learning tactic for many subjects where students are expected to discover the current state of the knowledge in a given topic.

2. *Students' learning styles and world view*: Students have different learning styles and world view. By selecting appropriate learning tactics, it is possible to provide suitable opportunities to every type of learner to actively participate.

3. *Teacher's personality, instructional style, competencies, and world view*: Since teachers have their unique personality, each one of them cannot effectively manage all types of tactics. For example, certain tactics need a lot of organizational and leadership skills, whereas certain others require more of critical reflection. In general, an extrovert teacher may fit in well with tactics that require organization and leadership skills while an introvert teacher may find himself/herself comfortable in dealing with tactics involving critical discourse.

4. *Evaluation system*: Examination and evaluation system is a reality that should be taken into consideration. The type of examination and questions, for example, multiple choice questions (MCQs), short answers, very short answers, essays, assignments, practical sessions, workshops, reports and journals and so on and their expected learning outcomes must guide us in the selection of appropriate learning tactics.

5. *Facilities and infrastructure:* Certain learning tactics may require special facilities. For example, group discussions and team learning activities can be better around a round table rather than in a theatre style class. ICT-enabled learning requires easy access to certain kinds of infrastructure besides high-speed Internet facilities. Thus, the choice of learning tactics has to be guided by the available facilities or whether they can be mobilized without much difficulty.

6. *Ethics and values:* Ethics and values refer to issues related to undesirable discrimination among students and communities, such as poor aesthetics, unequal opportunities to learners, gender inequity and so on.

Creating a competent learning design involves plotting the learning tactics in a pattern or sequence that could help the students to move towards developing higher-order thinking skills and thereby ensure effectiveness. See Table 7.2 for an example.

Table 7.2:
Elements of a Learning Design

Learning Activities/Tactics	*Level of Thinking*
a. Showing digital content with necessary instructions to students to find answers to a few questions given in advance. This could also facilitate to gain their attention and make them focus on the given task.	Knowledge and understanding
b. Asking the students to find answers to the questions collectively in groups through discussions.	Deepening understanding, application, analysis, evaluation and synthesis
c. Conducting experiments, surveys, games, simulations, role play and so on.	Application, analysis, evaluation, construction and so on.
d. Construction of theories and designing experiments to verify the theory	Creative thinking

Source: Author.

I must reemphasize that lower-order cognition is essential to move to higher-order cognition. Second, creating a competent learning design challenges the creativity of a teacher and requires considerable amount of thinking and practice. Third, it needs conviction that such student-centric learning is more effective than classroom lectures.

Relevance and Generic Graduate Skills

As mentioned earlier, an important parameter of quality instruction is the development of generic skills. Some of these skills include the following:

- Managing one's own affairs, including daily chores
- Communicating effectively—both oral and written
- Relating to others
- Working in teams
- Providing leadership/displaying leadership skills

- Thinking critically and creatively
- Sharing and cooperating with one another
- Recording and documenting learning and findings
- Calculating and keeping accounts
- Using computers and other applicable/relevant technology when necessary

Many of these skills can be developed by adopting Cogitagogy. For example, the use of ICT-based learning tactics develops skills to identify, access and utilize information and ICT. Collaborative learning tactics create opportunities to work in teams, build leadership skills, share and cooperate with others as well as communicate effectively within the group and class. Projects and group assignments lead to the development of problem-solving skills, essential language and communication skills, such as documentation and recording, and working in teams.

Take Away

As a take away from the chapter, Table 7.3 presents a few sample learning tactics belonging to each of the five categories. This should help a teacher create his/her own learning design.

Table 7.3:
Sample Learning Tactics for Each Category

S. No.	Category	Learning Tactics
1.	Active reception	Listening to lecture, audio, video, observing, reading a text, surfing the Internet
2.	Collaborative learning	Group discussion, projects, group assignments, phone conferencing, tutoring and mentoring
3.	Exploratory	Research, survey, projects, brain storming, buzzing and problem solving
4.	Experiential	Games, simulations, case studies and field studies
5.	Technology enabled	Digital content, YouTube, Teacher Tube, Blogs, Wikis, websites, Chats

Source: Author.

Cogitagogy is discovery oriented. Hence, recommending any specific formula or a plan of instruction will be illogical. However, it is possible to provide certain samples to exemplify the kind of plan of action for implementing Cogitagogy (Table 7.4).

Table 7.4:
Sample Planner for Cogetagogy

S. No.	Levels of Cognition	Possible Choice of Tactics
1.	Remember	E-content, textbook, lecture, surf the Internet
2.	Understand	Collaborative, team, peer group learning
3.	Apply	Demonstrate, solve problem, individual and group assignment
4.	Analyse	Compare and contrast contents, examples, experimental results and so on from different sources
5.	Evaluate	Focused group discussion, debate, structured evaluative exercise
6.	Construct	Predict new relationships, formulate hypotheses
7.	Create	Propose new ways of working, create products and so on.

Source: Author.

1. Decide what should the student be able to do at the end of the session/theme/chapter. The deriving out of principles of competency--based education, we should be able to say that students will be able to explain; analyse, compare and contrast between two concepts, ideas, practices, experiments, et cetera; evaluate the benefits, advantages and disadvantages of a given practice, solution, product and so on; propose and test a hypothesis based on data and experiments; design alternative examples and experiments to prove a scientific theory; create alternative ways of solving problem, complex models and theoretical constructs and so on.

2. Choose appropriate learning tactics to engage students so that the competencies specified are achieved. For example, the prerequisite of a student to be able to explain certain concepts and practices there has to be a minimum level of information and knowledge on the subject that may require either reading a book, watching a digital content or listening to a lecture, surfing internet and so on. Out of all these, digital content is more efficient in terms of quality, cost and time.

3. You may like to follow it up with a series of learning assignments to be solved by groups; such groups may discuss issues together, work on projects to find new ways to solve problems, construct models and theoretical constructs and so on.
4. Students may be encouraged to take field surveys, laboratory experiments, data analytic research and so on.
5. Students can undertake collective and mutual evaluation of learning and take remedial actions.

Conclusion

The ultimate objective behind emphasizing about increasing the quality of higher education is to nurture students to think critically and creatively instead of just becoming a mere storehouse of relevant or irrelevant, outdated or updated information. Only then higher education can extract the real potential of students and move towards knowledge creation. An effective teaching–learning process has to support this goal. It has to be tuned to the styles and needs of 21st-century learners. It has to exploit the benefits of emerging technological developments wherever applicable, especially what has come to be known as EdTech. Cogitagogy serves as both the means and ends for achieving the desired impact in the teaching–learning process. Cogitagogy not just skilfully builds into it the sciences of andragogy, technogogy, heutagogy and MCLS, but goes beyond them in order to nurture higher-order thinking skills among the young women and men.

8

Quality of Examination and Student Assessment

Introduction

Examination is by far the most criticized and debated issue in higher education in the context of quality. Irrespective of the criticism, examination is a necessary, even if it is an evil, component of higher education. Examination cannot be wished away from education. Its intrinsic value is the assessment of learning outcome of students—validation of whether desired learning and change is happening. Extrinsic or tangible value is certification of candidates based on examination that acts as the passport to higher-level courses and job opportunities. The issue is whether the certificate as an indicator of learning is reliable and valid. Did the examination measure what it intended to measure, and whether the candidate would be able to show consistency of results over either parallel or delayed tests. There is a huge gap between levels of learning and certification.

The primary reason behind criticizing examination and student assessment is that conventional examination does not actually serve the purpose for which it is meant. For example, a human being lives in four planes, namely intellectual, physical, mental and spiritual. Conventional examination measures only the academic achievement (intellectual domain). The learning and development in physical, emotional and spiritual domains remain unattended. There is increasing evidence affirming that individuals with same IQ succeed differently in life because of differential emotional quotient (EQ) and spiritual quotient (SQ). I prefer to define 'spiritual plane' as one that implies exploration, inquiry and knowledge enterprise that leads to research and invention. It does not find any place in the schema of examination in higher education. This is also obvious by the nature of examinations that evaluate only knowledge assimilation or lower-order cognition in higher education.

Again, from the perspective of multiple intelligences, conventional examination evaluates only mathematical–logical and verbal intelligence. It does not include the assessment of other domains of intelligences. Even within the logical–mathematical intelligence, the conventional examination and student assessment system evaluates learning at the lower level of cognition like memory and understanding, whereas the aim and emphasis in higher education is on achieving higher-order cognition, namely application, analysis, synthesis, generalization and creativity. As a result, the outcome of examination in the form of scores and marks is highly unreliable in terms of assessing the actual capabilities and potential of students. By adopting non-scientific tools for the assessment of students without a blueprint, conventional examination does not even comprehensively assess the learning from the coursework by the students. This is besides the subjectivity in the assessment as indicated by inter-examiner variability studies.

As mentioned earlier, learning of the course can be either fragile or sustainable. Fragile learning is the outcome of cramming facts, concepts and principles without either understanding or application and is stored in the temporary memory; much of it is lost as soon as the examination is over. Compared to that, sustainable learning is integrated with the existing (knowledge) schema and stays with the learner. The purpose of higher education is sustainable learning. There is enough empirical evidence to prove that the examination scores are not very dependable indicator of sustainable learning. The fact that a large number of college graduates actually forget the subject in which they score very high within a very short span of time indicates their fragile learning. The examination system and the student assessment practices do not necessarily demand sustainable learning. They only provide a distorted picture of the graduate according to the marks scored in the university examination. Though the graduate may appear to be sound on the basis of mark sheet and certificate in, say physics, his/her actual learning and understanding of physics cannot be certified immediately after the examination. Thus, these graduates display some knowledge of the subject matter without developing a disciplined mind (Gardner 2010) or understanding of the epistemology of the subject.

Human being cannot just be viewed as a cognitive configuration.[1] An individual is much more than that. The conventional and contemporary student evaluation and assessment does not assess students' emotive, psychomotor or social skills like leadership, cooperation, interpersonal relationships and so on. In reality, it assesses only one component of the budding human being, that too, the lower level of cognition. In other words, it serves very little purpose for student assessment. Since higher education graduates assume leadership roles in various fields like economic, social, political, cultural and so on, it is necessary to develop a comprehensive system of assessment for students in higher education. This would require laying down a framework for assessment.

The new assessment framework must include both academic assessment and assessment of life skills, which include emotional and social skills as well. There have been several policy initiatives in setting up academic assessment frameworks for modernizing examination and evaluation. In 2009, the UGC directed all the central and state universities as well as deemed universities to adopt a semester system within a time frame of three years. The reforms policy also recommended introducing facilities for credit system and credit transfer. In another circular, the UGC instructed universities to introduce certain reforms and make it public (known to students). These reforms intended to allow students to take courses of their choice from one university and move on to another for accumulating credits. A large number of universities have posted their semester systems and student assessment frameworks on their websites.

In this chapter, we propose to deal with techniques for improving quality of students' assessment in the academic domain and introduce scientific techniques for the assessment of life skills.

---

[1] Human beings have been called a 'mind configuration in a physical body' in the interpretation of The Gita.

Assessment of Academic Achievement

There are several issues in modernizing assessment of academic achievement. These are periodicity and types of evaluation (namely formative and summative assessments), planning for evaluation like assessment blueprint, tools and techniques of tests, forms of tests (online, offline, walk-in assessment, etc.).

Formative and Summative Assessments

The purpose of academic assessments is twofold. Conventionally, assessments have been used to make judgments about the quality of learning or the level of attainment of learning outcomes and were measured by conducting term-end examinations. This is called summative assessment. Another important purpose of academic assessment is to help students to learn better or improve their quality of learning, and most importantly, develop a self-organizing learning system. This requires intermittent assessment coupled with regular feedbacks that help students to identify their learning styles, learning gaps, strengths and weaknesses and improve upon them. This is largely the function of formative assessment. Formative assessment is not common in the Indian higher education system, although it figures prominently in a majority of universities in the Western countries. Formative assessments are the milestones for students during their learning journey. The emphasis of formative assessment is on the feedback that helps students to improve learning. Nicol and Macfarlane-Dick (2006) provided a comprehensive review on formative assessment, a theoretical model and seven principles of good feedback.

Good Feedback

- Helps clarify what good performance is (goals, criteria, expected standards).
- Facilitates the development of self-assessment (reflection) in learning.
- Delivers high-quality information to students about their learning.

- Encourages teacher and peer dialogue around learning.
- Encourages positive motivational beliefs and self-esteem.
- Provides opportunities to close the gap between current and desired performance.
- Provides information to teachers that can be used to help shape teaching.

Indian higher education needs to introduce formative assessment—at least two or three in each semester. Formative assessment can be done through a number of ways like individual and group assignments, short tests, project works, laboratory practical sessions, conducting survey, research, experiments and so on. Formative assessment can be practised at the individual or teacher level by those who are keen on experimentation and innovation. A teacher can design a few assignments that a student is expected to complete during the academic year. For each subject, a teacher can propose, say 6 to 10 assignments, out of which each student will be expected to complete at least 4 or 5 assignments. This can be made a prerequisite (like or instead of 75 per cent attendance in the class) for clearing the final examination. Another smart alternative or complementing assignment-based evaluation can be an online test. Teachers can construct an objective type test on her/his subject and post it online with the facility that students can respond online and get his/her score with qualitative comments like very satisfactory, satisfactory, not so satisfactory or not satisfactory.[2] With growing access to technology and Internet facilities, online tests are more possible today than before.

Planning for Assessment

The purpose of conventional examination and testing is to measure the learning outcomes of students. Revisiting sample question papers

---

[2] We created a multimedia training programme on comprehensive and continuous evaluation for teachers that included formative and summative evaluation; along with the programme, we created a 100-item/objective-type test and posted it on the website. On the completion of the training programme teachers take the test; computer gives the feedback in the form of scores and qualitative statements; and a teacher who scores 60 or more out of 100 can print his/her certificate.

and old question papers of various universities indicate a usual pattern characterized by long-essay and short-essay-type questions asking students to answer three or four out of seven or eight questions.[3] Some universities add short notes.[4] Smart students carry out such trend analysis to guess the questions and prepare themselves to answer only those that are highly probable to appear in the examination. This way, if they are expected to answer, say, three questions out of ten, they can get through by preparing just 30 per cent of the syllabus and eliminating 70 per cent. This gives rise to a serious learning gap. Further, the common verbs used in the question papers include 'write down', 'mention', 'bring out', 'examine', 'what is' and so on. Students reproduce answers to such questions from their notes by meticulously memorizing them through repeated practice and drill. Such questions actually test memory rather than deeper learning. There is every possibility that the contents that are reproduced in examinations are not integrated with the knowledge of the students. No wonder, students forget (learning loss) much of what they 'learnt' almost immediately after the examinations are over. Quite often, there is no relation between the quantity and quality of knowledge with that of the score in the examination. This indicates fragile learning. The challenge of improving quality in assessment is to evaluate sustainable learning—learning at the higher levels of cognition.

The basic assumption that supports conventional methods of examination and test papers is that human cognition and learning is a mono-level function, namely information storage and retrieval. As mentioned in the earlier chapter on the teaching–learning process, human cognition is a multilayer function where information storage and retrieval form the lowest level of cognition. Other levels are (just to recollect) understanding, application, analysis, synthesis, evaluation, construction, generalization and creation. It is important to note that the lower the level of cognition, the higher is the fragility of learning. Therefore, sustainable learning is achievable only through higher-order cognition. In order to achieve higher-order cognition, a student has to resort to thinking while interacting with others, solving worksheets and problems, conducting experiments and surveys, and analysing and

---

[3] www.keralauniversity.ac.in/
[4] http://www.nagarjunauniversity.ac.in/syllabus%5Cartsmq.pdf (accessed on 3 May 2014).

interpreting data. All these seriously engaging activities, help in subsuming the new knowledge with the existing old knowledge.

> A primary process in learning is subsumption in which new material is related to relevant ideas in the existing cognitive structure on a substantive, non-verbatim basis. Cognitive structures represent the residue of all learning experiences; forgetting occurs because certain details get integrated and lose their individual identity. (Ausubel 1963)[5]

Quality examination endeavours to assess sustainable learning (or, meaningful verbal learning!), and thus test learning at higher levels of cognition.

There are certain action verbs that provide the basis for understanding the level of cognition that a question intends to measure. Generally speaking, when a student is asked 'what is', 'list', 'describe', 'write down', 'mention',[6] the test asks for *recall* or *recognize* a memorised concept, principle, examples and illustration and so on; it intends to assess knowledge and information. When a question asks to explain, the intention is to assess 'understanding'. 'Application' level of cognition is tested through problem-solving, illustrating and giving examples and so on. Comparing, relating and contrasting between two or more sets of information test 'analyses'. Formulating hypothesis or deriving conclusions based on the given data or information tests the 'synthesis' level of cognition and learning. 'Evaluation' level of cognition and learning is tested by questions intended to assess a theory. However, all these verbs are futile if students memorize the answers from study guides available in the market. Irrespective of the action verbs, the entire assessment then finally boils down to testing only the lower-order cognition. It requires teachers' creativity to overcome the barriers of study guides.

It should be evident that measurement of learning at different levels of cognition cannot be achieved by one single type of question, namely essay or short essay-type questions. It requires a wide variety of test items like objective tests, very short answers, short answers, short and long essays, projects, assignments, discourses and so on.

---

[5] http://www.instructionaldesign.org/theories/subsumption-theory.html (accessed on 3 May 2014).

[6] These action verbs have been picked up from actual university question papers for B.A. examination.

Thus, a quality examination has at least three dimensions, namely learning goals in terms of the levels of cognition, complete coverage of the curriculum and content as well as the types of test questions. By properly combining these three dimensions, it is possible to generate a blueprint for a more scientific system of evaluation. Also, the blueprint allows application of relative weightages to various units of the curriculum and content. Table 8.1 presents a template for an assessment blueprint.

Table 8.1:
A Sample Format for Assessment Blueprint

Content/ Units	Relative Weightages	Knowledge	Understanding	Application	Analysis
One	10				
Two	10				
Three	05				
Four	05				
Five	20				
Six	20				
Seven	10				
Eight	10				
Nine	10				
Total	100				

Source: Author.
Notes: 1. You can add more columns to include Evaluate, Construct, Generalize and Create.
    2. Each cell has to be filled in with types of questions and number of questions for each type. For example, for Unit 1, there will be three objective-type tests[7] under knowledge, one short-answer question each for understanding and application and none at the level of analysis.

Question papers that are set with such blueprint ensure complete coverage of the curriculum and evaluate students at different levels of cognition simultaneously. Thus, they reduce subjectivity because of testing through different types of questions, particularly objective-type and short-answer-type questions. Short-essay and long-essay

---

[7] Objective type tests are not very popular in higher education, largely because their potential and power have not been adequately explored. A short note on objective type test is attached at the end of this chapter.

questions facilitate testing of expressions besides higher level cognitions of learning (analysis and synthesis).

A large number of research studies indicate inter-examiner variability (different examiners assign different marks for the same answer). This implies that a student's score in the examination depends upon the examiner, which again reflects subjectivity in student assessment. In order to reduce inter-examiner variability, certain examination agencies[8] develop model answers and get it verified by groups of experts. Then, the students' answers are actually compared with the model answer that is prepared by the group of experts. By developing such a question bank, the elaborate examination process can be substantially made scientific without leaving this burden to the teachers.

Assessment of Employability Skills and Certification

In Chapter 6 on Curriculum in Higher Education, there is an elaborate discussion on generic graduate skills. A large majority of these generic graduate skills overlap with employability skills. Also, we have referred multiple times to the contemporary research on employability skills of Indian graduates conducted by Aspiring Minds, which revealed that more than 80 per cent of Indian graduates and more than 47 per cent of engineering graduates lack employability skills. We also attempted to draw attention to the fact that employability skills not only enhance job prospects of young graduates, but also become a key determinant to the national economic growth. Hence, for individual employability and national economic growth, it is rather essential to develop employability skills. Let us examine some of the ways of assessing generic graduate skills and employability skills.

---

[8] Many universities develop several question papers by different paper setters primarily to meet with contingencies like leakage of question paper. Several boards/councils of higher secondary education not only develop several question papers, but also each question paper is answered by the paper setter, and then moderated by a team of subject experts. These moderated answers are used as model answers. Students' answers are checked against these model answers to increase objectivity.

Although there is a wide variation in selecting the generic graduate skills from one university to another, let us pick up a few skills that are common across many universities in the world, and those that find their way into the list of employability skills.

The University of Sydney lists the following generic graduate skills[9] (as updated in March 2015) for graduates of Faculty of Arts and Social Sciences:

- Research and inquiry
- Information literacy
- Personal and intellectual autonomy
- Ethical, social and professional understanding
- Communication

On the critical assessment of policy options on generic graduate skills, Barrie (2004) may be referred to.

Each item in the list has been further elaborated in the form of enablers. (The reader is recommended to visit the university website[10] for details.)

Another list provided by Minerva[11] contains the following skills:

- Mathematical skills
- Adopts the principles of reflective practice and lifelong learning
- Knows the limits of professional competence
- Presents information clearly in all formats
- Is an effective teacher/mentor
- Capable of self-management
- Applies research principles and audit and studies topics in-depth
- Can deal with uncertainty
- Manages information retrieval, presentation and manipulation electronically

For details on each skill, please visit the university website.[12]

---

[9] http://sydney.edu.au/arts/teaching_learning/academic_support/graduate_attributes.shtml (accessed on 5 May 2014).
[10] See note 9.
[11] Source https://www.minerva.shef.ac.uk/outcomes/generic.htm (accessed on 6 May 2014).
[12] See note 11.

There are several skills that are classified as employability skills, which reflect 'what the employers are looking for in their potential employees'. Mukhopadhyay et al. (2015) carried out a comparative analysis of employability skills suggested by various authors and studies. A detailed analysis reveals a total of 32 skills (Table 8.2).

Table 8.2:
Consolidated List of Employability Skills (in alphabetical order)

Employability Skills	Employability Skills
1. Business and customer awareness	17. Learning
2. Citizenship skills	18. Negotiation skills
3. Commercial awareness	19. Numeracy
4. Communication and listening	20. Planning and organizing
5. Coping with emotions	21. Problem solving
6. Coping with stress	22. Professionalism
7. Creative thinking	23. Reasoning
8. Critical thinking	24. Reflective skills
9. Decision making	25. Science
10. Empathy	26. Self-awareness
11. Handling information	27. Self-management
12. Influencing skills	28. Team work
13. Initiative and enterprise	29. Technology/computer application
14. Interpersonal relationship	30. Thinking innovatively
15. Investigating and analysing	31. Thinking
16. Leadership	32. Time management

Source: Mukhopadhyay et al. (2015).

Some of the skills that occur frequently at various lists are as follows:

- Initiative and enterprise
- Self-management
- Learning (to learn)
- Communication
- Teamwork
- Problem solving
- Time management

- Planning and organizing
- Technology (ICT) skills
- Using information

A careful examination will indicate the common elements between the list of generic graduate skills and employability skills. The exception is about research skills. For our purposes, in the contemporary context of Indian higher education, our focus should be on the employability skills.

From the standpoint of quality management in higher education, there are two important issues with respect to the assessment of employability skills. These are (a) concepts and psychological meaning of the identified skills and (b) the tools and techniques for measurement of various employability skills. Let us discuss a few examples from the employability skills listed above.

Problem Solving

Problem solving (also listed under life skills by the World Health Organization) is an important employability skill as it is required at home, in social groups, as well as on the job. Problem solving is considered as a life skill especially because the nature of problems will change with time and a graduate will be expected to innovatively solve problems as they arise. Problem solving involves being aware of a problem, being concerned about finding a solution (since it may not be possible to solve all problems within a given time frame by an individual), understanding the details of the problem from various perspectives, finding as many solutions as possible, weighing each solution in terms of pros, cons, consequences and long-term implications, choosing the optimum solution that best fits a particular situation and (maybe) carry out a trial run. Quality in education (as well as in other fields) suffers largely because of lack of awareness, sensitivity and concern for quality. An interesting case on hand is developing employability skills and generic graduate skills among graduates. Although the issue of generic graduate skills is common in higher education in many developed countries, Indian higher education (in general) and universities (in particular) is yet to recognize this as an issue of quality in higher education.

Problem-solving skills can be assessed in more than one way. First, there are several tests available online for assessing problem-solving skills.[13] Second, peers (classmates and college mates) can mutually rate each other on problem-solving capabilities. Third, teachers can create/construct a number of real-time situations based on daily life issues and ask students to come up with their own solutions to these problems.

Communication

To start with, communication skills matter a lot, especially during interviews for the young graduates. These also matter later on the job to develop interpersonal relationships, maintain record and file management, initiate and facilitate upward and downward communication of information and decisions in the organization and, of course, in the day-to-day management of life. Communication skills comprise written and oral communication. Further, oral communication comprises verbal and non-verbal communication. Communication can be effective as well as ineffective. When the person at the receiving end is able to make out the meaning of what is being communicated, only then the communication becomes effective. Communication is considered ineffective if the person who receives the communication is unable to decipher the message. A 'good teacher' is most often a good communicator.

However, there are various layers of communication. At the lowest level, it is communication of information. The next level is communication for influencing. An indication of influencing through communication is apparent when a communicator develops conviction or a belief in a particular way of thinking or mode of working

---

[13] The Passi-Usha test of creative problem solving (http://www.npcindia.com/contact_us.html).
- Problem-solving ability test by L.N. Dubey. Source: http://www.npcindia.com/contact_us.html/ (accessed on 7 May 2014).
- Mckinsey problem-solving test: Yale Graduate Students, www.yalegradstudentconsulting.org/resources/ygcc.../mckinsey_pst/ (accessed on 6 May 2014).

among others. At a still higher level, communication is to inspire. On a day-to-day basis, spiritual discourses delivered by (genuine) saints are quite inspiring.[14] Communication during a selection interview is the typical case of 'impressing' or influencing the selectors by the candidate.

Besides observation and peer rating, communication can be assessed by some readily available measurement tools. Tools on the assessment of communication can be found on various websites.[15]

ICT Skills

ICT skills dominate the list of employability skills as this has been found to immensely contribute to national economic growth (OECD, 2006). There are generic ICT skills and specific or professional ICT skills. Generic skills involve word processing, using presentation software like PowerPoint or Prezi, working with spreadsheet programmes like excel and so on. Professional skills include cyber security, designing and so on. Generic skills have been further classified into three categories—basic, intermediate and advanced. Every job seeker today is expected to have ICT skills. ICT skills are no more considered professional skills; these are life skills. ICT skills can be measured by developing certain in-house theory and practical examinations. Or, students can be encouraged to take the required ICT certifications from any of the recognized certifying agencies.

ICT skills are tested and certified by several agencies like ECDL, Microsoft, Oracle and so on. Since certificates issued by such IT giants are better recognized and preferred by the employers, colleges and universities can tie up with such certifying agencies and encourage graduating students to take the test.

There are various free online or downloadable tests on the Internet on all the employability skills listed earlier. Higher education institutions are well equipped with computers and high-speed Internet connectivity. Students can take these tests twice a year or once every semester to assess whether their skills are improving.

---

[14] Swami Vivekananda's Chicago address is by far the most outstanding event of inspiring communication. Available at http://www.youtube.com/watch?v=p4Nmvbm4WYM.

[15] http://www.youtube.com/watch?v=p4Nmvbm4WYM

Assessment Portfolio

Students step into the professional world after graduation. Except in the case of teaching and a few other selective professions, the professional world hardly requires the knowledge of the subjects which a student learns and takes the examinations. The employee productivity depends largely upon certain other life skills and behavioural qualities. There is an interesting incident to highlight this. Because of the reputation of the Ramakrishna Mission Vidyamandira, Belur, Howrah, West Bengal, students were taken for granted about their knowledge and skills in computers; they were tested on their life skills, especially values and ethics (read as prospective work ethics in future) (Mukhopadhyay 2012a). This is an important question, particularly because the employment market is steadily changing from the organized government sector to an organized or semi-organized private sector. The evolving job market will demand much more of such job-related skills, life skills and skills that enable smooth transition to work. In other words, the selection processes can be facilitated in a much better manner if there was comprehensive information about the candidates on their physical, emotional and intellectual attributes of life besides details about the marks that the candidates scored in the examinations. An individual student portfolio would be a better alternative over the prevalent practice of issuing a mark sheet; student portfolio would provide a more holistic assessment of a student. Let us illustrate this a little further to indicate the kind of information that can be there a portfolio.

Physical data: Photograph, height and weight, identification marks, colour of the eyes and skin, blood group, any chronic ailment, general state of health, any special disability or deformity and so on.

- Physical skills: Any special talent in sports, games, gymnastics, dramatics, dancing and so on. The description could also include specific events, such as participated or represented the college/university in inter-college or inter-university competitions, district, state and national level.
- Psychological: Details on a host of psychological attributes like aptitudes, personality, intelligence, creativity, self-motivation, emotional maturity, emotional intelligence and so on.

- Intellectual: This highlights the subjects studied during pre-college and college, performance in the subjects during different years, special skills and interests like creative writing, debates and group discussions and so on. This should also include a range of other information like books other than course material read during the graduation or postgraduation programme.
- Social skills: Cooperation, leadership, organization, helping others, social service, hobbies and so on.

This is only a sample list. It can be extended depending upon the requirements in different situations. What is important is to appreciate that such a portfolio will provide a comprehensive view of the student and stand as a landmark in the life of the student.

The student portfolio should also contain data on employability skills. Since these skills do not change very often, students can take online tests twice every year. Each time a test is taken, he/she can write his/her name and the date of the test and file it in the portfolio. Over a period of three years of undergraduate or two years of postgraduate programme, a student would have taken six or four of such tests, the results of which will help to compare and examine whether he/she is improving on the employability skills. As mentioned earlier, feedback is an essential component of mentoring students. The portfolio assessment will be incomplete without portfolio conferences held jointly by the teacher and the student along with the peer group members.

Let us re-emphasize that good quality assessment must be holistic and provide comprehensive information about all aspects of the student. Accordingly, the mark sheet will be included as a part of portfolio itself. These reforms in student assessment may require an institutional mechanism like an assessment centre.

Assessment Centre

Developing a comprehensive portfolio requires a comprehensive mechanism of assessment. Assessment centre is a viable and useful alternative. Although it is not common in India so far, certain corporate houses have set up assessment centres for their own employees. Many progressive schools in the private sector have set up examination and assessment unit. Universities have Controller of Examination heading a full unit on examination.

The basic requirement of an assessment centre is to have a repertoire of relevant online assessment tests along with standardized psychological tests, a trained psychologist with experience in administering such tests, scoring and interpreting scores and providing feedback to the students. Every college and university should be able to set up such an assessment centre. The University of Kent maintains its own assessment centre. For details, please refer to the university website.[16]

In operational terms, computer labs can be used as assessment centres as most of the tests are available online; even in case of offline tests, test data have to be stored, analysed and retrieved from computers. Subject to affordability, one terminal can be dedicated for this purpose within the computer lab. Students can volunteer or are asked to take different kinds of tests on their own (according to their preference). The assessment centre will administer such tests, score them as well as interpret and enter the results/scores on the student portfolio. Setting up assessment centres is not very expensive because a majority of the psychological tests are available online and free; and printed tests are not very expensive except certain tests of global repute. Moreover, they are reusable.

Conclusion

Quality student assessment warrants a conceptual overhauling. The essential requirement is to move from 'only scholastic' to comprehensive scholastic and co-scholastic assessment, especially by including assessment of employability skills. As part of the scholastic assessment, there is a need to introduce a judicious combination of both formative and summative assessments. Formative assessment with the right kind of feedback will help students to improve their quality of learning. This will further lead to sustainable learning when tested through the summative assessment. Formative assessment, in particular, will demand considerable amount of innovativeness and

---

[16] http://www.kent.ac.uk/careers/selection.html (accessed on 10 May 2014).

creativity on the part of the teachers as they would have to invent different types of tools for assessing progressive learning. To make summative assessment more reliable and valid, the use of different types of tests (questions) against a blueprint is recommended. Finally, higher education institutions should become more innovative and resourceful to source various types of online and offline tests for assessing employability skills.

Note: Objective Type Tests

Objective type tests are not very popular in Indian higher education; as a technique or tool, it is looked down upon as trivial or pedestrian. It is often equated as tick, tick, tick, meaning thereby a guess work. One of the major reasons is the unfamiliarity of this powerful instrument of testing.

Objective tests, by the very name, suggest objectivity—one of the important psychometric properties of a good test. By implication, it also means lack of space for subjectivity, thereby eliminating interrater (examiner) variation. In objective type tests, a student/candidate is required to respond to a question by choosing the correct answer provided with the question—whether the question is true/false. Matching, fill in the blanks or MCQ.[17]

Misconception emanates from the idea of one correct and three wrong answers (MCQ) without understanding the purpose of wrong answers. Wrong answers are called distracters. The issue is how powerful the distracters are so that unless a student is sure about the correct answer, she/he would get distracted and resort to guess. The guess element can be eliminated by introducing correction factor—correct answer minus wrong answers. Correct answers can be a combination of actually knowing and guess. Wrong answers are exclusively because of not knowing, but answered by guessing. Thus, guessing is there both in correct and wrong answers. Logically, to eliminate the effect of guess, in the correct answers, the number of wrong answers is subtracted. More importantly, where candidates know that this

---

[17] caacentre.lboro.ac.uk/resources/objective_tests/index.shtml (accessed on 8 May 2014).

correction factor will be used, they avoid guessing, and leave the questions unanswered.

Another issue is about the level of cognition that can be assessed using objective type questions. Objective type questions can be used for assessing higher-order cognition. 'You can design MCQ tests to assess higher-order cognition (such as synthesis, creative thinking and problem solving), but you must draft questions with considerable skill if such tests are to be valid and reliable. This takes time and entails significant subjective judgment'.[18] Assertion reasoning type of MCQs assesses higher-order cognition. Almost all standardized aptitude tests (especially verbal) use MCQ to test higher-order cognition.

---

[18] https://teaching.unsw.edu.au/printpdf/543

9

Quality of Research in Higher Education

Introduction

The concept and role of universities have evolved from the days of John Henry Newman's *Idea of a University* (Newman 1854). The central theme—universities as the melting pot of fresh ideas and innovations—remains unchanged. Higher education or a university is a knowledge enterprise: one that not only dispenses knowledge, but also creates, archives and disseminates knowledge. Mitra and Mandke (2003) proposed this knowledge enterprise concept as the 'theory of higher education'.

Knowledge creators are world leaders. Time for military colonization is thing of the past. The era of economic colonization too is behind us. The next era will be known for 'knowledge colonization'. Knowledge is the premium. Knowledge creators will colonize the world. Knowledge creation is the function of research and development activities. That precisely is the reason why knowledge creation should form the backbone of higher education as knowledge enterprise. Not surprising, hence, is the evolution of the idea of 'research universities'. Research universities are a classification by the Carnegie Classification of Institutions of Higher Education. It lists top 50 research universities in the United States.[1] Such universities

---

[1] http://www.bestcollegereviews.org/top-research-universities/ (accessed on 7 March 2014).

focus much more on doctoral and postdoctoral research, pre-doctoral courses as preparation for research, rather than on undergraduate education. The mission of research universities is to promote and generate research and train students who can take research as the profession.

> Some of the world's most famous discoveries have been made through university research. From the invention of the telegraph, the discovery of AIDS, the origination of the internet, and current advances in stem cell research, our nation's universities are the hub of knowledge and discovery, 56% of our nation's basic research is being conducted at universities. Students are an integral part of university research; studies show that students who engage in research are twice as likely to graduate, five-times more likely to go on to graduate school, and have more successful careers after graduation. These students go on to become the next generation of scientists, engineers, teachers, and leaders in government and industry.[2]

Indian Institute of Science (Bangalore), All India Institute of Medical Sciences, New Delhi, IITs, and a few of the universities are credited as research universities because of their contribution to research.[3] Knowledge creation is the main function of a research university; knowledge conservation and dissemination are extension functions. This brings in the issue of quality of research in higher education. In this chapter, we will deal with what constitutes research, how and where are research conducted, research documentation and publication, assessment of quality of research, and organization of research with an eye of improvement of quality of research.

What Constitutes Research?

What constitutes research is a naive but fundamental question. Naive, because research is being done for ages. Fundamental, because there are important professional statements that indicate what is not research. Standard dictionary (*Chambers, Concise Oxford, Webster,* etc.) definitions refer to investigation as equivalent of research,

---

[2] http://www.bestcollegereviews.org/top-research-universities/
[3] http://www.careers360.com/news/9725-top-100-institutions (accessed on 7 March 2014).

qualifying clause being 'systematic', indirectly though. Such definitions also indicate the purpose of research, namely, increasing the 'sum of knowledge' or 'discovering facts'. By another definition, 'research is an organized and systematic way of finding answers to questions'. This definition has been further elaborated with explanations of the key words, namely, systematic, organized, finding answers and questions.[4]

Research got a more elaborate definition in the context of research assessment exercise (RAE).

'Research', for the purpose of the RAE, is to be understood as original investigation undertaken in order to gain knowledge and understanding. It includes work of direct relevance to the needs of commerce, industry, and to the public and voluntary sectors; scholarship; the invention and generation of ideas, images, performances, artifacts including design, where these lead to new or substantially improved insights; and the use of existing knowledge in experimental development to produce new or substantially improved materials, devices, products and processes, including design and construction.[5]

This new definition is an improvement over the definition provided for RAE (Jones 1989).

The University of Queensland, Australia (Office of Research and Postgraduate Studies [ORPS] 2004), for the purpose of both external and internal funding defined research as: 'Research and experimental development comprises: Academic pursuits that add new knowledge and increase stock of knowledge for potential new applications'.[6]

Any activity classified as research and experimental development is characterized by originally theory; it should have investigation as the primary objective and should have the potential to produce results that are sufficiently general for humanities stock of knowledge (theoretical and/or practical) to be recognizably increased (Kerlinger 1973 cited in Olaewe and Bashiru 2009).

According to Olaewe (2006), "research is an active, diligent and systematic process of inquiry in order to discover, interpret or revise

---

[4] http://linguistics.byu.edu/faculty/henrichsenl/researchmethods/RM_1_01.html (accessed on 7 March 2014).

[5] http://www.rgu.ac.uk/credo/staff/page.cfm?pge=9471 (accessed on 7 March 2014).

[6] The OECD definition of research and development.

facts, events, behaviours or theories or to make practical application with the help of such facts, laws or theories".

According to the definition of RAE, the following do not constitute research:

- Routine testing and routine analysis of materials, components and processes such as for the maintenance of national standards, as distinct from the development of new analytical techniques (RAE, ORPS).
- Development of teaching materials that do not embody original research (RAE, ORPS).

ORPS provides a more comprehensive list of activities that are excluded for research funding. These are:

- Scientific and technical information services
- General purpose or routine data collection
- Feasibility studies (except into research and experimental development projects)
- Specialized routine medical care
- Commercial, legal and administrative aspects of patenting, copyright or licensing activities
- Routine computer programming, systems work for software maintenance (research and experimental development into applications software, new programming languages and new operating systems would normally meet the definition of research)

There are also common grounds about what constitutes research and what does not. There is, however, a strong argument against excluding preparation of teaching learning material as research. The leading open universities in the world, UK Open University (UKOU), as the pioneer and leader, invests huge amount of money on research and development in refining self-instructional material in print and electronic media. This sophistication and high quality put the UKOU as the world leader. This, hence, needs serious consideration.

From the perspective of managing quality of research, the processes, purpose and output of research differ from one subject or discipline to another. For example, research in certain disciplines of science and technology may lead to a product development; in the same discipline or elsewhere, the purpose and the product can be discovery of a new principle or finding or constructing a new way of working, or solving a problem. Research in sociology or anthropology, say, ethnographic studies, among others, aims at converting tacit knowledge (organizational culture, group processes, rites and mores of the aborigines etc.) into explicit knowledge; certain other studies that provide a better understanding of the state of art of a set of characteristics amongst a given population and so on. Accordingly, then, it would be difficult to develop a common set of criteria for evaluating quality of research.

Research Scenario: Where and How are Researches Conducted

Researches are conducted primarily at four levels—postgraduate, M Phil, doctoral and postdoctoral levels. A large number of research projects are conducted by faculty members funded by various governmental and non-governmental agencies. There is a divergence of opinion regarding the aim of research at the postgraduate level—whether it aims at training in research or at knowledge creation. It is, nonetheless, an important activity at the postgraduate programmes. Ignoring quality concern runs the risk of creating wrong impression in the beginning researchers about the rigour of research and concern for quality. Negligence of quality concern at this level has serious implications. In fact, it is here that the seed of poor quality of research at higher levels is sown.

At the MPhil and doctoral levels too, the debate does not completely wither away; it only changes in intensity. Some universities put premium on the MPhil programmes as entry qualification to the doctoral programmes. With a combination of coursework and dissertation, MPhil aims at equipping researchers for their serious 'knowledge-creating' endeavour at the doctoral level. Doctoral research forms the backbone of research in higher education in most of the developing countries, since for most doctoral researchers, doctoral dissertation is the first and last research conducted in their entire career. Resultantly, this becomes almost one-time investment in research in higher education. Hence, this needs serious attention.

The fourth category of research comes in the form of research projects—institutional and individual. In the research universities, senior and eminent scholars directly involve themselves in the research projects; they also involve young researchers in the projects. The young researchers work on some aspect of the comprehensive large project and use it, sometimes, for their doctoral degree. This provides a sound framework for quality management as well as capacity building of young researchers. In the teaching universities, however, teachers primarily act as research guides. More often than not, they enrol a large number of students as permitted by the statutes of the universities, which may or may not be in their own area of specialization. The problem is more acute in the case of social and behavioural sciences.

There is a widespread perception that quality in research in almost all branches of knowledge is declining in Indian universities. This sentiment and perception found a voice in the Association of Indian Universities (AIUs) seminar on Supervision of Research in Universities in 2000 in Goa. The publication also devoted an entire section on the issue of quality of research (Powar and Shafi 2001). In the revised situation, due to global competitiveness, new universities, especially the central and deemed universities, articulate their aspiration to have 100 to 500 research students in campus, primarily following the Western research university model. In the absence of an adequate number of academic staff in the university departments and very few really qualified to guide with some kind of specialization, the quality of research in the foreseeable future stands challenged. Academic staff without experience in research and publications in quality journals is being called upon to guide students. Let us take two examples. One, during one of my personal conversations with a professor in a central university, I learnt that he guides six doctoral students and several postgraduate and MPhil students. On further inquiry, he mentioned the research problems of his six doctoral students. Each topic belonged to different domain of the concerned subject. I asked him what his specialization was. He had none; no major research projects or no major publications to his credit. Two, NIEPA is a reputed research institution and think tank in educational policy, planning and management. It was converted into a deemed university (NUEPA) in 2006 and had to fall in line with others in the system. The situation changed. Those serious and senior scholars (professors) who preferred to concentrate on research now guide MPhil and PhD scholars constraining on their time for serious research that they were engaged till recently. On the other hand, some faculty members who preferred to spend time in the library make notes and bring development in their respective fields to classrooms, and those not interested in research publications have to guide MPhil and PhD students. It burns the quality of research at both ends.

Much of the research, available from universities, is criticized to be imitative; many of them are charged of plagiarizing. If these criticisms are taken seriously, much of the research will not qualify to be considered as research according to the definition of research quoted earlier. That is a serious matter since a large amount of research is not research at all, no use debating on its quality and quality assessment.

The AIU seminar, referred to earlier, concentrated on supervision, which is an important instrument of quality assurance in research. There are several other factors, too. The most important among them are research facilities in the universities and evaluation of research theses. The selection of examiners for the assessment of a research thesis is guided largely by consideration other than its actual purpose. The friendly nexus of mutual support between research guides and examiners does not facilitate quality assessment of research thesis. The issue is of poor professional standard in assessment of research. There are exceptions, though. Some conservative universities and dynamic heads of departments engage distinguished scholars from globally reputed universities in the world to test the 'depth of water'—quality of research.

Another important bottleneck in managing the quality of research is research facilities in the universities. Research in science and technology suffers most heavily due to inadequacy of scientific equipments and gadgets; poor library and learning resource facilities constrain research across disciplines.

The third problem is the lack of dissemination of research. There are not many journals coming out from the developing countries; and Brazil, China, India and Mexico, the emerging economic giants, are no exceptions. Refereed international journals are difficult to enter, besides the long cue before a paper can be published. What is, however, intriguing is the poor quality of research work when almost the only criterion for promotion of academic staff in the colleges and universities—both through open selection and time-bound promotion (CAS)—is research publications.

India Vision 2020, popularly known as the Technology Information, Forecasting and Assessment Council (TIFAC) report, is a response to this challenge, where it identified frontline areas of science and technology and created the road map for future research. The concentration or focus of TIFAC is on research laboratories with a window to service and upgrade capabilities of universities and other institutions of higher education. Despite the offer of funding support for high-quality research, not many universities have shown enthusiasm. As a case in hand, only 21 of about 900 engineering institutions responded to the REACH programme of TIFAC that intended to assist technical institutions.[7]

However, TIFAC-type visioning is almost absent in other spheres of research like sciences, social and behavioural sciences. Equally absent is the road map for 'education' as a subject of research. For example, the Internet has emerged as a major learning tool globally. The United States, the UK, Australia and Canada appointed expert committees to explore the 'Power of Internet for Learning' (title of the American Report) in the late 1990s. Although India is promoting use of the Internet at all levels of education, there is no planned initiative; some kind of research and development perspective on the Internet for research is completely missing. The poor quality of research and poor planning of research and quality management will continue to hold back countries like India from getting the competitive edge with the developed world.

Quality of Research

Quality of research as an issue has its own intrinsic worth across time and space. The new economic order and globalizing world provide a new thrust. Under General Agreement on Trade in Services (GATS) and intellectual property rights (IPR) in the World Trade Organization (WTO) regime, quality of research takes a new turn. The new world order is a knowledge economy sustained by the knowledge workers. Like all other countries with ambition to emerge as a developed nation, India has also expressed its ambition to emerge as a knowledge

---

[7] www.tifac.org.in and www.missionreach.org.in

society and a knowledge superpower (Planning Commission 2001). This new social order—knowledge society and knowledge superpower—is the function of quality of research. In the new regime (IPR), cross-border knowledge transfer can happen only at a cost, and a huge cost at that. No wonder, Japan White Paper on Education in the 1980s decided to 'reinvent wheels' to create knowledge that can be converted into technology and used for production and services.[8] Without high-quality research, India will fail to generate knowledge and will continue to depend upon knowledge import at a formidable, if not forbidding, cost. Depending upon the economic and political opportunities and compulsions, the possibility of blockade to flow of knowledge is a definite possibility. Indeed, it risks ambition of emerging as a developed nation within a time frame.

Collaboration between industries and research institutions is a common feature world over, particularly in the industrialized nations. The main trend is: industry finances research that can contribute directly to enhance productivity, product-cost cutting through new technology and techniques. There are debates about the patenting rights between the industries that funded the research versus the institutions that invented the new product or the process. A related event in these collaborative researches is the outsourcing of smaller components of research, for example, software development or data processing to equally competent but less expensive institutions and individuals in countries like India and China (Johnson and Onwuegbuzie 2004). Similarly, cross-country collaborative research is steadily increasing. The UK–India Educational Research Initiatives, which began in 2006–2007, is an important example. Matching of quality is the backbone for meaningful participation in such collaborative research programmes. These newly developing trends indicate globalization of research.

Research Productivity: Publication-based Evaluation

Research productivity is an important issue in Indian higher education for more than one reason. First, the total number of funded research

---

[8] http://www.mext.go.jp/english/whitepaper/ (accessed on 7 March 2014).

projects, research papers and publications is far too few compared to the size of the higher education system, with more than 700 universities and 36,000 colleges housing a few million teachers. Second, with the introduction of the Career Advancement Scheme (CAS), it has become necessary to refine the criteria of selection. Publication during the last five years has been introduced as one of the main criteria. Many candidates submit chapters in textbooks and textbooks as evidence of research. Faculty members in some of the universities have started their own journal; they probably get easy access to publish their own papers. Such journals are often not refereed, nor are they able to maintain specified periodicity. In the same category come some of the e-journal initiatives. However, there are welcome exceptions where some of the distinguished scholars have set up refereed e-journal. Hence, at this stage of the development of Indian higher education, there is a need to emphasize and expand research activities among the faculty members in both colleges and universities, and in government-funded and private institutions. For, teaching, research and innovation should be a composite culture of all higher education institutions.

There is another important viewpoint and practice—evaluation based on a variety of publications by the same author over a period, normally five years. Publications for such evaluation can be monographs, research papers, review papers, edited research volumes, edited conference proceedings, authored books, chapters refereed in edited books, short communications to journals, unpublished research reports, addresses to learned gatherings and so on. All these publications can be from either international or national outlets. Each such publication can be given a value depending upon the rigour of scrutiny before publications. Ramsden and Moses (1992) proposed an Index of Research Productivity (IRP). It is the five-year sum of (3 × the number of single or multi-authored books) + number of papers published in refereed journals + number of edited books + number of chapters in edited books.

In this model, IRP of any academic unit would be the total of the IRP of its academic staff. Ramsden and Moses (1992) proposed that it is best to divide the credit equally among all the authors in a multi-authored publication. Powar (2001a) suggested a revised IRP suitable for Indian environment. This is: five years sum of (4 × number of research monographs and postgraduate-level books) + (3 × research and review papers in international journals and chapters in refereed books of postgraduate level) + (2 × research and review papers in national journals, edited research volumes and short communications in international journals) + (1 × short communications in national journals, proceedings of seminars, papers/review papers in university journals and unpublished projects/technical reports). Powar also proposed a formula for calculating departmental IRP by summating values of all members of the department.

There is usually an emphasis on publication in international journals. There is a serious problem if journals published outside the boundaries of a country are recognized as international journal. For an Indian scholar, a journal published in Turkey, Sri Lanka, Bangladesh as much as in the UK, the United States, Canada, New Zealand and Australia may fall in the category of international journal. The identification should shift to refereed journals whether published from India or outside the country. As a precaution, it may be advisable to examine the panel of referees.

It will be necessary to identify different types of research documentation and publication. An exemplar list may comprise the following:

- Authored technical/professional books
- Edited thematic volumes
- Research monographs
- Chapters in technical books
- Research papers in journals
- Review papers in journals
- Short communications in journals
- Research papers in e-journals
- Research papers in conference/seminar proceedings
- Reports of funded research projects
- Addresses to learned gatherings

We have not included textbooks in this list of publications, though good textbooks for undergraduate and postgraduate programmes are an important input for the overall quality of higher education.

Practices in Research Assessment

Quality of research has been voiced as an important concern from time to time in various countries. In the recent years, the quality of doctoral studies has been a subject of investigation. The report 'Evaluating Research Excellence: The 2003 Assessment' conducted by the Tertiary Education Commission studied the pattern of quality of academic research in New Zealand. The Performance Based Research Fund (PBRF) report[9] reveals significant strength in managing the quality of research in most of the universities and in many subject areas. The PBRF 2003 evaluation showed that there were a substantial number of academics in tertiary educational institutions undertaking research of a world-class standard. As many as 165 people from New Zealand and other countries were in the review panels of 12 subject areas that assessed and assigned ratings to the thousands of academics who took part in the PBRF process. The research studies are rated on A, B, C and R. There is a significant amount of high calibre research in a good range of subject areas (Tertiary Education Commission of New Zealand (2004), PBRF: Evaluating Research Excellence: The 2003 Assessment[10]).

In the UK, every four to five years, an RAE was used to take place. The main purpose of the RAE was to enable the higher education funding councils to distribute public funds for research selectively on the basis of quality. It also gave an indication of the relative quality and standing of UK academic research. It provided benchmarks that were used by institutions in developing and managing their research strategies. RAE provided quality ratings for research across all disciplines. Ratings ranged from 1 to 5*, according to how much of the work is judged to reach national or international levels of excellence.[11]

RAE was a peer review process, but not mechanistic. Panels used their professional judgment to form a view about the quality of research. Judgments were formed in the context of statements of criteria for assessment that were published in advance (Table 9.1).

The RAE's criteria were guided by two parameters—national versus international and proportion of research studies submitted for evaluation—'more than' and 'less than half', 'two-thirds' and 'virtually none'. One common feature in the assessment of research across the UK, the United States and New Zealand is the peer group involvement and assessment.

---

[9] https://www.tec.govt.nz/.../PBRF-Evaluating%20Research%20Excellence-th.. (accessed on 17 March 2014).

[10] http://www.tec.govt.nz/

[11] http://www.reading.ac.uk/Study/study-rae.asp (accessed on 7 March 2014).

Table 9.1:
Assessment of Quality of Research

Level	Criteria
5*	Attainable levels of 'international excellence' in 'more than half' of the research activity submitted and attainable levels of national excellence in the remainder.
5	Attainable levels of 'international excellence' in 'up to half' of the research activity submitted and to attainable levels of national excellence in virtually all of the remainder.
4	Attainable levels of 'national excellence' in virtually 'all' of the research activity submitted, showing some evidence of international excellence.
3a	Attainable levels of 'national excellence' in over 'two-thirds' of the research activity submitted, possibly showing evidence of international excellence.
3b	Attainable levels of 'national excellence' in 'more than half' of the research activity submitted.
2	Attainable levels of 'national excellence' in 'up to half' of the research activity submitted.
1	Attainable levels of 'national' excellence in none, or virtually none, of the research activity submitted.

Source: RAE (2001).

The RAE framework mentioned earlier was last used in 2008. A process was initiated in 2007 to find alternative ways of assessing 'excellence in research'. RAE was replaced by Research Excellence Framework (REF). A 2010 document listed the following grading criteria of research (Assessment Framework and Guidance on submission, July 2011, p. 43).[12]

- Four-star: Quality that is world-class in terms of originality, significance and rigour.
- Three-star: Quality that is internationally excellent in terms of originality, significance and rigour but which falls short of the highest standards of excellence.
- Two-star: Quality that is recognized internationally in terms of originality, significance and rigour.
- One-star: Quality that is recognized nationally in terms of originality, significance and rigour.

---

[12] http://www.ref.ac.uk/media/ref/content/pub/ (accessed on 2 January 2015).

- Unclassified: Quality that falls below the standard of nationally recognized work. Or work which does not meet the published definition of research for the purposes of this assessment.

The first REF was conducted in 2014. The assessment of quality of research under REF was conducted jointly by the funding councils of England, Scotland, Wales and Northern Ireland. Results were announced on 18 December 2014. Thirty per cent research output obtained 4-star; 46 per cent 3-star, 20 per cent 2-star and 3 per cent-1-star rating. A detailed account is available as Key Facts.[13]

However, REF is not without criticism (Martin 2011, Smith et al. 2011). Martin (2011) expressed his apprehension whether this initiative is creating a 'Frankenstein monster.'

The National Research Council (NRC) studies the quality of doctoral research in the United States from time to time. The system argues:[14]

> Graduate education is the key driver of quality in U.S. higher education. This latest study speaks to the importance of doctoral education as a key component of our system of education as well as the graduate education community's efforts at continuous improvement.

A detailed mechanism of the study design of quality of doctoral studies and the outcome has been published in 2011.[15] The NRC Report (2010) contained both rating and ranking of 4,838 programmes in 212 institutions.[16] This NRC practice of periodic evaluation of quality of doctoral research helps in maintaining and improving quality. Furthermore, by making this doctoral research evaluation database accessible to public, it builds in transparency and social accountability. For improving quality of research, attention is needed on doctoral research. India does not have any such mechanism as yet. It will be useful to commission studies on assessment of quality of doctoral and funded projects.

---

[13] http://www.ref.ac.uk/media/ref/content/pub/REF%20Brief%20Guide%202014.pdf (accessed on 9 March 2014).

[14] http://www.rackham.umich.edu/nrc/background (accessed on 7 March 2014).

[15] https://grants.nih.gov/training/research_doctorates.pdf (accessed on 9 March 2014).

[16] http://www.gsas.harvard.edu/faculty/national_research_council_report_2010.php and https://grants.nih.gov/training/research_doctorates.pdf (accessed on 9 March 2014).

Criteria for Quality Research

Evaluating quality of research is not easy. It is also demonstrated by various critical scholarly publications (Martin 2011, Smith et al. 2011). Also, developing one set of criterion for research in all disciplines and at all levels may not solve the problem. It will be necessary to develop a multiple set of criteria and relevant benchmarks.

> A variety of indicators are being used to evaluate the quality of research. These include publications, research support received, peer opinion, overall research activity, and honours and awards received. Ideally, an appropriate mix of all these should be used while evaluating a department, but this is not always possible. One may have to consider not only the quality of research but also the way the institution manages the research environment, and the way research impinges on both postgraduate and undergraduate teaching. (Piper 1993, as cited in Powar 2002)

There have been some interesting efforts in setting up criteria for assessing the quality of research. In one such study, quality aspects have been divided into scholarly output and social quality. The scholarly output has been spelt out in terms of scholarly publication or output, scholarly use of research output and evidence of scholarly recognition. The social quality issue has been seen as societal publication/output, societal use of research output and societal recognition. Each one of these six criteria has been further broken down into a total of 21 criteria (Royal Netherlands Academy of Arts and Sciences, 2011[17]).

A comprehensive framework of assessment of quality of research should search for external and internal criteria or indicators of quality. External criteria are the following:

External Indicators

Some of the external indicators of quality are as follows:

- Sources and size of funding
- Patenting and patent registration

---

[17] https://www.knaw.nl/en/.../quality-indicators...research.../20111024.pdf (accessed on 9 March 2014).

- Publication in reputed refereed international journals
- Citations, impact factor, h-index and so on.
- Honours and awards
- Peer review

Internal Indicators

Four internal indicators of quality are as follows:

1. Relevance and problem solving
2. Process quality
3. New thesis—Knowledge creation
4. Originality versus plagiarization and imitation

Sources and Size of Funding

External funding of research—both size and source of funding, especially in science and technology research, has been considered as one of the criteria for evaluating research. The main argument in favour of external funding as a criterion is: the funding agencies carefully evaluate the proposal as well as the capability of the researcher/ research institution before taking the funding decision. However, there are limitations as well. Research in science and technology receives greater funding support from the state. For example

> During 1993–94 the distribution of research grants given by the central government was 51.99% for science, in agricultural sciences 16.21%, engineering and technology 25.80% and medical sciences 6%. Within the allotment in science, the biological sciences received 59.67%, chemical sciences 1.88%, the physical sciences 11.78 5%, other sciences 13.01 per cent and the mathematical sciences 3.66%. (Powar 2001a)

Because of high cost of research in science and technology, compared to research in social sciences, languages and humanities, funding as the only criterion cannot be used to compare quality of research across disciplines. However, this can be used as an important criterion within a particular field when one research project, for example, in physics, competes with another from the same discipline. Finally, this criterion will be better used for external funding of research projects rather than funding from the internal resources of the university.

Patenting and Patent Registration

Patenting and patent registration is an important indicator of quality of research, particularly in science and technology. Patents can be registered only when the product is original. As far as we know, there are very few patents registered by Indian researchers.

Patenting is covered by the Patents Act of 1970, as amended in 2005 by the Department of Industrial Development (Industrial Policy & Promotion) under Controller General of Patents, Designs and Trademarks, with its head office in Kolkata and branches in Delhi, Mumbai and Chennai. The Department of Education covers the Copyright Act of 1957 as amended in 1999. The salient features of patent law are as follows:

- Both product and process patent are provided
- Term of patent—20 years
- Examination on request
- Both pre-grant and post-grant opposition
- Fast-track mechanism for the disposal of appeals
- Provision for protection of biodiversity and traditional knowledge
- Publication of applications after 18 months with facility for early publication
- Substantially reduced time lines

The patents law defines invention under Section 2(1)(J): '"Invention" means a new product or process involving an inventive step and capable of industrial application'. It further defines invention:

- Relates to a process or product or both
- Be new (novel)
- Involves an inventive step
- Be capable of industrial application
- Should not fall under Section 3

Section 3 provides details of exclusion—what is not patentable. Patenting does appear to be a slow and cumbersome process. It takes several months of incubation, normally 18 months from the date of application.

Publications

Publication is one of the most commonly accepted criteria for quality research. There can be more than one type of publications—a research report as it is, a paper based on a research project, a review paper or a meta-analysis on the theme of research, a theory generating paper cutting across several studies of the author(s). Harris (1990) proposed (a) quantity, (b) impact, (c) quality and (d) importance as four measures for evaluating research publications. Quantity can be established simply by counting the number publications. According to Harris, 'Impact is a measure of the influence of the publication on fellow workers and can be quantified by using Impact Factor analyses', and 'Quality and importance are subjective, value based, measures that cannot be estimated by bibliographic means'.

Number of publications by itself may not be adequate a measure. For example, publication in a peer-reviewed journal cannot be compared with that in a seminar proceeding or a journal that is neither reviewed nor indexed by any major international indexing system. While evaluating the quality of research publications, it is necessary to examine the reputation of the journal. As can be seen in Table 9.1, there is an overwhelming emphasis on publications in international journals over national journals. This should be acceptable as an important principle, since competition in international journals is far fiercer than that in the national journals.

The only caution is about the national journals of high quality. For example, NIEPA's *Journal of Educational Planning and Administration* fetches some of the outstanding journals from all over the world on exchange basis. Even without reference to citation index and impact factor assessment, this is an important criterion for quality. I founded and edited a journal, *Media and Technology for Human Resource Development—A Journal of Educational Technology*—for several years. Despite best efforts of my editorial team to maintain high quality, I was not sure of the quality of the journal. Hence, I did not publish my own writings in this journal. I received a communication from a distinguished U.S. scholar appreciating the quality of our journal. Waking up, I sent complimentary copies and invited world leaders in educational technology to write, and we received research papers from many eminent scholars from all over the globe, including Alex Romizowaski, Fred Lockwood, Steve Downey, Michael Barbour and many others

A widespread view is that only the contributions published in refereed journals should be considered since such journals have greater citation index and impact factor. This exclusive criterion needs further exploration. Instead, different values or weightages can be assigned to different types of research publications (Table 9.2).

Table 9.2:
Values of Research Publications

Types of Research Output	Points
1. Refereed authored technical books backed by research from international publishers	5
2. Authored technical books backed by research from national/local publishers	4
3. Refereed edited thematic research volumes from international publishers	4
4. Edited thematic research volumes from national/local publishers	3
5. Research monographs and reports	3
6. Reports of funded research projects accepted by funding agencies	3
7. Addresses to learned gatherings, for example, keynote addresses	2
8. Refereed research-based technical chapters in edited books	2
9. Research papers in indexed journals—Indian and international	2
10. Review papers in indexed journals—Indian and international	2
11. Research papers in indexed/refereed e-journals	2
12. Research papers in non-refereed e-journals	1
13. Short communications in indexed journals—Indian and international	1
14. Research papers in non-refereed journals—Indian and international	1
15. Research papers in conference/seminar proceedings	1

Source: Author.
Note: If available on web, add 0.5 to the score.

Not many publications from Indian researchers are traceable on the Internet. This is one of the important reasons for poor citations of Indian research work. I tend to propose an additional value of 0.5 for all kinds of research publications that are available on the web.

A further refinement and global comparability will be to bring in internationally accepted criteria like citation index, impact factor, h-index and g-index, Eugene factor, altmetric and scientometrics 2.0 (Kumar 2011). We will return to some of these criteria in a little while.

Citation Index

Good quality research is referred by researchers, and their research gets impacted. The citation analysis can be used to determine the number of times a study has been referred by other scholars as an index of impact of authors, articles and journals (Kumar 2011, UIC 2014). This, hence, provides an objective quantifiable index of quality assessment. There are, however, certain limitations. All journals are not indexed and covered by citation facilities. This is particularly true for social science journals and journals published from small places. Besides, 'citations do not differentiate between a complementary and non-complementary reference; researchers can have bias for or against certain individual or institution; omission of a reference can be due to ignorance of their existence; the researcher may prefer citing works of eminent workers and ignoring significant work of little-known researchers; may not distinguish between major works and short communications. Furthermore, publications in languages other than English are likely to be less accessible; citation to multi-authored papers is recorded under the first name; no credit accrues to the second and the third authors' as listed by Powar (2001a).

There are different types of citation indexes. Google scholar citation index helps a scholar to keep track of citations of his/her works.[18] There are social science, science and data citation indexes available separately.[19] There are Indian citation indexes for Indian Science

---

[18] www.scholar.google.co.in/intl/en/scholar/citations.html (accessed on 9 March 2014).
[19] www.thomsonreuters.com

and Technology, Indian Social Science and Humanities Citation Index (ISSHCI) and Indian Journals Citation Report (IJCR).[20]

Impact Factor

The impact factor is also called Garfield factor in the name of Eugene Garfield, who devised impact factor. Impact factor indicates the number of citations of recent articles published in a journal. Impact factor is calculated annually starting from 1975 for the journals indexed in the Journal Citation Report. Journal Citation Report for 2015—a massive volume—is also out.[21] Journal Citation Report can be consulted for the impact factor of all journals indexed. Alternatively, one can Google Impact Factor of journals in one's own area of specialization. Table 9.3 presents an example of impact factor of education journals from 1981 to 2009.

Table 9.3:
Impact Factor for Some Education Journals

Journal	Impact Factor (1981–2009)
Review of Educational Research	41.04
Reading Research Quarterly	24.74
Sociology of Education	23.54
American Educational Research Journal	21.97
Review of Research in Education	18.98
Harvard Educational Review	17.48
Journal of Educational Statistics	15.91
Journal of the Learning Sciences	15.49
AIDS Education & Prevention	12.94

Source: http://archive.sciencewatch.com/dr/sci/11/jan2-11_1/

Australia has its own ranking system, Excellence in Research for Australia (ERA) Outlet Ranking. The latest document available

---

[20] www.indiancitationindex.com/

[21] http://about.jcr.incites.thomsonreuters.com/full-titles-2015.pdf (accessed on 9 March 2014).

on the website is ERA 2012.[22] Gerald Burke of Monash University, Australia, wrote in a personal mail to me (on 19 March 2011) about the Australian ranking of journals overall criterion: 'Quality of the papers'.

- **A*:** Typically, an A* journal would be one of the best in its field or subfield in which to publish and would typically cover the entire field/subfield. Virtually all papers they publish will be of a very high quality. These are journals where most of the work is important (it will really shape the field) and where researchers boast about getting accepted. Acceptance rates would typically be low, and the editorial board would be dominated by field leaders, including many from top institutions.
- **A:** The majority of papers in a Tier A journal will be of very high quality. Publishing in an A journal would enhance the author's standing, showing that they have real engagement with the global research community and that they have something to say about problems of some significance. Typical signs of an A journal are lowish acceptance rates and an editorial board that includes a reasonable fraction of well-known researchers from top institutions.
- **B:** Tier B covers journals with a solid, though not outstanding, reputation. Generally, in a Tier B journal, one would expect only a few papers of very high quality. They are often important outlets for the work of PhD students and early career researchers. Typical examples would be regional journals with high acceptance rates, and editorial boards that have few leading researchers from top international institutions.
- **C:** Tier C includes quality, peer-reviewed, journals that do not meet the criteria of the higher tiers.

h-Factor

h-Factor is a method of quantifying scientific research output of a scholar (Hirsch 2005). 'I propose the index h, defined as the number

---

[22] https://research.unsw.edu.au/excellence-research-australia-era-outlet-ranking (accessed on 9 March 2014).

of papers with citation number $\geq h$, as a useful index to character-
ize the scientific output of a researcher' The h-index is calculated by
extrapolating four sets of data, namely number of papers (N) published over certain number of years (n), number of citations of each
paper (j), the journals where papers were published and their impact
factor. Hirsh proposed the 'h index' of a scientist is h 'if h of his or
her N_p papers have at least h citations each and the other ($N_p - h$)
papers have $\leq h$ citations each'. Thus, it simultaneously measures
research productivity and impact on fellow scholars in the field.
The h-index can be found at Web of Sciences, Scopus and Google
Scholar.[23]

Peer Review

Peer review is the most extensively used technique for quality assessment of research. It works wonderfully well in the hands of professionally competent and committed reviewers. Otherwise, there are
several risks. It is not free from biases, either. Maintaining anonym-
ity, multiple peer evaluation, using a set of criteria and such other
practices can substantially reduce such biases.

Awards and Honours

Awards and honours have been recommended as tools for evaluating research quality. There are two kinds of awards—specific to
a particular piece of research work and for cumulative (lifetime)
contribution. It is an important indicator, provided other extrane-
ous factors are reasonably under check. Awards are significantly
influenced by extra-academic considerations like political and
administrative affiliations and connections; then there are other
aberrations like commissioned/ghost writings where the actual

---

[23] http://researchguides.uic.edu/content.php?pid=163124&sid=5366832 (accessed on 9
March 2014).

author is different from the award winner and so on. It is good not to use this as the only criterion; it is better used with other criteria mentioned earlier.

Building Quality

Building quality of research in higher education, particularly where the system is large and diverse, is a major challenge. Research scholars at the postgraduate level are directly enrolled in research programmes independent of the quality of education at the undergraduate and postgraduate programmes in universities. The quality check at the entry point goes largely unattended. The introduction of National Eligibility Test (NET) and Junior Research Fellowship (JRF) by the UGC is a step forward in screening candidates. Universities vary widely in the quality of academic programmes— both research and teaching. India provides an outstanding example of this wide diversity of quality where IISc., IITs, IIMs and a few universities stand at one end of the continuum matching international standards, while a large majority of the universities continue to produce graduates of indefinable quality on the other. Again, within the same university, the quality of academic programmes, including research, differs from one department to another. With more than 700 universities, including private universities, any centrally controlled mechanism for quality management would violate the academic autonomy that the universities are used to. Further, with the new regulations of career promotion, teachers in the colleges are also expected to carry out research and publish. With limited research facilities and environment in colleges, research is crowded with poor quality output.

The AIU seminar, mentioned earlier, focused exclusively on supervision. This is an important instrument of quality improvement in research, particularly for the postgraduate and doctoral levels. For an overall improvement of quality of research, we must, however, consider a few more parameters, namely, organization of research programme, supervision, infrastructure and research facility, including funding, evaluation and research environment.

Organization of Research Programme

Research programmes are organized differently in different universities. There are a few visible patterns.

Research students are enrolled under a university teacher who is an approved guide according to the university's regulations. Depending upon the regulation of the university, a guide can have six to eight doctoral students, often working on unrelated topics and themes. In sharp contrast to such practices, and to build quality in research, departments in certain universities adopt a planned research approach. The university department identifies few areas of research as thrust areas. Through detailed analysis of each of the thrust areas, the department identifies a few interrelated research themes or topics; the department also identifies teachers to lead each of the identified thrust areas of research. In such a situation, postgraduate and doctoral students work on interrelated themes.

1. The entry requirement for doctoral research varies from university to university. For many universities, entry qualification is a postgraduate degree, whereas in some other universities, it is MPhil degree.
2. Although full-time research has been made as a prerequisite for doctoral studies in many universities, it is not necessary in a good number of universities.
3. A majority of universities stipulate postgraduate degree in a particular subject as the eligibility criteria for admission to doctoral research programmes in that particular discipline; some of the universities have now introduced interdisciplinary research for doctoral programmes.

There are great many such diversities. These are only a few examples. In order to build quality, what is necessary is to design a research programme so that students may join doctoral studies with a sound foundation in research methods and some experience in researching. In the United States, coursework forms a significant component of the doctoral work. This model is being increasingly adopted in Indian universities while introducing MPhil programme. For building quality, it will be necessary to go beyond the MPhil programme as preparation for doctoral research. Instead, quality of doctoral research can be significantly improved by introducing coursework, making it interdisciplinary full time, and part of a teamwork on a planned research. Online education can be powerful means of coursework for MPhil and doctoral students.

Supervision and Evaluation

Several university professors, vice-chancellors and research guides have deliberated on the issue of supervision of research in the AIU seminar. There are two important considerations. First, a very large majority of supervisors are completely disconnected from research, their last research being their own doctoral studies. Many of them remain largely unfamiliar with the new developments in research methods and research processes. For example, many of the research guides are unfamiliar with the use of the Internet as a source of research referencing, data analytics and that it has become a requirement for successfully completing doctoral research. As a case in hand, a bright doctoral student of one of the reputed Indian institutions submitted her doctoral dissertation on a problem of self-learning material with hypertext. One of the evaluators from a reputed British University appreciated the thesis, but insisted on incorporating references from the Internet. The researcher worked for a few more months and then resubmitted her thesis, and then she was awarded PhD.

Second, supervisors enrol students working on a variety of different themes and topics; in such a situation, specialist guidance is hardly possible. Such research guides are hardly able to influence the quality of the research process of their doctoral students. Further, supervisors rarely interact with students. There are many occasions when the students write the thesis in consultation with others, even with private service providers (agencies) against payment of huge amount of money.

A large majority of the teachers in universities do not undertake research projects themselves. As a result, many of them do not stay connected to the field situations and lose contact with contemporary developments in research methodologies. In order to improve quality of supervision, universities should

- recognize teachers as research guides who are actively engaged in research themselves;
- offer refresher programmes on research methodologies, particularly for the social science research guides;
- recognize each guide for identified two/three areas of her/his specialization and
- stipulate interactive and collaborative learning requirements between supervisor and researcher and among the researchers.

Quality assurance and management must begin right from the beginning; research students may begin with scanning a broad field—the theoretical foundation and research studies in the field—and steadily converging at a problem that fills the gap, explores the contradictions, or moves into experimentation to find new products, processes, etc.

Just as research supervision is under scanner, management of quality of research will necessitate scanning of the process of evaluation of research theses, dissertations and research reports. As mentioned earlier, there is a nexus of mutual support between the research supervisors and research examiners. This nexus must be broken. It will be useful to develop a panel of examiners for each field with specialization, depending upon the published work of the experts, may be using IRP proposed earlier. For achieving greater professionalization, universities should introduce public defence of thesis. This practice is already in vogue in some universities, but it needs to be extended to all.

As a case in hand, the Centre of Advanced Studies in Education (CASE) in the M.S. University of Baroda, under the leadership of Prof. M.B. Buch, practised a very effective peer group technique for quality improvement and assurance in research. At the initial stage, a (fresh entrant) researcher is encouraged to interact with his/her peer freshers as well as seniors (researchers with two or three years of experience), facilitating freezing the problem of research and then moving on to drafting the proposal. After the proposal is drafted, the first discussion is held with the supervisor; the proposal is then presented in a seminar attended by the faculty members and the research scholars. On the basis of the feedback, the proposal is revised and submitted to the university.

Interactions, in informal mode, continue throughout the period of doctoral research for next two to three years. A major event takes place when the thesis is ready for review before submission to the university. Though not common, Professor Buch would ask two other senior research students to critically examine the thesis from the angle of research methods, organization of the thesis and language of the thesis. On the basis of this peer group exercise, the research student would normally carry out serious revision and modification. Only after that, the thesis is submitted to the research guide for his personal review and clearance. Professor Buch would go through every word of the thesis—examining research methods, analysis, thesis organization and communication, especially the interpretation of research outcome. As a research student myself then, submitting my thesis to others' scrutiny, and participating in reviewing other peer researchers' thesis, I found this practice very useful.

Infrastructure and Research Facility

There are several Nobel Laureates in science and social sciences of Indian origins but not necessarily Indian or resident Indian. Most of them have had their schooling and early collegiate education in Indian higher education institutions. But they shifted to Western universities, where they engaged in serious research and distinguished themselves with the prestigious international awards. Western universities offered them the research facilities and infrastructure that helped them to optimize on their talent.

Although not the only condition, the quality of research is significantly influenced by the quality of infrastructure, funding and research facilities. Research facilities include libraries, particularly the availability of national and international journals (often extremely expensive), access to international referencing systems and databases, computers for large data processing, individual work space/

station or office, state-of-the-art equipments and laboratories and so on. In most of the Indian colleges and universities, teachers share one single staffroom, leave alone computers and Internet facilities and international referencing resources, including international journals. They lack minimum basic facilities for study and research.

Funding is another weak area in promoting quality research. This is particularly true in case of research in science and technology. The research in science and technology requires not only heavy one-time investment but also heavy recurrent expenditure for the maintenance and upgradation of equipments and for removal of obsolescence. A majority of the university institutions are singularly constrained with research facilities. Some of the government policies have added further to this problem. Instead of supporting the universities to come up with modern facilities, the government decided to set up laboratories and research facilities outside the university system. Most of the university laboratories do not have the modern equipment and gadgets that are available in the national research laboratories. Resultantly, universities rarely contribute any significant scientific research. For improving quality of research, there is no choice but to enhance research funding in universities.

Research Environment

Finally, in order to improve the quality of research, it is necessary to develop a research environment in the university departments characterized by enthusiasm and professionalism. In the teaching universities, research is only by default; the main thrust is on teaching. One interesting indicator is workload definition. Workload of a higher education teacher is defined in terms of teaching load. A majority of the teachers do not take part directly into research. Their research contribution comes in the form of guiding research students, evaluating postgraduate and doctoral dissertations. It is rather rare to find research publications from senior scholars (associate and full professors). As mentioned earlier, guiding research students is another routine matter. More importantly, because of the lack of emphasis on research, the environment is missing.

Conclusion

Quality of research has been expressed as an area of concern for quite some time in India; several steps have also been taken. However, there is still a long way to go. The UGC has as its mandate for control and management of quality, including research. One of the missions of NAAC refers to quality of research. During the last 20 years since its establishment in 1994, NAAC has done very well on the quality assessment of teaching programmes and infrastructure. However, it is still to take up seriously the issue of quality of research.

Fresh efforts are needed for improving and sustaining the quality of research. It must start right at the beginning. The focus of attention should be placed on doctoral research, if not on MPhil level research. The sustainability of research can be ensured only when the foundation is well laid. This will require careful selection of research students, not based singularly on the marks in the postgraduate examinations. Students need to be tested on their research aptitude. Further, they need to be groomed through intensive engagement in interactive peer group learning, technology-enabled learning (TEL) and expert guidance. Expert guidance can come only when teachers engage themselves directly in research projects, and not through their students. In order to attract brilliant students and retain them for a period of three to five years for research, they need to be adequately financially compensated.

Evaluation of research dissertations is another important tool of quality control. Given the professionalization of research and research evaluation in many of the universities in the Western countries, it is important to involve, along with Indian evaluators, professionals from other countries. Indian concessionalism comes from the sympathy to the conditions in which a researcher works; Western counterparts, irrespective of the research conditions, look at the quality of research and output. Also, they seem to compare the research output with global standards. This cross-country evaluation of research will also bring in a globally comparable level.

In order to build quality of research, it is necessary to stipulate a mechanism for research assessment based on certain benchmarks. Also, it will be necessary to encourage journals from India and other developing countries to improve their quality and steadily emerge as refereed international journals in order to attract eminent scholars from all over the world to publish in India and generate a constructive competitiveness among Indian scholars.

Last but not least, an important issue is funding and research facilities. The grants for library for a majority of higher education institutions are miserably low; teachers' access to technology is extremely limited; research funds are in short supply for most of the institutions. Quality improvement in research cannot be accomplished only by improving process quality, must be matched by quality of material and financial inputs.

The issue of quality of research could have been considered as a luxury a decade ago, but not now. Also, there will be long-term implications of quality of research on national development since research is the means of knowledge creation. As long as knowledge creation remains function of the few countries, flow of knowledge can be restricted or allowed at a high cost. For global competitiveness, improving quality of research is necessary

10

Quality Infrastructure

Introduction

Infrastructure is an important item of quality of higher education institutions. The importance is duly recognized by the fact that there are specified norms of infrastructure, including total land space as prerequisites to affiliation of colleges and recognition of universities by the UGC. Infrastructure is also an item of quality assessment by the NAAC. The United Nations Educational, Scientific and Cultural Organization (UNESCO), as early as 1979, published Planning Standards for Higher Education Facilities: Examples from National Practices (UNESCO 1979). The UK had a Higher Education Space Management Project for Review of Space Norms in 2006.[1]

Very often, infrastructure planning is left to planners and architects, technologists for ICT and so on. No wonder, the civil works of hospitals, hotels and colleges and universities look so similar—some square or a rectangular room. Most often, the building, laboratory, library designs miss the inputs of teachers, science teachers and librarians. Fortunately, the trend is changing. A private university hired a reputed British architect firm for designing the university. Architects asked an unusual question to—what will be the instructional strategies or pedagogy of the university? As the likely or preferred pedagogy was explained, the architect company requested

---

[1] http://www.smg.ac.uk/documents/spacenorms.pdf (23 July 2014).

for drawing—a 'pedagogues architecture'. Fortunately, the trend is changing, and such consultative processes are taking place.

The institutional infrastructure should not only be functional in conventional terms but should also be innovative to fit to the purpose. Further, just as human beings cannot live with bread alone, simple rugged functionality is not enough to nurture the softer sides of the human mind. It needs aesthetics: beauty, sobriety and attractiveness that make students feel proud of their institution.

I was recently invited by my Alma mater (a rural degree college) for a seminar of the alumni; I guess this was to fulfil the requirement of NAAC assessment. When I was being escorted to the seminar hall, I expressed my wish to visit the staffroom. The staffroom is a large hall as large as the seminar room at the first floor. It had a long table and about 20+ wooden chairs strewn casually on both sides of the table. The table was full of chalk dust and a few pages of newspaper. Within the hall there was a partitioned cubicle with a glass door to house one of the clerks of the college. Two other scenes flashed through my mind. One is 1969 when I joined my first college teaching in another rural college. There was a long wooden table and wooden chairs, at least 10 fewer than the number of teachers, we were. We, the juniors, always stood to make space for the seniors out of sheer respect. I realized that nothing has changed for the college teachers in 44 years; the same apathy, same indignity, except the UGC wants them to spend five hours daily in the college without even a place to sit down.

The second was my days as a lecturer in 1974 (now called assistant professor) in the M.S. University of Baroda. All of us, junior or senior, had at least a small cubicle good enough to accommodate a three-feet-long table and a chair and two spare chairs for guests, to ourselves with a wooden swing door curved out of a large hall. We had the privacy and exclusion to study and research, if we liked, even when we were just a few days old in the profession. I wondered how would a teacher in my own degree college read, leave alone research even if he/she wanted to, when he is asked to wait on a 'railway platform' for the next train (read as class) to arrive!

An important issue is the convenience and homeliness of the infrastructure.

During my days at the M.S. University of Baroda, I happen to read a small amateur poster pasted in the study room of my teacher's teenage son; it read, 'a room should be clean enough to be healthy, but dirty enough to be comfortable'. I guess this was to keep his mother's scrutiny at bay. For me, it was a great wisdom. It is an important hallmark of a good infrastructure for educational institutions like colleges and universities. Institutions are places where the teachers live, at least in Indian situation, 25 to 30 years of their life—from their prime youth till the sunset days; the period of their stay would further increase with enhanced age of superannuation. Students spend three to four best years of their life. Hence, college infrastructure has to be a homely, indeed a home away from home. The hallmark of a good home is the convenience and warmth; these criteria should be extended to colleges and universities as well. Another major issue for educational institutions is the safety and security.

Thus, there are five major parameters of quality infrastructure. These are:

1. Adequacy
2. Functionality
3. Comfort
4. Safety and security
5. Aesthetics

There are two major phases or dimensions for consideration of quality of infrastructure. These are new construction and constructed space. In this chapter, I will focus on existing institutions and constructed facilities and not the upcoming infrastructure that should better be left to the planners, architects and engineers. My primary effort will be to flag certain issues of quality of infrastructure in existing higher education institutions. Since almost 90 per cent of the students in higher education are enrolled in the 36,000 plus colleges and less than 10 per cent in the universities, my emphasis will primarily be on the colleges.

Components of Infrastructure and Quality Indicators

Physical infrastructure of a college or a university has several components like classrooms, library, laboratories, office rooms, staffrooms, washrooms and conveniences, principal/vice-chancellor's office, corridors, wellness rooms, meeting rooms, students' union rooms, sports, games, gymnasium and so on. Superimposing the quality indicators against each of the components generates a matrix structure (Table 10.1)

This is just a sample exercise. If you follow organizational micro-analysis, we need to identify each classroom, each laboratory, each corridor and so on separately for the assessment and improvement of quality. For this chapter, we will pick up a few items from the infra-structure list.

Classrooms and Group Learning Space

Classrooms are the most significant component of a college infra-structure; in many cases, the college infrastructure is equated with the classroom itself, because college education is equated with the trans-action of the syllabus in the classrooms through a series of lectures. As pointed out in the chapter on quality of teaching–learning pro-cesses, this very approach to collegiate education is a serious threat to the development of higher intellectual and emotive capabilities of the young students, and hence, quality improvement.

Classrooms are organized in theatre (gallery) style in a square or a rectangular room; such an arrangement is meant for one-way com-munication, namely, teacher lecturing and students passively listen-ing somewhat similar to what we witness in an orchestra or a drama, and occasionally taking notes. Usually, space per student in such arrangement is less than 10 square feet. Changing the instructional strategy from such one-way communication with passive students to participatory learning, group interactivity and other varieties of active learning by the students will require change in the classroom organization. This would require approximately 25 square feet or more space per student. For example, the necessary physical condi-tion for effective interactive learning is seating arrangement, where students can face each other in semicircles, circle, a triangle or a rec-tangle with different arrangement. Of course, it requires a very dif-ferent norm of per-student space in the classrooms. Hence, current

Table 10.1:
Infrastructure and Quality Criteria

Items of Infrastructure	Adequacy	Functionality	Comfort	Aesthetics	Safety and Security
Classrooms					
Library					
Laboratories					
Office room					
Staffroom					
Washrooms					
Principal/vice-chancellor's office					
Wellness room(s)					
Student union rooms					
Store room					
Gymnasium					
Common/recreation room					
Corridors					
Media/AV room					
Staircases					
Electricity					
Water supply					
Sports and games facilities					
Others					

Source: Author.

classroom organization is not functional for interactive learning and space is not adequate for altered classroom organization.

For interactive learning, there has to be much better per-student space provision. New generation, especially private, institutions have ushered in new classroom organization. In BITM, Noida (Uttar Pradesh), a classroom is usually large where seating for students is arranged in U-shape with large free space at the centre for students to come out for discussion and academic networking.

As the government policy moves in to make TEL mandatory for quality improvement, classroom organization will also need changes in order to make full use of audiovisual aids and facilities. When I joined Katwa College (Katwa, West Bengal), in 1969, I had to deliver lectures in a pretty large hall with about 125 students; the only aid in the classroom was a huge vertical wooden frame with two sliding wooden chalk boards to be manually pushed up or pulled down. Indeed, it required a lot of physical strength. The classroom had very scanty natural light (of course, no electrical light of any meaningful illumination), compelling the students to make special effort to read what was written on the board. In sharp contrast, when I joined TTTI, Bhopal (now National Institute of Technical Teachers' Training and Research, NITTR) in 1978, I found each classroom was equipped with an overhead projector (OHP) and a tilted screen, a magnetic board, a flannel board and a white board. LCD projector, film and slide projectors were available on asking. The instructional aides have moved from wooden chalk boards to glass boards to whiteboards and smart boards and magnetic board and flannel boards as supplementary aids. A variety of projected aids like OHP (almost gone now), LCD projection, rather LCD screen, have increasingly become common. A few of Delhi colleges have taken a step further to equip classrooms with interactive smart boards. EDUSAT proposed to provide satellite interactive terminal to each college and university comprising a computer and LCD projector and associated equipments. This, however, did not happen largely due to unimaginative leadership where it mattered most, mismanagement of technology and vested interest within academia. Such a great opportunity was lost (Mukhopadhyay 2002, 2006b). The existing classroom organization and structure, including the furniture, are largely incompatible to accommodate the new-generation instructional aids as well as instructional strategies, particularly participatory learning and group interactivity.

Many colleges have installed smart electronics board at considerable costs. Such electronic boards provide dynamic support to lecturers. And, to that extent, these are useful. The quality of classrooms will be determined not only by the installation of such audio-visual aids and facilities in the classrooms but also by the way they are organized for the convenience of viewing, listening and taking notes, as well as the convenience and ease of interaction with one another whenever necessary. Since quality curriculum transaction is identified with opportunities for students to explore and discover knowledge and invent solutions, technology choice for classrooms is equally important.

Although the normal classrooms with new arrangements mentioned above can facilitate interactivity, though limited, depending upon the instructional style and strategy of the teacher, it will be necessary to create opportunities for small group interactivity where students can collectively solve problems in smaller groups. This will require small group rooms or facilities where students can meet formally or informally in small group discussions. A simple and low-cost way out would be to equip classrooms with (plastic or fibre optic) round tables and five or six light weight chairs around.

The corridor corners of IIM are an interesting innovation for informal group discussion among five to 10 students. Big shady trees are effectively used in Rabindranath's Shantiniketan for such group interactivity. Ideally, each large classroom should be supported with a few group rooms. Human ingenuity is unlimited; it should be possible for every college to find its own solution. What is important is to develop facilities for group interactivity.

In classrooms with stark deprivation, I have tried to generate group interaction by asking students in every alternate row to take 'about turn' in their own benches. Then, four or five students in one row faced four or five students in the next row, and engaged themselves in discussion, though not very comfortable.

Spacious classrooms that are well lighted and ventilated, cooled or heated for the physical comfort, furnished with flexible furniture that can be quickly reorganized to facilitate listening to a lecture or viewing a video, to form groups and so on with appropriate techno-logical installation are quality classrooms.

Library

One of the most important components of academic infrastructure in colleges and universities is a library, especially for the improvement of academic standards and learning outcomes. The current invest-ments in libraries are rather poor. Library grant for a college is a paltry sum of ₹ 20,000 to 30,000 annually on books, magazines and journals (hope it has increased in real terms!). Even if ₹ 15,000 is spent on books, on an average, a college can add hardly about 50 to 100 books annually. Most of the budget is spent on textbooks for the students; very little is left for reference books for the teachers. This issue of reference books and journals assumes new significance, especially with the new regulation for promotion under CAS, where teachers are expected to research and publish. Hence, there is a case for rethinking about the modernization of college and university libraries.

First, a quality library must have enough funds to add a good number of books, journals and magazines feeding to the intellectual needs and requirements of both students and teachers. It is difficult to lay down the annual budget for the library, which would vary depend-ing upon the number of students and teachers in a college. The basic principle should be to provide adequate funds. The second important criterion for a quality library is the provision of a reading room, with furniture that allows students and teachers to read independently. Just as there can be large reading tables for a group of students and teach-ers to sit down, read and take notes, there should be cubicles par-ticularly for the teachers to create semi-private space for prolonged use of the library for research and serious studies. Ventilation and lighting, cooling and warming or weather management are the two important physical requirements for a comfortable reading room.

Print materials like books, journals and magazines are no more the only source of referencing and learning. Learning materials are also available in the form of audio- and video-cassettes, CD-ROMs and so on. The new-generation quality library must become a multimedia learning resource centre. In many of the Western universities and colleges, it is a common practice to record the lectures of the teachers in some video format and transfer the video to the library so that students can revisit the class if they need to at their convenience. The development of the college and university libraries as a multimedia learning resource centre will remain incomplete without the Internet facilities. The Internet has emerged as a major learning tool. It provides access to free and open-source learning material in textual, video, audio and graphic formats from all over the world. Even in remote locations, it requires a telephone connection and a router for wireless connectivity. With this minimum facility, teachers as well as students can create subject blogs and post their lessons and comments, creating an interactive flexitime interactive learning mechanism.

Cataloguing, accession, issue and return of books, referencing and citations are the major functions of a library. Digitization of print materials is the added new dimension. To make library management more effective and user friendly, computerization is necessary. Many college and university libraries have been computerized. The computerization has also helped getting connected to library networks and thereby accessing documents across libraries. A large number of journals are also now available online. The UGC has been trying to provide the support through INFLIBNET. With such handy technology, libraries can introduce book or journal article alert for students and teachers through mobile phone-based delivery through an SMS. A good library must have provision for adding enough number of books, journals and magazines for both students and teachers, a comfortable reading room for both group reading and intensive individual reading, viewing material in multimedia format, Internet and INFIBNET connectivity supported by professionally competent and responsive staff.

Finally, a library must be attractive—aesthetically sound. I have seen libraries that are beautified with a number of decorative items of various kinds. It changes the ambience of the library from the jungle of books to a pleasant place for 'intellectual tourism'.

There are several strategies that a library can be improved. First, howsoever small is the budget, a proportion must be allocated for teacher resources. Digital resources are either free (OER and Free Open Source Software, FOSS) or cheaper than printed material. A certain portion of the budget should be allocated to digital content and technology (hardware). The second important way to improve the library within the given limited budget is to prepare medium-term (3 years) and long-term (5–7 years) plans. Allocation of annual budget can be done with a perspective plan. For example, a college decides to have five reader terminals in the reading room. It can add one or two terminals every year to reach the target in two to three years.

Library management is a major issue. It is often left with the librarian. There are at least two dimensions of library management for quality higher education. These are day-to-day routine management and visioning. NIEPA (now called NUEPA) is a good example (Box 10.1).

Box 10.1:
Case of NIEPA (NUEPA) Library

Eminent scholar directors like professors Moonis Raza, Satya Bhushan and Kuldip Mathur looked after the library themselves. They actively participated in book selection processes and visited library very often and sat down there to study. Most of the senior professors of NIEPA spent many hours in reading right in the library. Good library management is indicated by its services. To cite one such case, I was in the library and searching for some books when my librarian came and asked me whether she can help. I told her that I was working on a book on TQM in education, and I wanted to read some relevant material. She offered to search for me the relevant material and share with me; she asked me to go back to my office. I went back. Within half an hour, she placed before me a list of about 200 titles that may be useful to me. Like in NIEPA, a library should be attractive enough for the faculty and students alike.

Source: Author.

Laboratories

Only about 20 per cent undergraduate students enrol in science courses. Very few, even out of this small enrolment, imbibe a scientific attitude, aptitude or scientific bent of mind. This is primarily because of the way science courses are transacted in colleges and universities. Exceptions apart, science courses are transacted like any other subjects like history or philosophy or language and literature. The primary and dominant method is lecture. Science education deserves intensive hands-on practical work in laboratories and workshops. Today's catchword is 'science through experimentation'. Essentially then, one important element of infrastructure is a high-quality laboratory. There are several quality issues in a laboratory, namely space, equipments, ICT support, safety, laboratory organization and overall environment and ecology. The UGC stipulates norms for laboratories as a precondition for affiliation.

The existing laboratories in physics or chemistry or biology in colleges are rather poorly equipped. To build a quality laboratory, it will be necessary to develop and or revise norms of undergraduate and postgraduate laboratories in each subject area from time to time. In order to ensure that science education becomes globally competitive, such norms must match global standards. That would require a careful study of laboratory settings, equipments, instruments, chemicals, samples and so on in developed countries and/or in Indian institutions where science education has achieved high quality. The IISc Bangalore, Physical Research Laboratories (PRLs) and such other frontline science institutions should be able to provide leadership in this regard.

The second important requirement of a quality laboratory is the ICT support for experimentation as well as processing of data. A large number of experiments can be carried through computer simulation, and the sophistication that can be achieved through computer simulation may not be possible through actual on-the-table conventional experiments. ICT offers opportunities of manipulation of a large variety of variables and large amount of data that can be processed for meaningful conclusion. Besides computer simulations, computers can be connected to a variety of experiments so that data generated may directly be fed into the computer for processing of data and generating results. Slovakia's study on integrated science through computer-aided instruction is a good example (Holec et al. 2004). Jeskova and Onderova (2004) presented computer-aided experiments in several areas, including wave optics diffraction, kinematics, notion and method of black box and so on.

iLab, initiated by MIT, provides an important opportunity. According to the MIT website:

> iLabs enriches science and engineering education by vastly increasing scope of experiments that students have access to in the course of their academic careers. Harnessing the Internet, it enables students to use real instruments via remote online laboratories. Unlike conventional laboratories, iLabs can be shared across a university or across the world–and today, they are.[2]

There are some iLab initiatives in India too in collaboration with MIT.

It is not unusual to find laboratories choked with fumes, gases and pungent smell. This is primarily because of poor ventilation. A quality laboratory must design ventilation, provision of exhaust fans, as much as right illumination and lights, particularly where the experiments involved decisions and conclusions on the basis of colour like titration in chemistry.

Another important dimension of a quality laboratory is its eco-friendliness. Chemistry and biology laboratories make use of a large amount of chemicals for experiments. These chemicals, at the end of the experiment, are thrown into the basins, which often accumulate in the small drains within the laboratory due to poor maintenance and cleaning; even if it flows out of the laboratory, it accumulates just outside the laboratory. Cumulatively, it affects the environment. A quality laboratory must carefully plan waste disposal to prevent deterioration of ecology within and around the laboratory.

Finally, it is important to look into the overall laboratory organization so that it does not only support functionality—facilitating conduct of experiments—but also becomes an interesting place attracting the students to the laboratory.

Sports and Games

Institutions of higher learning cannot be a place for munching the subjects of their courses and reproduce it in the examination. This is

---

[2] http://web.mit.edu/edtech/casestudies/ilabs.html (23 July 2014).

the last phase of students' life in the campus before they enter into the world of work. Students must get opportunities for exercising and optimizing their physical skills and well-being. 'Healthy mind in a healthy body' is an age old maxim. Hence, quality higher education institutions must include reasonable and fair amount of facilities for sports and games—outdoor and indoor games, gymnasium and so on. In order to encourage girls' participation, sports and games facilities and gymnasiums should be specially designed. Such facilities should also be available for the teaching and non-teaching staff in the college.

There are two different purposes for creating the facilities for sports and games in colleges. One such purpose is to nurture hobbies among the students during the college days. The second purpose is creating sportspersons. Sports and games infrastructure in colleges can substantially support talented young people to excel in sports and games. Despite more than a billion people, India finds it difficult to win a few gold medals in the Olympics. The major reason is a lack of culture of sports and games in schools and colleges, as well as lack of facilities. At that high level of competitiveness, every small detail matters. The sports and games facilities must be created in colleges and universities not only to nurture hobbies but also to nurture talents in sports and games for district-, state-, national- and international-level events.

There are some outstanding examples in the school sector. For example, there is a modern cricket academy in Shreyas High School in Baroda coached by Nayan Mongia, former Indian cricketer and alumni of Shreyas. For the optimum utilization of such facilities that are normally pretty expensive, facilities can be created for a cluster of colleges. In metropolitan cities and other urban areas, there are colleges within short distances from one another. It should be possible to set up common gymnasium and sports facilities for use of students from other colleges.

Art, Craft and Music

Just as it is important to create sports and games facilities in colleges, facilities for music, art, painting, dramatics and other creative arts are equally important. These facilities are almost absent in a majority of our colleges. Many of the large private schools in India have separate rooms and facilities for music, painting, clay modelling and a variety of other creative arts centres. These are necessary to develop hobbies and optimize potentials among the students. Most of the U.S. universities have art galleries. Indian higher education institutions should create facilities for cultivation of music and art.

Staff Amenities

The UGC has issued instruction that every teacher must spend at least five hours in the college; another stipulation provides for teaching load of 16 periods for an assistant professor, 12 periods for an associate professor and 8 periods for a professor. The duration of classes varies between 45 minutes and one hour. It means that a teacher is expected to spend two out of five hours in the classes; three hours outside the class reading, preparing lecture notes, researching, counselling students and so on. Academically, it is sound. But one shudders to think how to spend three hours in the college (if I was back to Katwa) without even a place to sit down and be able to concentrate on reading or writing or even counselling a student.

Teachers continue to be the most important determinant of quality in higher education. It is necessary to take cognizance of the relevance and role of staff amenities in the colleges for quality improvement in higher education. The minimum requirement is a cubicle with a table and a chair, and preferably a guest chair. In the changed scenario, computing facility with Internet connectivity to each teacher cubicle is a necessity. This may appear to be a tall order which is really not the case. It is a case of redesigning. Usual staffrooms have a long table at the centre with chairs strewn around, leaving a lot of space behind the chairs on both sides. Instead, a college staffroom can be converted into about 40 demarcated spaces with a light-weight partition for working privacy, a working table and a chair, and a laptop with the Internet and an overhead storage space. Centre space can be furnished with a decent sleek conference table with comfortable chairs for college teachers to discuss, share some light moments and relax with a cup of tea/coffee between the classes (Figure 10.1).

Figure 10.1:
An Alternative Design for Staffroom

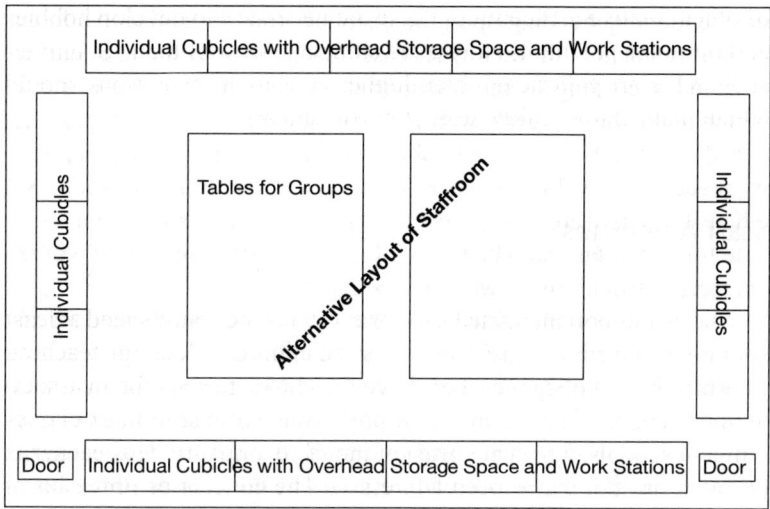

Source: Author.

I have not come across staffrooms that have attached washrooms, although almost every office of vice-chancellor and a college principal has a washroom, sometimes quite lavish one. For the sake of dignity and convenience, it is necessary to create such facilities. Special provision should be created for lady colleagues in the staff.

Each laboratory has enough space to accommodate two to three cubicles. Even if it would not have solved the complete problem, the college had enough space to provide at least 40 to 50 cubicles for the teachers.

During my discussion with college and university authorities, I learnt that what was missing was the sensitivity that teachers in higher education need and deserve a better place to work. Hardly, there is a plan document that identifies staffrooms and amenities as an area of expenditure. The building grant, contingency and maintenance grants that are used for furnishing offices of heads of institutions and other administratively important officers, for example, registrar and controller of examinations can also be used for staff amenities.

Staff housing is another important component of staff amenities, particularly for the rural colleges. A large majority of the teachers in rural colleges belong to the cities. In the absence of staff housing, they either travel up and down to the college every day or become weekenders, depending upon the distance from the college and their natural residence. In the former case, teachers' arrival and departure is timed according to the transportation systems like train or bus, which make them eagerly wait for leaving the college. This, I experienced as a teacher in a rural college; a majority of the teachers were weekenders, travelling from Kolkata or Burdwan and beyond. So, when students were free to consult teachers, teachers were not available for consultations. The issue is far more serious in case of women teachers, particularly in women's colleges.

Another important related issue that is far more complicated for any solution is the educational facility for the children of college teachers. In urban areas, college teachers have the choice to send their children to good schools. In rural areas, the only choice is to send them to government schools, which are often of indifferent quality. This perennial problem has not so far been addressed. The concept of provision of urban facilities in rural areas (PURA) may provide a solution unless colleges decide to run an experimental school within its own campus.

Although staff amenities may not be the only condition for quality improvement of teachers, it is one of the most important requirements for quality upgradation of teachers in higher education.

ICT Infrastructure

ICT has emerged as a dominant issue in college and university infrastructure. UGC and the Ministry of Human Resource Development have provided ICT facilities to higher education institutions. There are several issues with regard to ICT infrastructure for quality higher education. These are choice of technology, technology installation, access to technology for teachers and students, utilization of technology and monitoring and evaluation.

There are several types of technologies in education, like computers, laptops, iPads, mobile phones, video conferencing facilities and satellite-based facilities. There are debates about connected classrooms versus distributed classrooms. Hence, technology choice is a major issue in ICT integration in quality management in higher education.

Although in a large majority of higher education institutions, the teaching–learning process is restricted to classroom lectures with passive students listening and taking notes, some conventional laboratory work, quality education depends largely upon multichannel learning Systems (Anzalone 1994). Students tend to make up for the institutional deficiencies by adopting multichannel learning environment using classroom lectures, textbooks and notes, private coaching, mutual consultation and sometimes watching educational television programmes broadcast of the countrywide classroom. However, this variety of learning channels is not built into an organized system. Also, despite tremendous power of the Internet, use of the Internet for learning is still to be common. There is a huge gap between penetration of mobile phones and android phones and Internet connectivity in India, indicating non-utilization of Internet facilities (ETMA 2015). Rashtriya Uchchatar Shiksha Abhiyan's (RUSA) policy of TEL will require quality ICT infrastructure for institutions of higher education. There are several facets of ICT facilities for higher education.

India launched EDUSAT, a dedicated satellite for education on 20 September 2004. The proposal was to provide a satellite instructional terminal to every college and university; the universities will have additional provision for uplinking programmes (Mukhopadhyay 2002). The main idea is to generate a virtual classroom through networking of universities and colleges. The uplinking facilities will provide national channel from UGC, All India Council for Technical Education (AICTE), Indira Gandhi National Open University (IGNOU) and so on. In addition, there will be state channels that can broadcast programmes in regional languages; programmes can be specifically broadcast by universities for their own affiliated colleges using state channels. The teaching–learning process visualized through EDUSAT is to generate interactive learning through video-conferencing between the teaching ends and the students at the learning ends. Each college must have the satellite interactive terminals. However, this massive innovation remained largely an unfulfilled dream due to lack of vision and poor management by those who mattered then (Mukhopadhyay 2006b).

Another important item of ICT infrastructure is broadband connection and the bandwidth. Students should be able to access the Internet in the library and computer lab for enriching their learning. Internet facilities need to be extended to the teaching community.

Many major institutions have extended Internet facilities to staff quarters so that teachers have uninterrupted access to the Internet.

Unlike yesteryears, the use of computers is no more a specialist skills for computer professionals. It is a set of life skills. Accordingly, every teacher and student in higher education must develop basic computer skills like using word processing, use of spreadsheets, databases, PowerPoint presentations, Internet, Web 2.0 tools and so on. In addition, students should be encouraged to learn as hobby certain special software like Director, Photoshop, PageMaker, Corel Draw, Multimedia, Web Designing and so on. In order to build up life skills in computing, institutions of higher education should be well equipped with computing facilities. Under a scheme, the UGC has promoted computers in higher education institutions, and almost every college now possesses five to 10 computers. This is to be enhanced to set up a large multimedia computer lab with 40 to 50 terminals with broadband Internet connectivity.

Computing facilities should become part and parcel of the culture of an organization. In order to achieve this, it is necessary to ensure deep penetration of computers in the institution—use of computers in the library, laboratory, office management and so on. It is equally important to ensure that teachers have 24 × 7 personal access to computers. The ICT application cannot be in piecemeal. It must cover and support all areas of operation, namely, academic management, personnel management, infrastructure management, financial management, student support services management, office management, linkage and interface with outside agency and so on. Unless the computers are really on the desktop, it is unlikely that people will move out to use computers. With the reduction of costs, it should be possible to generate greater depth of penetration of computers and IT facilities in colleges and universities.

Safety and Security

Safety and security have emerged as major concerns in colleges and university management, especially after certain disasters like Kumbakonam school fire in 2004. There are several security issues in higher education institutions. Some of them are campus violence, including ragging, destruction of institutional properties, fire hazards, outside elements forcibly occupying hostel space, safety and security of women students. Other issues of security and safety are unsafe old buildings, old exposed electrical connections and so on.

As a measure for the safety and security, a large number of colleges and universities engage security agencies. However, a majority of them engage unskilled cheap labour as security personnel. As a result, there is no real impact on security. Higher education institutions may do well to include this item as part of the strategic plan for quality improvement.

Infrastructure Norms

There are certain norms of infrastructure for the affiliation of colleges and universities. Infrastructure is one of the areas of assessment for accreditation by the NAAC. Nonetheless, the prescribed norms are hesitant and conservative, meant for hand-to-mouth kind of operation of higher education institutions. Quality cannot be guided by 'needs', but must go beyond.

Conclusion

Quality of education is influenced by a multiple set of factors. One group of experts emphasizes on the teaching–learning process often at the cost of infrastructure, while others take a reverse view. In order to achieve quality in higher education, it will be necessary to look at every component of an institution of higher education since they are interrelated and affect one another. For example, there is enough evidence to infer that achieving higher order cognition necessitates collaborative and interactive learning. Collaborative and interactive learning does not happen in a theatre-style classroom. ICT-integrated blended learning results into better learning outcome. It cannot be achieved without ICT facilities in the classrooms. Similarly, in order to modernize scientific experiments, use of ICT becomes necessary. It cannot be achieved unless computers are available right within the laboratory. Multichannel learning is the hallmark of developing sustainable learning with higher order cognition. This cannot be achieved without videoconferencing facilities, Internet-based learning facilities and so on. It is hence necessary to seriously examine the issue of quality of infrastructure as an important determinant of quality of higher education. Quality infrastructure is the necessary condition for quality higher education but not the sufficient condition. A sufficient condition is the proper and effective use of such facilities.

11

Human Resource Management

Introduction

Education is all about human beings—for and by the human beings. Its performance depends almost exclusively on quality of human resources. As they say, smart boards do not make smart classes but smart teachers do. There is ample empirical evidence that what happens to an institute is who is at the helm—leadership position. The reputation of an institution is built by people who graduate from an institution.

In financial terms, human resources cost almost 85 to 90 per cent of the total expenditure in higher education. Whatever else is done, say, civil and electrical works, maintenance and upkeep, is done through human beings. In fact, the organizational growth and decay of higher education institutions are directly related to quality of human resources. However, human resources are not static. Quality of human resources needs continuous mentoring and monitoring through appropriate human resource management initiatives. Human resource management implies end-to-end management of human beings in the organization from personnel planning to personnel appraisal and reward and punishment linked to performance. In this chapter, we will restrict ourselves to the issue of recruitment, especially interview as a selection tool, staff induction, mapping human resources and staff development. Further, though quality management in higher education institutions requires attention and planned development of staff of all types and all levels, our emphasis here would remain largely confined to academic staff.

Recruitment in Education

Recruitment plays a very important role in quality management in higher education. The garbage in, garbage out maxim is equally applicable here; if you recruit less than good faculty, the institute has to be less than quality. A staff recruited today will be there in the system for the next 35 to 40 years (25 to 65 years of age). Recruitment can lead to either 40 years of asset or 40 years of liability. Hence, it is very important that higher education institutions pay greater attention to this issue that is largely treated as rule-bound ritual.

The UGC has prescribed norms for the recruitment of teachers in colleges and universities, which are preconditions for affiliation. The recruitment norms are now being backed by certain quality assurance mechanisms like NET and tests by college service commissions in different states.

Another serious issue is the lateral recruitment at senior levels like professors, principals, pro-vice-chancellors or vice-chancellors. During one of our conversations, Late Professor Moonis Raza (former vice-chancellor of Delhi University and director of NIEPA) justified an elaborate process of selection at the senior level as follows:

A senior professor is like a grown up tree. Before you transplant a grown up tree, you must check the soil condition and also the quality of the plant. Otherwise either the plant will die or it will crack and destroy the garden'. You must check whether this professor is the right professor for your institution. (Mukhopadhyay 2012a)

As mentioned elsewhere in this book, performance on the job, including academic profession like ours, is the function of qualification, technical skills and soft skills or employability skills. As our profession gets more and more complicated and challenging, it is necessary to verify all the three sets and not qualification alone. Our contemporary practice of verification of certificates and interview is not enough. It needs a more elaborate process of testing, observation, group exercises followed by interview.

With the introduction of NET and SET, there is some screening mechanism on ground. The NET and SET largely screen candidates on the knowledge domain. It is a good help especially when universities vary widely in their quality of curriculum and examination.

Colleges and universities will do well to test the employability skills of the candidates, especially on problem solving, critical and creative thinking, self-awareness, attitude towards the profession and students, working in teams, communication, emotional resonance or empathy, management of emotions and stress, ICT skills, reading range and habits and so on. There are online tests available on all these soft or employability skills. We have recently developed a Teacher Employability Assessment Scale (TEAS) standardized on school teacher sample (Mukhopadhyay et al. 2015). Although standardized on school teacher sample, the TEAS can be used for screening of teachers of higher education, although the norm will not be valid. Interview should be the last in this series of the selection process.

Interview

Let us first share what research has to say about interviewing as a selection tool. Nicholson (1989) points out how unreliable it is to depend singularly on interview for selection. Morgan et al. (1983) made a comparative study of recruitment in Education, Police Senior Command Course (PSCC), National Health Service (NHS) and Civil Services (CS). The PSCC, NHS and CS used most of the tested methodologies like prior training of selectors, appointment of specialist selectors, preparation of job specification, preparation of specific assessment exercises, tests and interview strategies, including designing and use of pre-structured interview schedule.

In England, Local Education Authorities (LEAs), in comparison depended only on interview without any preparation and structured schedule of observation. While many researchers have contributed in the area of personnel selection, I would prefer to refer to two major meta-analyses carried by Hunter and Hannah (1987) and Wiesnerf and Cronshaw (1988). Hunter and Hannah analysed more than 400 studies on interview, and the main findings are as follows:

- Interview is a grossly unreliable instrument for selection. It is highly subjective and has very little relevance to job performance. They recommended it to be discarded.

- On an average, an interviewer makes up her/his mind within first three/four minutes. Rest of the time he/she creates situations within the interview board to justify the decision.
- Reliability of an interview can be improved, by nearly 40 per cent, through professional training in interviewing.

The major findings of the Wiesnerf and Cronshaw (1988) study are as follows:

- Structured interview is significantly better (more reliable) than unstructured interview.
- Panel interview is more efficient than individual interviews.
- Individual structured interview is more efficient than unstructured panel interview.

It is rather paradoxical that unstructured interview by untrained selectors is empirically proven to be a non-dependable tool, and educational recruitment in India and elsewhere, including the UK, is largely dependent upon this particular approach. It is hence no wonder that a large proportion of candidates selected through such interview fail to fulfil the job roles and expectations.

Training in interviewing need special mention as reliability can be improved through training of the interviewers and using structured interview. It is possible to identify by name the people who frequent selection committees, and training programmes can be organized for them. I have been involved in conducting 19 national workshops on interviewing skills organized by the Staff Selection Commission (SSC), Government of India. These workshops drew more than 1,000 participants—chairman and/or members of the Union Public Service Commission (UPSC), SSC, state public service commissions, banking and railway service recruitment boards, Air India, Indian Airlines, ONGC, port trusts, oil corporations, Life Insurance Corporation, Indo Tibetan Border Police Force (ITBF), City Bank, Mahendra and Mahendra and many such other organizations; not many came from among the selectors in education sector. Members of selection committees in universities and colleges frequent various committees. They can be oriented and trained to increase reliability.

The obvious reaction to the above proposition is that it is too lengthy a procedure. Before getting into the question of whether it is lengthy or not, it is important to look at the need of the system from the professional angle. The issue is benefits in terms of cost of devoting time for selection: How much time is justified for selecting a person who will serve the system for 35 to 40 long years and influence lives of millions of students.

There are a few fundamental principles and practices that can improve the efficiency of selection interview.

- Knowledge cannot be tested in a few minutes; it is better tested through tests like NET/SET.
- Try to find out what the candidate knows rather than what he does not as the later domain is very large and not much of use.
- Create job specification, list the items of assessment, assess candidates specifically on those points.
- Assess the personal styles—communication, personal presence, attitudes and so on that make a teacher effective.
- Provide scores to each candidate on specific points—try and quantify assessment to create a reliable basis for discussion.
- The chairman should ensure that selectors do not overwhelm the candidates with their wisdom lectures.

Induction

Most often, and in most institutions, as soon as a person joins, he/she is given a class or assigned a specific duty without any opportunity to know the institution or the profession that was earlier observed only as a student. One of the important requirements of human resource management for quality is providing some space to the newly recruited faculty and administrative staff to get acquainted with the institution, figure out his/her role and how others in the same position are fulfilling their role expectations. Let us see a case.

A Case

Immediately after joining TTTI, Bhopal (now NITTR), the youngest member of the faculty with a degree in civil engineering met

Professor Y. Saran, then principal, and asked him, 'Sir, what am I supposed to do? What are my duties?' Professor Saran told him to spend a month visiting the library, observing training programmes and classes by senior faculty members, interacting with colleagues in various academic and administrative departments, and then come back for a discussion. After a month, when the young faculty member met Professor Saran, the principal asked him, 'What do you want to do here?' The young man replied, 'Make educational films, and take a few classes'. Professor Saran told him to report to Professor Dharap for educational film and to Professor Balu for classes in civil engineering.

There are two messages from this unconventional, innovative approach to induction. First, the new incumbent had ample opportunity to understand the institution—its culture and ethos, and had time to adapt himself to the institutional culture, norms and practices. He had enough time and opportunity to socialize and get him accepted as a colleague. Second, a person recruited today will be on the job for the next 35 to 40 years. If she or he does what she or he wants to do, she/he will contribute far more than if she/he is asked to do what she/he does not want to do. Further, if she/he 'has to contribute for 480 months, is it not worthwhile spending one month on inducting him/her to the institutional culture' was Professor Saran's argument.

There are several methods of inducting a teacher in an institution. These are:

- The principal provides information about the institute—its culture, practices, programmes, specialties and so on.
- Pre-induction training—The candidate can be provided a pre-induction training by organizing a training programme, provided there are several people joining more or less during the same period. For example, IGNOU provides pre-induction training for its newly recruited academic staff on a regular basis.
- The newly recruited teacher can develop a schedule and, with permission, observe other teachers teaching. This will give him/her an idea about not only the teaching practices but also the composition of classrooms and ethos of the students as well. Similarly, he/she can observe other activities in the institution.

- A young teacher can be attached to a senior teacher to team up on course design and delivery and research and publications. This was quite common when we joined the M.S. University of Baroda. Several of my initial articles were with Professor M.S. Yadav, a senior member of the faculty; and, I thought, it was a good training and experience.

Mapping Human Resources

The prerequisite of human resource management in an institute of higher education is to understand each member of the staff—both academic and non-academic—because each one of them is unique. Their collective character changes with the composition of the group creating 'crowd', 'groups', 'teams' and 'cliques', or purposeless to purposeful positive or negative clustering of individuals. Understanding others is a complex process since human beings are a multifaceted construct with physical, intellectual, emotional and spiritual self. As this four-fold self fuses into each other, they create the most complex configurations.

Because of these complexities, common sense is far too inadequate to justify the claim of understanding colleagues and peers. There are several ways of describing human beings, for example, Cattell's 16 personality factors, introversion–extraversion, ego states and life positions, or in terms of the three qualities, namely *Sattwa* (goodness), *Rajas* (passion) and *Tamas* (destruction). A more meaningful and useable description can be with respect to roles and factors affecting role performance.

Role analysis of a teacher in higher education indicates the following roles—some are major while some are minor:

- *Planning*: Planning of annual calendar and curricular plans, laboratory and workshop activities, examination and evaluation, personal leave (holidays) and so on.
- *Guiding*: Each teacher helps students both inside and outside the class in academic, examination, career choices and even on personal matters.

- *Teaching*: Classroom teaching, tutorials, group activities, laboratory practicals, field trips and other such learning activities.
- *Research:* Conducting research for teaching, action research, funded research projects, participating in collaborative projects and so on.
- *Publication:* Authoring and publication of papers, book reviews, research papers, research reports, books and monographs and so on.
- *Student assessment and examination:* Paper setting, planning the examination schedule, invigilation duties, evaluating answer scripts, tabulating marks and declaring the results several times in a year.
- *Management:* Classroom management, laboratory, library, field trips and educational tours, time management and management of examinations.
- *Human relations*: Relationship with the principal, colleagues, students, alumni and other professionals.
- *Professional development*: Reading, writing, attending conferences, seminars, extension lectures, training programmes, Internet browsing on professionally relevant material, participating in education-related social media and networks and so on.
- *Extension and social service*: Delivering extension lectures, writing and publications, participating in social action programmes, community development and so on.

These roles can be classified into three categories, namely content competencies, competencies related to science of human learning and managerial competencies. The role effectiveness will be guided by commitment and competence. The competency–commitment plotted in a matrix provides an interesting situational study.

Competency-Commitment Matrix

The competency (ability to do) and commitment (willingness to do) do not necessarily go together. Plotted on two axes of a matrix (Figure 11.1), there are four categories of teachers and non-teaching staff in colleges and universities.

Figure 11.1:
Can Do–Will Do Matrix

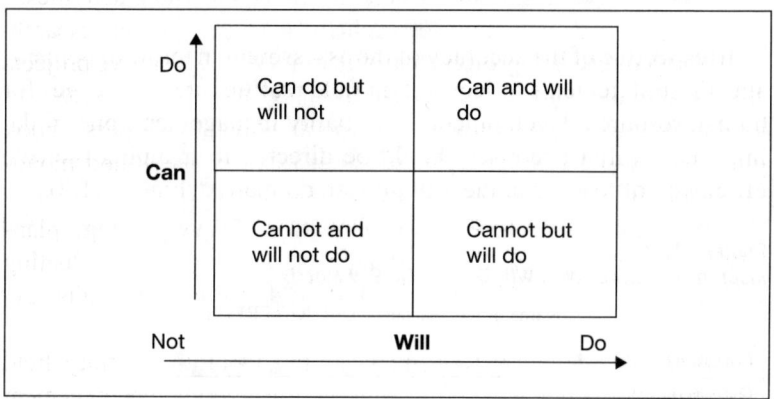

Source: Author.

Competence is the cognitive attribute of a human being, whereas willingness or motivation is the affective attribute. From the standpoint of development or behaviour modification, it is easier to develop the cognitive component when backed by affective attribute, but the reverse is not true.

This matrix provides four categories of teachers as follows:

- Competent and committed: The safe and trusted lieutenants of the institution
- Committed but not competent: Potential resource
- Competent but lack commitment: Threat to the system but a hidden potential
- Neither competent nor committed: Liability

During my workshops with principals of colleges, spread over 30 years, there was a near unanimity of opinion on the following:

- Quality component of colleges is on the shoulders of will do–can-do teachers who are not more than 15 to 20 per cent.
- Day-to-day management and routine are supported by another about 50 per cent from the second and third categories.
- The most difficult are the ones who are competent but not committed or willing to work.

- The fourth category is a definite liability, but fortunately they are not too many—not more than 5 to 10 per cent.

Irrespective of the accuracy of the assessment in terms of percentage, these statements reflect certain field realities and challenges for human resource development. For quality management, one of the important initial exercises should be directed to mapping the role efficiency of teacher in the will do–can do matrix (Figure 11.2).

Figure 11.2:
Mapping a Teacher on a Will Do–Can Do 9/9 Matrix

Name of the Teacher... Dr UJG TERFDS

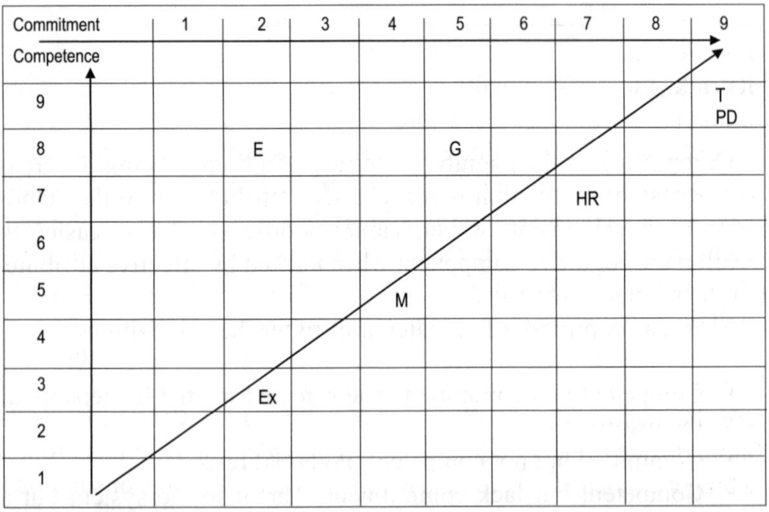

Commitment	1	2	3	4	5	6	7	8	9
Competence									
9									T PD
8		E			G				
7							HR		
6									
5					M				
4									
3			Ex						
2									
1									

Source: Author.

Notes: G=Guiding; P=Planning; T=Teaching; E=Examining; M=Managing; HR=Human Relations; PD=Professional Development; Ex=Extension.

The mapping will indicate that the role efficiency or role preparedness is different for the same teacher in different roles.

For example, in the case of teaching and his/her own personal development, Dr UJG has the highest level of competence and commitment; he/she is capable of good teaching and willing to do it to his/her best. The exactly opposite is his/her role preparedness for extension—neither competent nor willing to improve. Managing is in the middle of the road—not averse to doing it but no specific enthusiasm; not very competent, but can manage. Examination is another area where the teacher is very competent but does not like to do the work and not willing to do.

This profile can be the basis for developing individualized development plans. Again, these plans should have data indicating state of the art of capabilities of a teacher vis-à-vis the eight identified areas. The initial data will provide the baseline on which the developments can be compared over the years.

From the angle of quality management in higher education institutions, it is important to recognize that people with commitment can, and will, find their own ways to build competencies. But the reverse is not true—'you can take the horse to water but cannot make it drink'. Hence, for quality management in higher education, the premium is on willingness or commitment.

Because of their willingness or motivation to learn, the second group can be developed. The developmental needs of every teacher have to be identified and a road map has to be created for development in a time-bound manner. With the development of this group, they will migrate and join the first group, increasing the stock of the will do–can do staff.

The third group can be a threat. For, without the commitment, competence can act like unguided or even misguided missile. These are the typical non-establishmentarian group. Motivating being far more difficult than building competencies, dealing with this group is a bigger challenge. There is no readily available formula or solution to this problem. May be the Involvement–Responsibility–Recognition Cycle (IRRC) will work with some people in this group. The hallmarks of management strategy are as follows:

- Involve them in decision making.
- Make strategic interventions so that they accept the responsibility for their decisions and implement them.
- Recognize their contribution, in private and in public, initially even if it is not significant.
- Continue with this cycle till they have settled down to take organizational responsibility and reorganize themselves.

It is within the reach of our experiences: how a perennial critique of the organization becomes organizational person after getting a responsible position like principal, head of the department (HOD), dean or pro-vice chancellor or vice chancellor. In one of my assignments, I came across one such colleague—critical about everything. I had the similar feedback from other colleagues. However, this critic never failed on his assigned work, rather finished it fast and used rest of the time for criticizing others, especially the establishment. I used the IRRC model. One of the activities in this organization was developing learning material in English and Hindi. I called upon him to get it rendered into other Indian languages. I gave him full freedom to choose his team for various language groups; the remunerations have to be within the specified norms of the institute. Within one year, he got all the material (huge) into seven languages. Just as I am doing it here, I personally acknowledged his contribution and showered praise—genuinely—on him in public.

It is important to distinguish within the same group between people who are shirkers and critics and those who are looking for responsibility and recognition.

The fourth group lacks both motivation and competence. It is difficult to motivate. Since they are not motivated, it is difficult to build competence. This group represents 'Task Immaturity'. Direct instruction should work, at least partially, by assigning them simple tasks and using 'authority' to ensure timely accomplishment. Insist on completion, and, if need be, concede quality to begin with. As they learn to complete on time, introduce the element of quality. As a matter of strategy, emphasize initially on development of competencies—take simple and one skill at a time and then move on to integration and complicated skills. As the skills and competencies develop, you can use the IRRC with them. The transformation of teachers in Mrinalini Devi College is an interesting case (note at the end of this chapter).

It is a spiralling process. Involving staff in decision making, allowing and encouraging them to accomplish and giving recognition can move from one level to another. The secret of staff motivation is making them feel important and recognize and realize what great things they are doing. According to Secretan (1999), an inspired person is self-propelled; the challenge of staff development is to create that inspired being within the staff. As we maintain, an outstanding professor is an inspired learner.

Human Resource Development

Let us remind ourselves that only those teachers and staff can be developed who want to change and develop themselves. Staff development programmes offer an opportunity to those who want to change. Opportunities of staff development can be created in several ways. Let us browse through a few.

Knowledge Management: Staff Seminars and Informed Discourses

In a large majority of higher education institutions, there are outstanding faculty members who work in isolation. Due to lack of interaction and synergy, there is poor knowledge management that could have given much stronger foundation for academic quality. Let me site two brief cases to draw home the point.

CASE (M.S. University of Baroda), then headed by Professor M.B. Buch, actively used two major techniques. In one, he invited outstanding scholars from various universities and institutions to deliver lectures in their own area of specialization to the members of the faculty and research scholars. Since the institution did not have enough money to pay for the travel, he would invite scholars travelling through or nearby cities, or visiting the university on some other academic duties. In the second intervention, he asked his faculty colleagues and research scholars to present seminars on their research projects.[1]

Let me share the second case from the college where I began my career in higher education.

Case of Katwa College

This is the story of Katwa College located in Katwa, small township 125 kilometres away from Kolkata and about 40 kilometres from Burdwan. This small college, situated on the beautiful confluence of two

---

[1] I was then a research scholar and later a lecturer (now, called assistant professor). All of us benefitted significantly from these two interventions.

rivers—the Ajay and the Ganges—runs in three shifts with 49 teaching staff. Though a degree college, this college had some outstanding scholars, though none of them were full professors (early 1970s). There were rich informal academic and intellectual discourses in staffrooms, staff quarters and elsewhere. However, such rich discourses were never inducted into formal mechanisms of staff seminars that Dr Ranajit (Mukhopadhyay, 2012a) tried in his college, and initiated the process of knowledge management. That could have enriched the intellectual ecology of Katwa College. Such talented teachers are there everywhere, though the number of good scholarly teachers may vary from one college to another. Optimizing their talents through scientific knowledge management of the faculty members, Indian colleges can change their faces.

Quality higher education institutions must find their own ways and mechanisms of brining the individual expertise on to the table for everyone to share and collectively get enriched.

Team Projects: Research and Development

With new promotion policies, career advancement scheme (CAS) for example, there is a lot of emphasis on research and publications. There is also a substantial increase of opportunities of research grants not only from the UGC but also from the Indian Council of Social Science Research (ICSSR) and various other ministries of the Government of India and corporate houses. Colleges and universities should encourage staff to prepare research proposal either on their own subject areas or on higher education and submit to funding agencies. Instead of individual projects, institutions should encourage group projects. Group projects help working in teams and synergy of knowledge and expertise.

How much fund is brought through research projects can easily be a criteria for staff evaluation as it is in many Western universities. NIEPA had good tradition of faculty research, where almost every faculty, including the directors, worked on funded research projects. That also complemented the requirement of young research staff.

Most of the social science research studies are carried out on small samples and within small geographic locations. Teachers should be encouraged to undertake collaborative research with colleagues from other universities. We completed a study on employability skills of teachers drawn from 12 Indian states; we involved one professor as co-investigator from one of the universities from each of the sampled states. Besides making it feasible, the collaboration of 12 professors contributed to the quality of research output (Mukhopadhyay et al. 2015).

Conferences and Seminars

Conferences and seminars provide a good opportunity for academic development. However, current regulations do not encourage participation unless one's paper is accepted for presentation. There are two implications of these regulations. First, teachers who are not used to writing, though read enough, have to miss participating in the intellectual discourses. Second, some make it a point to send something; they know that conferences need participants. So whatever they write will be accepted. During the last few years, the UGC has been providing liberal grants to colleges and universities for organizing conferences and seminars. Many higher education teachers make use of these conferences for presenting their papers and make their portfolio for promotion. The UGC has created a good provision, and efforts must be made to make best use of it for quality improvement. Some of the quality-conscious universities and institutions adopt a quality assurance mechanism by asking faculty members to present the paper in in-house staff seminars. Staff members are asked to modify and improve the paper on the basis of the discussion and feedback.

Training Outside: Face-to-face Training

Another approach in staff development is taking advantage of formal in-service programmes. Academic staff colleges offer courses for newly recruited teachers in higher education institutions. It has now expanded its scope to offer courses and workshops for senior academic colleagues and principals of colleges and deans of faculties. The programmes for the new entrants have been made compulsory and linked to job security (confirmation on the job). This provides a good opportunity for staff development. However, the effectiveness of the ASC is not beyond question.

From the standpoint of organizational design for human resource development, ASC is a poorly designed organization with relatively junior people on the staff with one senior professor as director. Often the director is drawn from the academic departments without any training and orientation on Training of Trainers. Usual practice is to invite number of speakers from different universities and institutions who deliver lectures. ASCs, due to their structural deficiencies, have not been able to differentiate between teaching and training. UGC norms are another barrier to quality. For example, the academic value of a trainer-professor is ₹ 1,000 per day, whereas his/her airlines value is unlimited, giving an impression that travel by air is more important than properly remunerating the academic preparation of a trainer.

Nonetheless, attending ASC programmes is useful because it provides an opportunity for peer group interaction.

The course design and content need special attention. Behaviour modification and personal excellence sessions that can actually open up the mind and contribute to the unwilling teachers are often missing from the programmes.

Open and Distance Education

The open and distance education has thrown up new opportunities. There are various direct-to home (DTH) channels offering programmes of relevance to teachers of higher education. More importantly, teachers interested in self-development can browse the Internet and access open education resources. Many universities, including Stanford and others, are offering massive open online courses (MOOCs). There are directories and lists of MOOCs offered by various organizations on the web.[2] Both OER and MOOCs are free courses. The OER and MOOCs do not cost the individuals except that they ought to have access to computers with Internet connectivity and strong bandwidth. Then, there are online courses.

Impact of Training

The training loss is a fact established by research. Average training loss is almost 80 per cent within first few months. That is one of the reasons why, despite so much of investments in training and so many training programmes, the actual impact is not visible. The difficulty is

---

[2] For example, www.moocs.com, www.mooc-list.com and many others.

with the training design and with the missing provision of follow-up. Research also reveals that training loss can be reduced substantially with follow-up. The follow-up can be through shorter duration face-to-face programmes or through online programmes. Journals provide an important mechanism of continuing education and follow-up. Training effectiveness can be improved significantly by introducing a monitoring and evaluation mechanism. Commonwealth Educational Media Centre for Asia (Commonwealth of Learning) CEMCA (COL) made an elaborate exercise on developing a plan for the monitoring and evaluation of capacity building of open and distance education (ODE) personnel in higher education (Mukhopadhyay and Parhar 2014).

Creating provisions for subject journals, educational and pedagogical journals in institutions provides support for in-house staff development.

Human Resource Development Blueprint

For a meaningful effort in human resource development, it is necessary to develop a human resource development blueprint. The following are a few suggested steps in developing the blueprint:

1. Each teacher and employee engages himself/herself in an exercise of task analysis, preferably using a work–time log sheet to document their day-to-day activities.
2. Every teacher and employee identifies the skills and competencies required to perform in each of the work areas identified. Further, let each one identify their relative strengths and development needs vis-à-vis their work areas.
3. Tabulate the training needs for all teachers and employees in a master sheet against each functional area. This should provide enough data for clustering the teachers and training areas, for example, a group of teachers may need one kind of training.
4. Discuss with the staff the master sheet and collectively decide the strategy of development—what skills will be developed through on-the-job training, where and in which programme can one be deputed for formal training and what can be done through organized and unorganized distance education programmes.

5. Create an annual calendar within a medium-term framework since all the training needs cannot be achieved within one calendar year.

6. Cost of development—Development schedule has to be managed within the limited resources of the institution.

7. Affordability to spare a teacher—It is necessary to negotiate between the developmental needs of a staff and the institution being able to afford to spare him/her from the institution.

8. Sustainability—One-time development effort will have to be followed for sustainability and further improvement of the competencies developed.

9. Review—Carry out review of staff development at multiple points—first immediately after the development activity/training, followed by review every quarter and an annual review.

10. Monitoring and evaluation—Mount a monitoring and evaluation framework to assess cost–benefit analysis and to find mechanisms for improving effectiveness and impact of staff development.

Conclusion

Human resource is the most critical of all the resources for quality management in higher education. Deming, Juran, Crosby, Ishikawa and all quality scientist recommended staff training and development as one of the cardinal principles of total quality management. Education as such is an human-intensive enterprise; over and above, teachers in higher education are, many a time, the only resource for students who have ventured into higher education but cannot afford to buy books. The critical role of teachers needs to be focused and not pushed under the carpet with lofty statements like 'Nation Builders' without corresponding support and recognition.

As mentioned elsewhere, 90 per cent students are in undergraduate courses and in affiliated colleges. Obviously, the largest single number of teachers is in such colleges. The focus of human resource management must shift to these teachers. There must be new ways of meaningfully empowering them, rather than confusing with some apology of staff training with undermanaged quality. The empowerment needs to be multifaceted, covering affective as well as cognitive dimensions.

SECTION III

Levers of Change

12

Student Involvement in Quality Management

Introduction

The world at large—employment market, community organizations, social and political systems as well as civil societies—gets
connected through students in higher education, especially at the
leading edges. Higher education produces leaders in all walks of life.
Hence, concerns about the quality of higher education from the point
of view of students are genuine.

With quality education, students can be pillars of sustainable quality of life in the society and at home. Further, students are the ambas-
sadors of institutions; they build reputations. Reputed institutions
around the world (top 100 universities) and in India, like the IISc,
IITs and IIMs, Presidency College (Kolkata), St. Stephen's (Delhi),
Ramakrishna Mission (Belur), Loyola College (Chennai), Lady
Shri Ram College for Women (Delhi), Birla Institute of Technology
and Sciences (Pilani), Faculty of Management Studies (University
of Delhi), The Indian School of Business (Hyderabad)[1] and many
others are known for their graduates. This institutional reputation and
graduate quality are mutually supportive.

---

[1] There are many others. These are just a few examples.

Students are the main stakeholders in higher education institutions. Hence, their voice concerning quality must find place and should matter. Students' involvement in quality management is not only logical and administratively ethical, but also necessary because they are mature and can contribute to quality improvement and assurance. They can not only construct quality, but can also act as quality watchdogs. They can be creative, out-of-the-box thinkers as they have 'no experience' to tame their thinking. Many peer-group assessors for NAAC have shared their perception that students can make meaningful contribution in quality in all the reputed institutions of higher education.

In this chapter, an effort has been made to discuss the issue of students' participation in quality management. We will deal with the quality framework, scope of participation of students in quality management and a series of action steps that have either been tried out somewhere or are feasible and worth trying. In the process, we will also review and refer to some of the international experiences on student involvement and participation in quality management.

Framework for Student Participation

Conventionally, it is believed that the job of students in a college is to attend classes, go to the library, conduct practical sessions in laboratories (science students) and sit for examinations. Their participation in college activities and student organizations is neither encouraged, nor seen positively. Participation in student organizations is often seen as an activity with an underlying political intention/motivation, often leading to (political) caderization. There is not much research in India on student involvement in co-curricular and extracurricular activities and their impact on student growth. Co-curricular and extracurricular activities and student participation do not find any meaningful place in the discourses on quality of higher education institution.

Verma (2007) identified class seminars and discussions, activities of subject societies/clubs, sports, cultural activities, intercollege competitions, NSS and National Cadet Corps, freshers' day and farewell functions, committees formed for discipline, cleanliness, and so on, political activities and student bodies, fairs and festivals, representation on other committees, awareness campaigns, tutorials and house activities in the institution as practices prevalent in student participation. Montelongo (2002), based on a comprehensive review of the literature on student participation in college students' organizations, spelt out governing bodies, Greek letter social organization, student government groups, academic clubs and professional groups, honour societies, publication and media groups, service groups, intramural sports clubs, religious organizations, and special interests and cultural groups as the categories of college student organization (Astin 1993, Craig and Warner 1991). Montelongo (2002) presented a useful review of literature on student participation in college students' organizations and examined from different outcome parameters, like students' background and participation, participation and college satisfaction, campus development and students' development. The findings are as follows:

1. Studies on student background and participation failed to find any specific pattern for any meaningful conclusion. In other words, students' background and personality are not related to students' participation (Berk and Goebel 1987, Burton 1981).
2. Studies also revealed that non-governing, non-Greek organizations attract more student participation (Craig and Warner 1991).

   There is a direct relationship between satisfaction in the college and students' participation in student organizations and extracurricular activities. The satisfaction is largely credited to peer-group interaction and social life in the college. Astin (1993) claims that the level of satisfaction is dependent upon the number of hours spent in clubs and other organizations for socialization. Astin's study finds an echo in Abrahamowicz's (1988) study that reveals the difference in the degree of college satisfaction between students who take active part and those who do not. In other words, there is a direct correlation between college satisfaction and campus involvement.
3. Pascarella and Terenzini (1991) reported that 'thinking in retrospect, college graduates perceived that their participation in

extracurricular activities has significant impact on their development of interpersonal and leadership skills, which is important for occupational success'.

4. Contrary to the conventional belief that student involvement in college organization adversely affects their learning outcome and development, several studies show positive cognitive and affective growth with the degree of participation of students (Astin 1993, Pascarella and Terenzini 1991). Also, studies found that students' participation improves self-confidence together with interpersonal and leadership skills. Further, increase in the number of hours spent on student organizations and activities reduces 'time and energy' necessary to invest in verbal and quantitative learning (read as learning outcome) (Anaya 1996).

NAAC declared 2006 as the year of the students and undertook an innovative exercise across the country. NAAC organized seminars in various parts of India. In all, 476 students participated in 11 centres. In these seminars, students were asked to voice their opinions and concerns on three issues:

1. My understanding of 'quality'
2. Students' views matter—Feedback mechanisms for quality enhancement
3. Students' participation in institutional quality assessment by NAAC

A detailed analysis of the responses is available in the report 'student participation in quality enhancement.[2]

International Experience

It may be worthwhile to examine the cases of student involvement in some selected countries. In Australian universities, the engagement between teachers and students is very intense due to guidance,

---

[2] http://naac.gov.in/docs/Students%20Participation%20in%20Quality%20Enhancement.pdf/ (accessed on 22 February 2014).

pastoral and other types of support (Krause and Armitage 2014). The depth of the engagement and the relationship is obviously more between the students and their teachers, and research scholars and their guides. This nature of engagement influences the culture of universities, making them a community of students, academic staff and administrative support staff.[3] Hence, there is some kind of collegiality among the students and the staff with different roles. Although this may not be a case of direct student involvement with the management, a deeper engagement between the faculty and the students has an impact on the quality of learning, which is the central theme of a university. There are formal mechanisms of student involvement in the management of universities, which is significantly influenced by the community culture.

Participation of students in university administration and management in Australia has to be seen from these organizational culture perspectives. In the formal mechanism, Australian universities have student representatives in governing bodies. The practice of student representation varies among the universities. In some universities, students' representatives of the governing bodies are elected directly; in some other universities, students are nominated/appointed from the students' association. Further, all universities have student representatives on the second-level decision-making bodies like academic board, faculty board and various advisory bodies. Thus, student

---

[3] While travelling from Paris to Delhi, two young people were seated next to me. They wore a T-shirt of the University of Illinois, Urbana Champaign. During our conversation, I learnt that they were pursuing engineering education at Urbana. They had done two years of engineering education in one of the Indian universities earlier. To my query about what was the difference between Illinois and their Indian alma mater, they made a very interesting comment. 'Teachers in Urbana are very caring'. What does that mean? They clarified that 'their teachers in the Indian institution were as scholarly as their teachers in Urbana. Indian teachers were bothered about their subjects and themselves, not about us'. Not sure, I understood, I pursued, especially because I am one of the Indian teachers and one of the Urbana inmates. They clarified those teachers in Urbana, wherever they meet, will stop and ask besides greeting, how are we doing on our coursework, whether we have any problem, whether they can help, and so on. If we had any problem, they will advise, even on the corridors, what to consult, what to do; and even fix time to meet them personally'. I realized how deeply teachers engage themselves with students. I knew that the engineering department in Urbana had quite a few Indian professors, at least when we were there. On my asking, the two young students clarified that the Indian teachers were as caring as their American and European counterparts. They said, 'this probably is the culture of the university'.

representation in these bodies follows the same or similar pattern as that in the governing bodies.

Stella (2007) refers to the creation of a 'listening strategy' by universities. Australian universities involve students in decision making through focus groups and surveys. This helps the universities to assess students' satisfaction and get their feedback to map views of students as major stakeholders. Like in some other countries, even in Australian universities, every course and course faculty is appraised by the students. 'The results are recorded, synthesized and used in a number of ways to improve the quality, content and relevance of courses and inform teaching. These could be considered as highly indirect ways to influence decision making within an institution, but they are—nonetheless valid' (Stella 2007).

Fletcher (2004) presented a wholesome analysis on meaningful student involvement in educational institutions. He cited several books to draw home his point about listening and partnering with students. Though his citations are from the context of school education, the implications are equally valid in higher education.

The survey of student satisfaction is quite common in a majority of universities in the United States, the UK and other developed countries. These surveys involving students are an effective source of quality audit. In India, the only example is of IGNOU (Parhar et al. 2010).

The case of Scotland—Student Participation in Quality Scotland (SPARQS)—is often cited as an interesting, effective mechanism of student engagement in quality management. SPARQS works with all the higher education and further education institutions in Scotland. It is an official mechanism of student engagement in quality management that is funded by the federal government.[4] Its mission is to 'assist and support students, their representative bodies and the institutions to improve the effectiveness of student engagement in quality processes' (Hensens 2007). Its aim is to have a quality engagement of students in quality management. SPARQS engages with all stakeholders—students, academic and administrative staff and the national bodies. Initially, SPARQS developed a work plan based on a large mapping project of student representation. It provides training to students, teachers and administrative staff. In addition, it collates

---

[4] http://www.sparqs.ac.uk/

information and runs the projects to develop quality across Scotland. SPARQS also develops and provides resources like information brochures, briefs, handbooks and online resources on how to involve students in quality management.

In a majority of the experiments and research carried out on students' involvement in quality assurance in higher education, the emphasis has been on academic excellence. In certain others, the focus has been on satisfaction and self-development, namely employability skills and generic graduate skills.

Student Involvement: Some Propositions

Let us continue with the holistic quality framework proposed in Chapter 1. We argue that indication of quality is the quality of life in the institution offering intellectual, emotional, physical and spiritual development of the students, teachers, non-academic staff and the institution as a whole. The basic parameter of holistic quality is the satisfaction of students, teachers, non-teaching staff and others contributing to happiness and performance in every sphere. This is important since we do not know what the real potential of a student is. We know of several qualified physicians who are equally good musicians; there are outstanding authors and novelists among civil servants, and a distinguished painter is an otherwise professor of science.

Long ago, I read an inspiring beautiful biography of such a case in the book section of *Reader's Digest* (I am unable to cite the exact reference). A senior citizen in an old-age home walked out in the afternoon to play Bridge with his friends. The receptionist informed him that his friends have gone out with their respective families and there was no partner to play Bridge with him that day. The gentleman felt miserable and completely lost about how to fight the time that stood like a mountain before him! The receptionist suggested to him to go to the hobby room and do some painting. The gentleman showed his annoyance as he thought that she was joking. He had been an engineer all his life. Undaunted, the receptionist warmly led the resident senior citizen into the hobby room, asked to try his hand and left.

Angry as he was, he started throwing colours on to a canvas that hung at a distance. Tired and exhausted, he sat down helplessly in a chair. After a while, he opened his eyes looking at the canvas that had a variety of forms created by the colours trickling down the canvas. To cut the story short, during the next 20 years, beginning at 80, he had seven solo international painting exhibitions!

From such a story, it becomes difficult to figure out whether this gentleman was originally endowed with the skills of a painter or an engineer. What certainly emerges is that he was a first-rate painter, and engineer by default or chance. His self-actualization happened through painting. This episode, and many other instances that we come across in life, argue for holistic development of students, teachers and others in the institution.

Carrying this argument further, our proposal for students' participation in quality assurance will also include all aspects of life in the college and university, namely academic management, management of the human resources, management of infrastructure, management of finance, management of student services, management of office, management of linkage and interface with external world in addition to managerial excellence and leadership. By implication, students can play roles in quality assurance in each of these departments of the institution in higher education.

Academics

Students are more grounded; their ears are closer to the ground. They also have their emotional affiliations and roots in their community. They can figure out the problems and invent solutions. Not yet bottled up within the disciplinary walls, they promise with their intuitive skills a better opportunity for multidisciplinary approach. The academic area comprises curriculum development, curriculum transaction or teaching–learning process, examination and student evaluation and co-scholastic activities. Students can make meaningful contribution in most of these areas to improve quality. In fact, students should be involved in curriculum development along with course transaction and assessment with the principles of standard referenced assessment.

One important instrument of quality management involving students is the student feedback approach. 'In some developed countries, student feedback is becoming more important in assessing quality, but there is little standardization in how it is collected or, perhaps more significantly, what is done with it' (Harvey 2002, Williams 2002). The quality assuring agency in Britain has reorganized student feedback as being central to quality improvement. As Somaiah (2007) contends, '...any educational program that believes in creating open systems, also consider students as an important sub system and stakeholders in the educational process'. This is a salient feature of some of the leading business schools across the country. Through such participation, students bring in their viewpoints, opinions, suggestions and comments, especially in the learning processes. These activities bring in enormous learning, which is outside the competencies acquired in the formal classroom.

Let us take the case of Mr Saigal's experiment in involving students in quality learning. Saigal used to teach metrology and instrumentation in a polytechnic institute in Madhya Pradesh in India. He would devote the first two or three periods at the beginning of the term for discussing the entire syllabus with the students, and then plan the transaction of the curriculum with them. This made the students familiar with the nuances of the entire curriculum right at the beginning. This also worked as an advance organizer for the students and thus made learning more meaningful.

Instead of the teacher deciding alone, the entire class collectively decides the weightages to be given to each topic/theme while covering the syllabus. After a detailed analysis of the curriculum, students were divided into teams of four each. Each team picked up one chapter/theme. Each team was responsible for covering one chapter. They prepared a plan of transaction of the chapter, teaching aids and evaluation questions. Except for the three most difficult chapters, all the other chapters were covered by student teams. Saigal himself taught these three chapters. Saigal used to prepare the student teams and then be present in the class to mentor himself. He practised it for several years, and in all those years, his students topped the state board. He took up this subject as a challenge when a majority of the students had failed in the subject. He turned it around by involving students themselves.[5]

---

[5] I had documented this case many years ago when I was in TTTI, Bhopal; Saigal taught at Shri Vaishnav Polytechnic in Indore.

Both these practices can be extended by involving students as teaching assistants. A group of students can help the teacher to prepare material for the concerned topics and actually deal with a certain portion of the contents. Teaching, as all of us might have experienced during our career, is a wonderful way of learning. Ancient Indian scriptures also prescribe teaching to learn.

Another important method of involving students is creating a mechanism of peer consultation and mentoring. When we first drafted our doctoral dissertation under the guidance of Professor M.B. Buch (the legendry teacher–researcher and head of CASE, M.S. University of Baroda), he would invariably ask us to get it reviewed by a few scholars—one from the same field, one who is good at research methods, and another one who is good in language and communication. We all mutually reviewed each other's dissertation. Then, Dr Buch would critically go through the dissertation. He gave his feedback not only to the doctoral student but also to all of us who happened to review the document. What an awesome learning experience it was!

In many universities, especially students in postgraduate classes form groups to study and prepare together. Such informal mechanisms can be formalized by creating appropriate platforms for students to participate in the teaching–learning processes in the colleges and universities.

Higher education institutions in many countries collect students' feedback to evaluate the teachers. This is still not a practice in a majority of the higher education institutions. In the early years of my university teaching days, I developed a tool for the assessment of my own classroom performance by the students. The objective was to get feedback for improvement. It was my private, rather individual initiative. Neither it was a practice in the department, nor did I share my personal evaluation with my colleagues or with Dr Buch, then head of the department. I found this to be extremely useful to fine-tune my content, communication and classroom management.

IIMs also gather student feedback about teachers at the end of the term (Somaiah 2007). She also mentioned that teacher feedback is sought after the results are out so that students have no fear, howsoever unfounded, of attracting teachers' displeasure and getting affected.

Many years ago (1981–1983), we worked on a project on student evaluation of polytechnic teachers in several states. The experiment was resisted by a section of the teachers. Interestingly, the teachers who had the reputation to be good and always prepared well for the class welcomed and actively participated in the project seeking feedback.

These days, students are much smarter, especially with technology, computer, mobile phone and the like. Students can be involved in content generation and generation of Apps on the contents of their courses. Such Apps can be out on the OER domain for larger dissemination.

Similarly, subject teachers can create a blog on their subject and post their lessons or views on the blog, including questions. Students can be encouraged to post their comments on the blog, thereby creating a discussion forum or a collective learning platform. A majority of the Indian higher education institutions cannot afford to buy either digital content or software. Students can be encouraged to create content, software and educational Apps. Even if students are rewarded with a token amount of money, these will be cheaper while encouraging students' creativity.

Resource utilization is a major issue in the Indian education system. Instruments may be available, but teachers are unfamiliar; very often, expertise to utilize these resources may also be missing. Also, teachers do not have the time to explore. Students can explore more easily and can contribute to better utilization of resources for their own benefit. Indeed, students can fill the gap in terms of manpower and knowledge generation, subject to the fact that institutions create provision for that.

One unwritten, but regularly followed practice in CASE referred to earlier was that selected doctoral students were asked to teach the postgraduate classes, when a qualified subject specialist teacher was not available in the department. Only a few of us got the opportunity, and we all appreciated the contribution it made to our own professional development.

Another aspect is the co-scholastics domain, especially important for developing generic graduate skills or employability skills. Students' own involvement in organizing and participating in co-scholastic and co-curricular activities can give them significant development opportunity.

One of the common features of colleges and universities is the student unions. Unions are elected bodies of the students.[6] Student

---

[6] Few universities have banned student union election and student politics in the campus. The wisdom is questionable. Do universities ban examinations because of mass copying? Malice has to be handled and eliminated. A positive example is arresting, though not eliminating ragging.

unions work like a cabinet. Besides president, secretary and treasurer, there are secretaries for various areas, like culture, sports and games and so on. In many institutions, each of these departments of student unions has a 'professor in-charge' who guides in planning and managing these activities. Fitting these activities into a quality management framework, teachers can act as mentors, while students organize, manage and evaluate various activities round the year. In the process, students develop planning and management besides leadership skills. Other students demonstrate their talent in various forms of sports and games or cultural activities. All these enrich the campus life.

Infrastructure

There are many dimensions of college/university infrastructure, like classrooms, library, laboratories, equipments, ICT facilities, corridors, conveniences, staffrooms, office, play fields, gyms, common rooms, music and cultural activity rooms and facilities, student union office, hostels, electricity and water supply and so on. Against each one of these components of infrastructure, there can be construction, repair and maintenance. And the third dimension is the adequacy, functionality, comfort and aesthetics. Can students contribute in any manner? For example, can they contribute to construction or mobilizing funds for construction? Can they support repair and maintenance? Can they inspect and evaluate infrastructure against the four quality criteria? Or, can they contribute to quality, say, enhancing comfort and aesthetics?

The first issue is the adequacy of facilities; adequacy of per student space in the classrooms, laboratories, gym and so on. From the viewpoint of adequacy are the issues of furniture and other facilities. Students may not be able to contribute directly to the issue of adequacy. However, they can contribute by carrying out, from time to time, surveys to figure out the differing needs of the institution in terms of infrastructure for the projected growth of enrolment of students and recruitment of staff. They can also work towards helping college and university authorities. Further, this will activate students' awareness about planning for the future, which will come handy in their working life.

The second important issue is functionality. There are several dimensions like light, ventilation, comfort level of the furniture in classrooms, laboratories, libraries, staffrooms and so on. More often than not, these get ignored and do not cope with the changing trends of the time. For example, classrooms are often dark and dingy, floors are broken, and there are very few electric lights and fans. Desks and seats are poorly designed and uncomfortable. Staffrooms are often crowded, looking more like a waiting room in an Indian railway station where teachers wait for the next train (class). In many cases, teachers are not provided with the minimum facilities and comforts to be able to read or write or participate in a serious academic discourse. Even if the classrooms are functional, corridors, toilets, sports and games facilities are often neglected.

Another chronic problem is the maintenance of infrastructure. People in-charge of maintenance, for example, caretakers, are often not properly trained. They do not have the right perception of quality benchmarks. Students can be involved (mobilized) to take charge of optimizing the functionality of the available infrastructure. They can divide themselves into small groups—each group with a defined responsibility for maintenance and management of quality of a particular space in the college.

Students can also make direct contribution through love of labour as mentioned in Chapter 5 the case of a DIET in Punjab. Let us take a look at another case of Centre of Advanced Study in Education (Box 12.1).

Box 12.1:
Student Participation in CASE

The department of education in the M.S. University of Baroda was upgraded to CASE by the UGC in 1969. The university hired the services of Professor M.B. Buch from the NCERT, who was known for his dynamism. The centre had hardly any human or material resources other than the usual staff of the department. The only difference was a few fellowships. The head of the CASE ensured that these fellowships attract the best of the student from all over the country.

Within a few years, CASE brought in 20 bright young men and women from various universities in the country into the doctoral studies programme. CASE had a circulating library of 10,000 books and financial provision for a few journals. The head of the department had no secretarial support. There was no computer; except for a huge calculator and a cyclostyling machine, there was no other infrastructure.

The centre introduced weekly seminars, guest lectures and attachment of young scholars with the guest speakers during their stay in Baroda. Without any direct intervention with the staff of the department, Dr Buch was able to generate serious academic interaction between young scholars and visiting scholars.

Young scholars were encouraged to cut stencils; they also ran the cyclostyling machine. There were repeated incidents when Dr Buch would call the scholars at the daybreak and say, 'Let's go to the library and clean it up'. Since there was no helping hand, the library used to get untidy over a period of time. A few students and the head of the institution would pick up books from the racks and clean them up with their own handkerchief.

Similarly, the scholars contributed journals in their respective professional fields subscribed through their own contingency funds. Thus, the range and the number of journals found in the library never matched the financial budget available for the purpose.

There are several other instances where the participation of the doctoral students made up for infrastructural deficiencies while simultaneously raising the level of intellectual debate and quality of doctoral education.

Source: Author.

Aesthetics of infrastructure is another dimension to be taken into consideration. There is a wide divergence in sense of aesthetics. There are many Indian higher education institutions where the walls of the corridors and classrooms are covered with posters, often political in nature. There are other institutions where the same places are beautified with paintings, sculptures and murals. Such creative displays accommodate pieces created by students as well. Instead of just being a drab collection of books and journals, libraries can also be lighted up with decorative pieces. A beautiful example is the NIEPA (now NUEPA) library.

It is now public knowledge as to how IIT alumni mobilize substantial funds and compliment on IIT infrastructure. Delhi IIT-ians have constructed an entire modern hostel in the campus. It is mutual. IIT-ians are proud of their alma mater and IIT ancestry, and IITs are also proud of their alumni. They keep in close touch with each other. Further, there are innumerable cases where earlier graduates of IITs and various other universities have helped in finding suitable placement opportunities for their juniors. Every Indian university and most colleges have some outstanding alumnus. Current students can create a database that could form a bridge between the alumnus and the college together with the current batch of students.

Higher education institutes cannot purchase much of the licensed software. Students can write those basic packages. Even if the institute pays them, those packages will become assets in the future. Similarly, most of the teaching materials are boring and soporific. Students should not only give feedback about a course, but should also actively participate in designing interesting courses.

Many institutes do not have proper lab set-ups. Students can contribute to creating virtual labs. Many resources are now available for free online (OER). Students are better explorers of the Internet sources than their teachers; also, they have more time at their disposal. Students should be encouraged to explore, sieve, archive and disseminate if they find something interesting to their counterparts and also with their teachers.

Human Resource Management

Another domain of quality management is human resource development and management. Students vary widely in their co-scholastic skills and life skills.

One of the most important life skills is the ICT skills. ICT skills do not imply only computational skills or the skill of using computers. It also includes use of mobile devices and technology management. During many of our formal studies, we came across students with highly developed ICT skills. Let me share one instance.

We were working on a project on ICT-enabled teacher training in Bihar. We were trying to ascertain the penetration of mobile phones among the school graduates and their skills in using the phones. Almost all senior state-level administrators were very sure that neither there was enough penetration, nor there was competence among the users of mobile phones.

When we visited a rural DIET in Nalanda District, we met 42 DIET students working with spades in the field. We got them to the classroom for an interaction. During our discussion, we asked how many of them had a mobile phone. We asked them to show their phones. Everyone (100 per cent) had one and some of them had better phones than many of us in the committee! Many of them had either laptop or access to computers at home. Also, they were well-conversant with the techniques of software and content downloading.

Most importantly, all of us learnt to use mobile phone through peer consultation and self-exploration, not through a 'short course on mobile telephony'. Similarly, colleges and universities can use this experience of skill development and enthusiasm of students in quality management of higher education institutions.

The adult generation is neither familiar with technology, nor does it put much effort to develop these skills. For quality management, it is necessary to identify and map these skills of students. For example, ICT-skilled students can be involved in ICT skill literacy programmes for office staff and other junior employees.

The vice chancellor of one of the universities got all their lowest cadre employees, such as gardeners, sweepers and security staff, to go through a one-week crash computer course. All of them learnt to create emails, send messages and photographs, type and print their own names and addresses and so on. The course was not only fun, but also a great motivation booster for the staff, who are always left out of developments in technology. Students can be effectively used for such orientation programmes. They can also be used to help academic faculty in generating content through video or audio, open a blog and maintain it.

Student Services

'Client satisfaction' is the key criterion in quality management. Total quality management has been described as satisfaction and beyond.

UK Open University conducts student satisfaction survey on regular intervals. High student satisfaction survey matches with its ranking among the top universities in the UK. Student satisfaction is seriously influenced by the quality of students' services.

A few important domains of student services are admission, monthly payment of fees, participation in classroom processes, examination and student assessment, various co-scholastics and co-curricular activities and student self-governance, namely student union formation. Admission into a college is a very important event in a student's life. How competent, how smooth and how warmly a student is admitted make the first impression of a college or a university. On the other end is the departure of the student from the college or the university after completing the course and appearing for the examination. Both these entry and exit moments can be made memorable or otherwise.

Students' involvement can be a great opportunity to make it memorable. Old brutal ragging that has cost several precious lives and has made many more to leave the institutions are justified as student interaction by the sadists. There can be better ways of connecting and interacting.

I can never forget our 'interaction' with our seniors when we joined the postgraduate class in Calcutta University. The seniors gave us a cultural evening. The challenge (read as ragging) was that we had to return every item of their music, mime acting, drama or skit, dancing or recitation, item by item. The major difference was that while they were prepared, we had to do impromptu. Our teachers were there to judge.

To our surprise, the teachers and our seniors encouraged us (the juniors) all the time, even when we did not actually match their talents. At the end of the cultural evening, the seniors hosted a simple dinner at their own cost for the faculty, seniors and juniors and for the subordinate staff. Similarly, we, the juniors, gave our seniors a farewell party when they finished their final examination. This kind of student involvement in managing student affairs leaves a great sense of satisfaction.

The second aspect is the leadership in organizing these activities, especially through student unions. As mentioned earlier, in many institutions, every department of the student union is mentored by a faculty in-charge. This brings closeness among the faculty and students. As Stella (2007) contends, student participation in university governance is seriously influenced by the culture of deeper engagement between students and academic staff as in the Australian universities.

Our final point of discussion about student involvement in managing student services is the community outreach and leadership. Unlike schools, institutions of higher education are often disconnected from the parent community and the neighbourhood. Students come from the community. The same students can be used for community services either in disaster management or even celebrating community festivals.

Engaging with the Alumni

Alumni are a powerful group that can contribute in a variety of ways for the growth and development of a higher education institution. Most often, colleges and university departments do not maintain any contact with alumni. Konana (2015) identified the following areas of engagement with alumni:

- Fund raising through individual contribution and corporate contribution.
- Quality improvement in education through academic collaboration with the alumni as individual as well as with her/his organization.
- Start-up innovative programmes, especially for new courses that have serious financial implication.
- Student placement in companies/organizations where alumni is in a senior position.
- Life skill development, like training in interviewing skills.

Network and Interface Management

With developments in technology and mass communication, the world is increasingly getting integrated. This social integration can be incidental or deliberately designed for quality improvement in higher education.

Networking and use of social media have emerged as the most powerful means of getting and staying connected, in addition to benefitting from 'knowledge management' through networking. Imagine free MOOCs from the best of the universities in the world!

There are several agencies that share information on a variety of vital areas. For example, a group of entrepreneurs, Buddy4Study, relentlessly inform prospective students about various types of scholarships through SMS. The Educational Technology and Management Academy (ETMA) created a Facebook page for ETMA where every small or big events are posted for feedback. Thousands of people from all over the world visit this page and now know more about ETMA and its innovative activities that were unknown to them until recently.

Students can be the captains of college or university social networks. They can create and maintain Facebook page for the college and post updated information. They can also use Twitter for this purpose. Similarly, creating an alumni web page and posting the movements and progresses of the alumni keep them connected to the institution.

Students can also create blogs on various subjects and help their teachers to maintain these blogs. Just like teachers can post their lectures or viewpoints on the blog, students can also post their comments either anonymously or with names, generating a healthy academic discourse on selected themes from subjects or beyond.

Conclusion

Students are the biggest stakeholders in higher education. They are not only 'customers' or 'clients', but also and more essentially, a partner in the enterprise called higher education. Further, they are mature, talented and capable of making contribution for their own interest. They need to be involved in quality management. Instead of the ritual of restricting them to student unions, there should be provision for students to participate in various decision-making bodies of colleges and universities like senate and syndicate, college governing body and so on. Students' involvement in modernizing and shaping academic processes is of paramount importance. NAAC's initiative in student involvement in quality management is a welcome initiative. This needs to percolate down to every college and university in the country.

13

Leadership for Quality Management

Introduction

Quality is a team exploration. Explorers have pathfinders, torchbearers, navigators and other members in the team. It is a difficult journey, often in the unknown terrains. Hence, pathfinders, torchbearers and navigators inspire people to take the journey. The team entertains to make the journey joyful to sustain the enthusiasm of all members of the team. They ignite, start and accelerate the journey vehicle. Leadership is all about 'Gung Ho'[1]-ing the quality journey involving all in the institution. Leadership is all about creating space for everyone to contribute, creating opportunity for everyone to display their talents and commitment to the quality journey.

The stories of rise, fall and again rise of educational institutions are stories of successful or unsuccessful Gung Ho-ing. Every institution has a story of growth, status quo and decay in its history. This shift in the inner life and status of an institution is because of a variety of factors that operate simultaneously to effect the change—either positive, negative or neutral. The common thread that binds all such factors together is leadership—people who occupy leadership positions like vice chancellors and principals, pro-vice chancellors and vice principals, HODs and other office bearers.

---

[1] *Gung-Ho* is the title of a brilliant book by Ken Blanchard and Sheldon Bowles (1997).

The quality of leadership in a higher education institution is the determinant of quality management, as borne out by research on educational leadership. Personality and management styles of the people in leadership positions are the single most determining factor for the organizational growth and decay. Organizational culture, ethos and innovativeness of an educational institution change significantly with the change of guard, while all other components—human resources, physical infrastructure, finance and so on—remain either same or similar. Thus, leadership is the central issue in quality management in higher education institutions.

We have divided this chapter into two sections. We will deal with theoretical issues of leadership in section I and practical aspects of leadership for quality management in section II.

Section I
Educational Leadership: Theoretical Considerations

Incumbents in the Leadership Positions

Educational institutions are complex organizations. There are tensions among the forces that stimulate each other as well as that cross each other's path. Because of the complexity and tensions, the era of a leader is over; it is time for leadership—collective leadership. It is a team game of people in leadership positions.

The people in leadership position in educational institutions are simultaneously administrators, managers and leaders. However, each person has certain dominant trends:

- Administrators (dominant trait) are responsible for facilitating institutional activities within a stipulated structure guided by rules, regulations and protocols. It has the disciplining effect, though it may resist change since rules were made in the past; and innovation being a creative activity cannot be bound by rule.
- Managers (dominant trait) operate in a relatively larger workspace dealing with 'here and now' situations; they manage day-to-day activities and ensure smooth and effective management of institutional activities. They refer to the past, but stay in the present.

- Visualizers (dominant trait) are merchants of dreams and visions. They stay in future and take the institution to that future. They innovate; they change; they break new grounds for the future. They lead to translate vision. Leaders are visualizers, but all visualizers are not leaders.

My preferred visual for the combination of administrator, manager and leader is different (Figure 13.1).

Figure 13.1:
Administrator–Manager–Leader in Inclusive Format

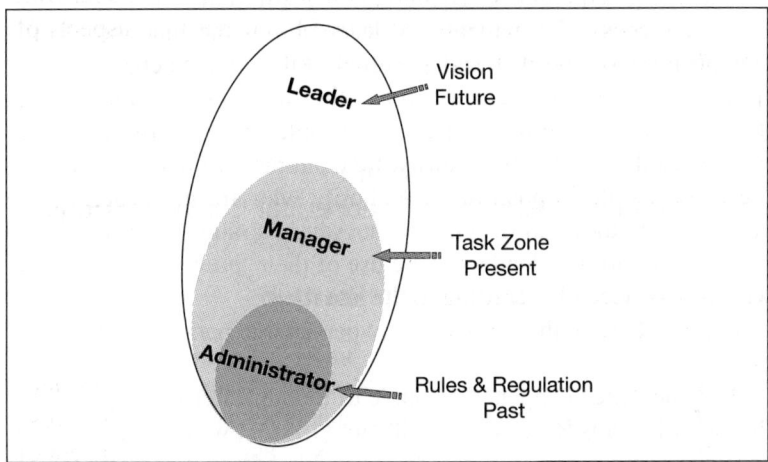

Source: Author.

By this presentation, the implications are as follows:

- Administrators are exclusive—almost abhor manager and leader qualities. Guided by rules and regulations, they (mind) live in the past and run the institution from past perspectives and experiences.
- Managers include administrators—they derive framework from past (rules and regulations) but run the institution from the present perspectives and experiences.
- Leaders include both administration and management—they derive from past, conscious about present but inspired by the future. They lead to the future but not disconnected from either past or present.

Administrators, managers and leaders complement each other and create synergy. The problem arises when people in leadership position behave as administrators or managers. Their decisions are guided by the most conservative interpretation of financial rules (FRs) and general rules (GRs). A large majority of people in leadership position manage tasks and people in the institution. They are the 'managers'. The third, and relatively small, group of heads nurtures a vision and a dream. Many colleges like Ramakrishna Mission College of Belur was transformed into a deemed university with the vision and leadership of Swami Atmapriyananda (Mukhopadhyay 2012a). The result of leadership is qualitative change in the institution.

Effectiveness of organizational leadership is the function of official position (authority) and personal skills of influencing others (power). A leader in a leadership position wields power and authority, but often uses power. There are people in the institutions who influence others without authority, for example, teacher leaders; also, there are people in position of authority who are not heard by the colleagues without an official order. Administrators tend to depend more on 'authority'; leaders make use of their 'power'; mangers use whatever is needed according to the situation.

Let me share with you one of my personal experiences of display of 'power'.

This incidence happened a couple of months after I joined NIEPA. Professor Moonis Raza was the director (1984). I was sitting with him and discussing a research project when his personal secretary came and informed him that a few employees wanted to see him. He asked her to send them in. They were about six, all from administration. One of them presented a paper and said, 'Sir, we want to present our memorandum of demands'. Since there were not enough chairs, Professor Raza was already standing, I too followed him. Professor Raza kept the paper aside and told them, 'I'm here, you are here. What is the need of such a memorandum? Come on, tell me what your demands are?'

One of them took the lead and mentioned the first demand. Professor Raza said, 'That's genuine. Let me call the registrar'. Professor Raza sent a message for the registrar. Within a few minutes, the registrar came up. Professor Raza repeated the demand of the staff and told the registrar that it was a genuine demand and should be implemented. 'Okay. What is your second demand?' The leader of the delegation read out the demand from his copy. He looked at the registrar and told, 'This should also be implemented'. Professor Raza looked back to the delegation. The delegation leader mentioned the third one. Professor Raza looked at him and said, 'This demand is in your interest but not in the interest of NIEPA. Hence, this will not be implemented'. The dialogue went on to cover all the five demands; three were accepted and two were not accepted. In the presence of the employees, Professor Raza instructed the registrar to implement the three immediately. The delegation left with a big smile, sincerely thanking Professor Raza.

The test of power occurs when the head of the institution is out of office (read as authority). Leaders live by the legacy they leave.

It may appear, then, that leadership is fait accompli—an institution either has a leader or it does not. Management of quality in colleges and universities, then, can only be incidental depending upon the nature of the head of the institution. Further, certain leadership positions are on contract for a limited time period, for example, term appointment of vice chancellors. Our search for management of quality cannot end with the chance meeting of a few who are endowed with qualities of a 'leader'. We must find ways to develop collective leadership for quality management.

Understanding the College or University Organization

There is more than one way of describing a higher education institution. It can be described in terms of its functions, roles or as a system comprising inputs, processes and output. The most useful way of looking at higher education institutions for quality management is through its various functional areas of management. Based on our earlier research on task analysis and training needs assessment of heads of institutions, we identified eight areas. These are:

1. Academic management
2. Human resource management
3. Infrastructure management
4. Finance management
5. Student services management
6. Interface and network management

7. Office management

8. Managerial excellence and leadership

Since quality is the agenda and ICT is the common denominator for all quality initiatives, these are not separately listed. As described in Chapter 4, each area can obviously be unbundled into smaller components. For example, academic management includes curriculum, instructional processes, examination and so on. Each one of these areas can be further unbundled into smaller and concrete areas of management through organizational micro-analysis (Mukhopadhyay 2005a). I have used this approach of organizational micro-analysis to develop a management of change model for higher education institutions (Figure 13.2).

Figure 13.2:
Model of Management of Change in Education

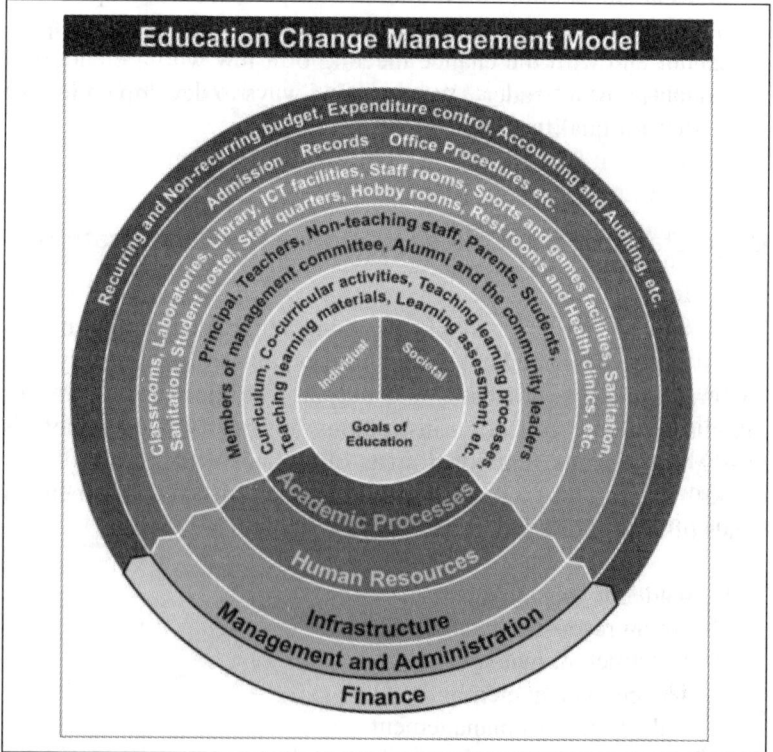

Source: Author.

The nucleus is the vision, mission, objectives, goals and targets of an institution because it guides all other actions. Just as there has to be goals for individual excellence, higher education institutions must have social goals irrespective of their source of funding.

This model lays down the following orbits:

- The first orbit is the academic processes comprising curriculum, teaching–learning process, instructional/reading material and examination.
- The second orbit is human resources—management, teaching and non-teaching staff, and students. Because educational institutions are human-intensive systems, human beings are either gateways or gatekeepers of innovation. No wonder, all quality scientists like Deming, Juran, Crosby and Ishikawa flagged staff development as one of the common cardinal principles of TQM.
- In the third orbit is the infrastructure—classrooms, staffrooms, laboratories, libraries, ICT facilities, sports and games facilities, student hostels and staff quarters and so on, where major management issues are adequacy, functionality, aesthetics and removal of obsolescence.
- The fourth orbit is about management and administration—especially personnel administration, and office management, management of admission, examination and so on.
- The fifth orbit deals with finance, which is necessary not only for maintaining the day-to-day activities but also for innovations and management of change.

Though normally, finance is put as the most important item for quality; this model focuses on academic functions that are central to educational institutions, and infrastructures and finance are enablers.

Another important way of looking at higher education institutions is on the basis of their stages of development (Klepper 1997), namely

- Formative
- Rapid growth
- Mature and stable
- Decline

Quality management at each stage of the institution's life demands different sets of skills to be effective. Some are more successful during the formative stages, whereas some others lead very well during the mature and stable state. The stage of decline and resurrection warrants yet another set of skills. For management of quality, it is necessary to understand the stage of development of the institution.

Leadership Styles

Leadership for quality management and institution building has been debated throughout ages. Let us briefly review a few leadership theories that have dominated the discourse in the modern times. I prefer to bookmark Kurt Lewin's theory of 1939 in this context.

Leadership Theories

The first set of theories was classified as 'great man theory', assuming leadership to be an inherent trait available only to a few and rare individuals. These theories portray leaders as heroic, if not mythic, who would definitely rise to the occasion and show the way to people. Also, it probably believed that only 'men' (please note the gender bias) can lead.

Next-generation theory was trait theory. The 'great man' leader has been portrayed in terms of certain personal traits like intelligence, integrity, drive, dominions, self-confidence, determination, proactive, trustworthy and so on. However, researchers found that all people with such qualities do not make leaders, although leaders may possess these traits. Hence, the trait theory of the 1960s was questioned.

Contingency theory is the third-generation theory. Its primary contention was that there is no single leadership style that is either good or bad. It depends upon the situation. The configuration of the situation is created by the personal style of the leader, qualities of the followers and the complexity of the situation. This became the basis of a number of theories built around people and tasks in organizations. Situational leadership theory is by far the most accepted theory in this school of thought. A major contention here is that effectiveness of a leader depends upon the choice of the style based upon the situational variables. In other words, different styles of leadership may be appropriate for certain situations of decision making.

The fourth-generation theory is the behaviourist theory that argues that leaders need not be born; they can be developed through appropriate training and education. Further developments in the leadership theory have been classified into relationship theory, participative theory, management theory, inspirational theory and so on. I will refer to Kurt Lewin's leadership theory, Blake and Mouton's leadership grid, Hershey and Blanchard's situational leadership theory, because these theories have some direct relevance to quality management.

Kurt Lewin's Theory

The most popular classification of leadership styles as authoritarian (autocratic), democratic and laissez-faire is the contribution of Kurt Lewin in 1939 when he was leading a group of psychologists working on leadership styles. Authoritarian or autocratic leaders clearly instruct the subordinates what to do, when to do, how to do and at what cost. It is essentially hierarchic where the status difference between the leader and the followers is carefully configured and maintained. The democratic leaders are also called participative leaders who provide not only guidance to the followers but also participate with them in defining, designing and accomplishing tasks. Participative–democratic leaders encourage members of the group to contribute their ideas, but often retain the right to decision making to themselves. Laissez-faire style has two interpretations. Linguistic meaning of laissez-faire is 'the policy of leaving things to take their own course, without interfering'[2] or 'a philosophy or practice characterized by a usually deliberate abstention from direction or interference especially with individual freedom of choice and action'.[3] The opposite of authoritarian style, here leadership, is least visible. The second interpretation is that laissez-faire leadership is delegative. In this style, the designated leader delegates rights and responsibilities of decision making to the members of the organization.

The hidden message in Kurt Lewin's thesis is the approach of the head of the organization to organizational tasks and people, rather approach to task accomplishment through people. Leadership, then, is the effectiveness with which these two variables are manipulated

---

[2] http://www.oxforddictionaries.com/
[3] http://www.merriam-webster.com/dictionary/

for organizational goals and visions. The variable task has multiple dimensions like complexity, relative importance, concern for task and so on. 'People' often meant 'relationships and concerns for people'. Later theorists largely moved around these two variables. Ohio studies led to identification of initiating structures and consideration for the study of leader effectiveness.[4] Initiating structure is primarily around task concerns and consideration around people or relationships. The Michigan State University research identified production emphasis and employee orientation—task and people concern expressed differently. Fiedler's contingency model recommends matching between leadership style and demand of the situation; according to path–goal theory (House and Dressler 1974), substantive tasks of a leader are managing tasks and people. Robert R. Blake and Jane Mouton (1964) proposed a managerial grid out of concern for production (task) and concern for relationships. By plotting both the concerns on a nine-point continuum, they created a grid (Figure 13.3).

Figure 13.3:
Blake and Mouton Managerial Grid

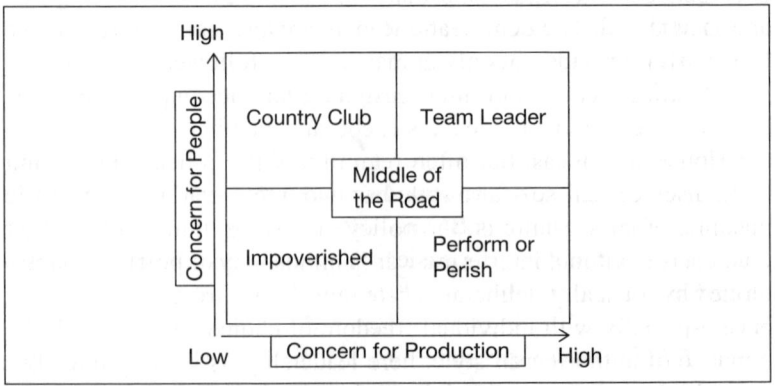

Source: Blake and Mouton (1964). The Leadership Grid® figure from Leadership Dilemmas—Grid Solutions by Robert R. Blake and Anne Adams McCanse (formerly the Managerial Grid by Robert R. Blake and Jane S. Mouton). Houston: Gulf Publishing Company, Copyright 1991 by Grid International, Inc. Available at https://www.mindtools.com/pages/article/newLDR_73.htm.

---

[4] https://www.boundless.com/management/textbooks/boundless-management-textbook/leadership-9/behavioral-approach-70/leadership-model-the-ohio-state-university-350-3483/ (accessed on 2 May 2014).

They identified the styles with five labels.

1. Produce or perish leadership (9,1): This is the authoritarian style. It also considers punishment as the most important tool for managing employee motivation. This coincides with McGregor's theory X assumptions about employees.
2. Team leadership (9,9): For Blake and Mouton, team leadership is the best. It has simultaneous emphasis on production as well as relationships. The assumption is that employees understand the organizational needs and involve themselves. Thereby, they satisfy themselves while satisfying the production need of the organization. This resembles the participative style.
3. Country club leadership (1,9): This is 'people happy' leadership style where the agenda is to keep people happy with the assumption that happy people will be more productive. Research evidence, however, does not support this contention.
4. Impoverished leadership (1,1): This represents the laissez-faire style of leadership. This does not generate a motivating ambiance for people to be productive.
5. Middle-of-the-road leadership: This style seems to buy peace while running an organization. The leaders compromise on both the competing concerns, namely people and task.

Hersey and Blanchard picked up from where Blake and Mouton left. They picked up the matrix of concern for task and concern for people. They dichotomized the two concerns, probably to make the classification of styles easier. They classified the four styles as follows:

1. *Telling style* (high concern for task and low concern for people) resembles Kurt Lewin's authoritarian and Blake and Mouton's produce and perish style.
2. *Selling* (high concern for task and high concern for relationship) matches Lewin's democratic and Blake Mouton's team leadership.
3. *Participating* (high concern for relationship but low concern for task): This is another style of Lewin's participative style and Blake and Mouton's country club style where leaders' agenda is to keep people happy even if it costs task accomplishment.

4. *Delegating* (low concern for relationship and low concern for task): In a way, this resembles Lewin's laissez-faire and Blake and Mouton's impoverished leadership. However, this has a different meaning for quality management.

Hersey and Blanchard called their theory situational leadership theory, close to contingency theory. Unlike Blake and Mouton, they did not indicate their preference for the style. They argued in favour of style effectiveness—what suits the demand of the situation. To assess leader effectiveness, Hersey and Blanchard created a situational test (Leadership Effectiveness and Adaptability Description—LEAD—questionnaire) comprising 12 situations—three situations each ideally suited for the four styles. They recommended analysis of leadership style and effectiveness in terms of style preference, style flex and style effectiveness. Style preference is indicated by the frequency[5] at which a leader opts for one of the four styles; style flex by the flexibility with which one can change and adopt styles as required by a situation; and style effectiveness as indicated by the right choice of a style according to the situation.

During many of the workshops with college principals, we found the LEAD questionnaire useful for data feedback. Principals discovered their style. There were certain basic trends. A huge majority (more than 92 per cent) prefer relationship (or concern for relationship) as the anchoring point of leadership. In other words, a large majority of them choose either selling or participating style. Very few principals choose telling style irrespective of the maturity of their colleagues/followers. Most significantly, almost none (less than 2 per cent) chose delegation as a style; those who choose, do not choose correctly.

People in leadership positions view organizational tasks differently. They visualize tasks from their own world view (personal style). They also approach human resources differently. Leader effectiveness is all about judgment of situations and making effective use of human resources for task designing (for vision accomplishment) and implementing. But, we must remember that every person

---

[5] Hersey and Blanchard (1992) developed a situational leadership questionnaire, called LEAD questionnaire. The questionnaire comprises 12 situations; three each are most suitable for each of the four styles.

in leadership position has a personal style and sees situations through the world view developed with the genesis of his/her personality. What is important for every head of the institution is to identify his/her native style and then make efforts to change suitably for improving effectiveness.

Section II
Leadership Practices for Quality Management

Managing quality is managing change. It is changing a complex tapestry of self and others, institution and tasks (Figure 13.4).

Figure 13.4:
Concept Map on Leadership for Quality Management

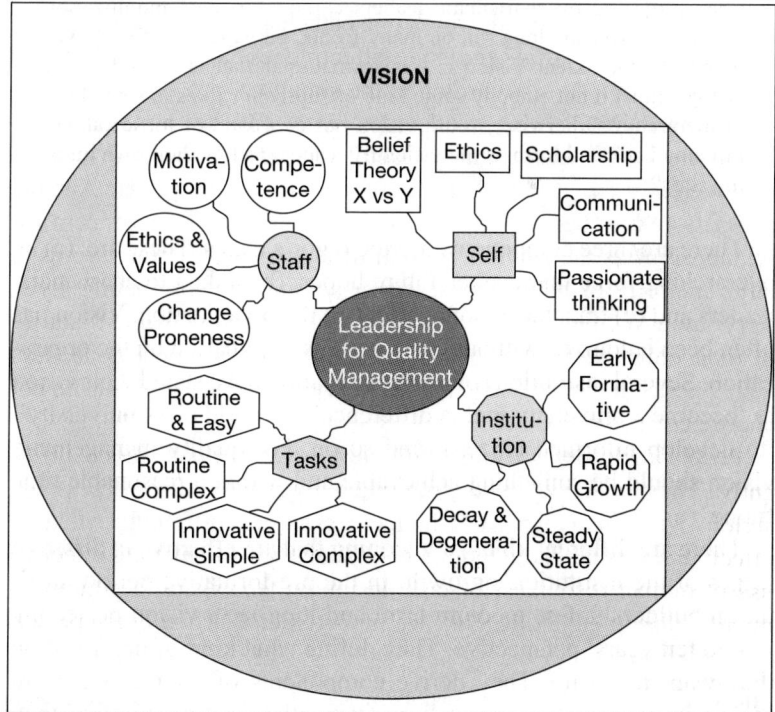

Source: Author.

The concept map (Figure 13.4) depicts self, staff, institution and tasks as the four dimensions of leadership. For quality management, these four elements are guided by vision.

Vision: Role of Visioning

Almost invariably, vision is associated with leaders. James MacGregor (2004), in his foreword to the book by Joanne B. Ciulla's *Ethics: The Heart of Leadership*, wrote:

> We think of vision as an overarching, evocative, energizing, moralizing force ranging from broad almost architectural plans for a new industry, say to an inspirational, spiritual, perhaps morally righteous evocation of future hopes and expectations of a political movement. Visions are often projected by charismatic leaders calling for mass mobilization and action over the long run on many fronts, perhaps even for a revolution. To the extent Vision is transformational–that is, calls for real change–must it not embody some kind of supreme values in some kind of hierarchy? Otherwise, would vision not be a kind of loose cannon lurching back and forth as the visionary leaders follow their own guiding stars?

There are three components in McGregor's thesis. These are: (a) an overarching force that evokes future hopes, (b) linked to charismatic leaders and (c) transformational effect on the organization. Vision has often been eulogized without much serious implication on the organization. Several institutions of higher education have stated their vision to 'become a university with a difference', 'a world class university', 'to develop informed citizens' and so on. For quality management, vision should be something achievable and within a reasonable time frame.

There are different kinds of visioning that are effective in different stages of the institution's growth. In the pre-formative period, institution builders define medium-term and long-term vision projecting five to ten years' perspective. They define what kind of organization they want to create. They derive components of their vision from their own imagination, as well as from other institutions that they want to emulate. For example, while designing the Andhra Pradesh

Open University as well as IGNOU later, (late) Professor G. Ram Reddy's vision was informed and inspired by UK Open University, as he shared with me in a personal discussion. During the formative stage, a qualitatively different visioning is a distinct possibility by synthesizing visions and vision statements filtered through one's own imagination. Just as an example, after I took charge of National Open School (NOS), I analysed vision or vision-like statements in all the available previous documents to understand how the architects of this institute visualized NOS. Times had changed. Subsuming all the vision components, I visualized NOS to be an R&D organization to lead open schooling movement within and outside India. In the process, I consulted visionary leaders of that time like chairman, UGC and doyen of ODE late Professor G. Ram Reddy, member of the Planning Commission and Comenius awardee educationist late Dr Chitra Naik, vice chancellor of the Yashwantrao Chavan Maharashtra Open University (YCMOU), known as institution builder Professor Ram G. Takwale, and education secretary Sri S.V. Giri (Mukhopadhyay 2001, 2012a).

Visioning undergoes qualitative change as the institute enters into rapid growth and a mature period. Most leaders identify a few improvements or innovations that can be carried out in the given situation, conscious of the possible resistance of the system and the people. Incremental visioning is common at this level. The leader adds on incrementally to the innovative activities; followers sum it up to credit their leaders with a long-term vision. '…everything the leader may do, however casual, is taken by staff as planned and meaningful' (Latchem and Hanna 2001).

However, there are cases where institutions are taken by storm because of and for re-visioning. Ravi Mathai's institution building in IIM Ahmedabad is a brilliant case in hand (Pareek 2012).

Take the case of St. Joseph's College, Vishakhapatnam. It is an autonomous college and accredited by NAAC with B grade. We (my colleague Professor Jaya Indiresan and I) conducted a two-day workshop on appreciative inquiry involving all 70+ academic staff, including the principal. Jaya also ran a complementary workshop on quality for the administrative staff. At the end of the first day's workshop, the staff collectively posted their vision at three levels spread over 10 years. Immediate vision or goal was to secure better NAAC grade—A+. Intermediate vision was to become one of the 10 best autonomous colleges in the country. And, final posting was to become a deemed university in 10 years.

The staff devoted entire second day creating action plan—departmental, cross-departmental and interdisciplinary projects to achieve the immediate, intermediate and long-term goals. They identified as many as nine projects.

In the case of organizational decay and decline, and organizations at risk, vision is to put the organization back to normalcy. In such cases, there is neither a long-term vision nor incremental vision; vision is putting back the organization on the track.

Depending upon the stage of development and health of the organization, people in leadership position in higher education institutions must take steps to construct meaningful and achievable vision involving all.

Self

Research on the management of change clearly indicates that 'whatever happens to a college or a university, everything else remaining the same or similar, is because of the person occupying the leadership position'. Although the leadership trait theory has been discarded, head's personal styles, especially beliefs, ethics and values, scholarship and communication, and thinking and passions cannot be delinked from the process of leadership in the institution. For, these beliefs and values influence head's perceptions about the staff in the institution.

According to McGregor, we either believe 'most people are good, responsible and matured' (theory Y) or most people are not straightforward, shirking, scheming, immature, selfish and so on (theory X). If the head of an institution subscribes to theory X, his/her leadership style will be control oriented. If theory Y is believed, leadership style will be participative and delegative. Whether the head believes people can be trusted or not, whether people are responsible or not, does not depend upon people alone. It is the prism of the world view through which the leader peeps out. As they say, trust begets trust.

Case studies on leadership for institution building (Latchem and Hanna 2001, Mukhopadhyay 2012a) indicate that none of the institution builders are suspecting Toms. They subscribe to theory Y, trusting and respecting the colleagues. This is the first lesson in leadership for quality management. Leader's inability to trust and respect others gets reciprocated by the followers.

Further, leader's faith in theory X or theory Y is deeply ingrained in the early childhood development of the person. Those nurtured in the environment of trust learn to subscribe to theory Y. Those who grew up into an environment of suspicion and doubts have unknowingly developed faith in theory X. Hence, your subscription to theory X or Y is largely a phenomenon of behavioural determinism. The pangs of theory X syndrome can be overcome first by recognizing your orientation to people, second by deciding to change, and third through continuous practice:

Ethics

Research also indicates that institution builders derive power out of their personal values and ethics. Values and ethics command emotive powers for influencing. Let us take a few examples to illustrate the point.

- The institution builders focus on developing the public space in the institution like classrooms, laboratories, libraries and so on when most of the heads of institution enrich their private space—his/her office, personal staff, guest room and so on. It is quite common to find office of a principal or a vice chancellor extraordinarily spruced up when staffrooms look more like railway platforms where teachers wait for the signal for the next train (class) crying for minimum basic facilities. While a majority heads of institutions ask for 'my entitlement', institution builders define 'entitlement of the institution'.
- The second important principle is the transparency creating a salutary effect on the staff and building the image of genuineness. Institution builders act with the belief that they are

custodians of public interest, property and resources. During a discussion with late Professor P.V. Indiresan (case of IIT Madras), he mentioned that distribution of German scholarships to staff used to be decided in a meeting of the HODs with the director. Staff had no opportunity to apply or a say. Indiresan met the HODs and created a set of qualifying criteria for the scholarship award and displayed in the notice board asking for applications. The applications were invited and evaluated against the set of criteria, and six members of staff were chosen. Swami Atmapriyananda's case of Ramakrishna Mission Vidyamandira provides a good case of transparency (Mukhopadhyay 2012a).

- Institution builders keep themselves equidistant from everyone, without allowing the coterie to grow around them, though they listen to all. The emphasis is on fairness to all in the organization.
- Appointments in leadership positions in educational institutions are significantly influenced by the political and administrative acquaintances and preferences. Average heads of the institution express their gratitude to his/her benefactor at the cost of the institution. Institution builders choose organizational interests above personal benefactor's interest.
- Another issue is academic ethics. Many heads of institutions either cannot write or do not have the time to write; they try to influence junior colleagues to include their names in books and papers not authored by them. Or, call for paid papers, stitch them with a preface to claim an edited book. Institution builders encourage colleagues and younger faculty members to author and publish (refer cases on CASE and TTTI in Mukhopadhyay 2012a); they extend their personal help in improving the quality of such papers without taking away the credits. Several of my senior academic colleagues in NIEPA helped and edited several state reports on administration prepared by junior colleagues without putting their names as authors. Many of the previous titles and reports carry the burden of name(s) of seniors depriving the junior the due credit.
- Institution builders put organizational agenda ahead of their personal agenda. In case of conflict between organizational interest and self-interest, they put a premium on the organization's interest. They enjoy basking in the organizational glory.

Dynamism-Honesty Grid

People in leadership positions are also classified as dynamic and non-dynamic (decision making) and honest and dishonest (ethics). These two attributes of people in leadership position generate an interesting dynamic–honesty grid to better appreciate the impact of a person at the top. A dynamic leader is one who is full of ideas, enterprising enough to take decisions fast. An honest leader is an ethical person as described above. Both dynamism and honesty can be plotted on continuums and posited against each other in a matrix (Figure 13.5)

Figure 13.5:
Dynamism–Honesty Matrix of Leadership

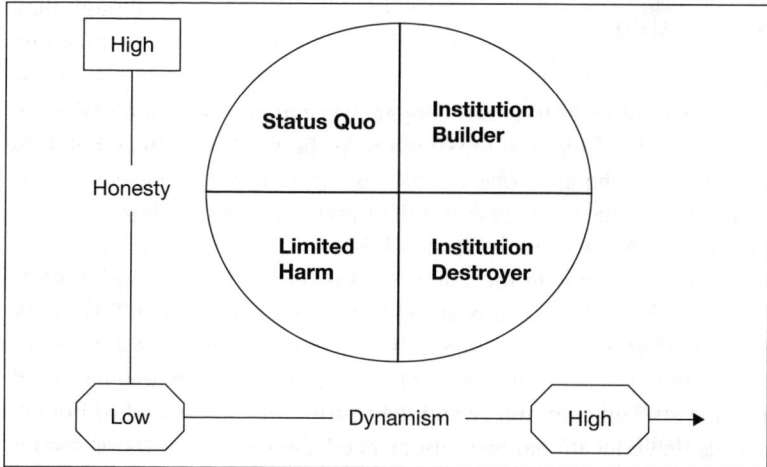

Source: Author.

1. Dynamism combined with honesty is the key to institution building. All institution builders that I have come across and documented are dynamic honest persons.
2. When dynamism is combined with dishonesty, it threatens and destroys the inner strength of an institution. Almost all cases of financial corruption are due to dynamic–dishonesty combination.
3. Non-dynamic honest leaders are not harmful, but not of much use either. They maintain the status quo with an eye on their reputation for honesty.

4. Non-dynamic–dishonest leaders can have a limited harmful effect. Because of the lack of dynamism, their dishonesty will have limited effect on the organization.

There is yet another category of people in leadership positions who are rigid in their values and principles with the combination of honesty with either dynamism or non-dynamism. They affect vested interests who gang up together against them. Such leaders hurt themselves, and indirectly their loved institutions. A number of cases of inquiry and court cases are shared by dishonest and honest leaders with rigid principles.

Scholarship

A majority of institution builders are outstanding scholars. The study on the heads of top 100 universities in the world indicates that they are reputed scholars—one of the best in their respective institution. This has also been the trend in India's prestigious technology and business management schools, such as IITs and IIMs. My case documentations also subscribe to the same conclusion. The position of heads of academic institutions is a position of academic leadership. Hence, the pursuit of academic excellence is a necessary condition for institution building. It also helps develop source credibility among the teaching and student community and the institution. One school of thought argues that educational institutions need a good administrator and not a scholar. Such arguments are often put forward by administrators who stray into education. Literature on institution building does not provide enough evidence to justify the argument. For academic leaders, reading, researching, writing and informed extension are passion. Hence, people occupying leadership position in an academic institution must lead in academic pursuits.

Communication

An associated quality of a leader is the communication skill. Case studies (Mukhopadhyay 2012a) indicate that all institution builders are good communicators. A majority of them are excellent class-room teachers. Further, for almost all institution builders, teaching is a passion. In NIEPA, all directors who came from academic profession conducted regular training sessions for the participants. Reasons for this are not far to seek. Higher education institutions are student centric. The reputation of a good teacher provides him/ her the academic source credibility that helps in organizations and management. The recent instance of Bombay University is a case in hand. When Professor Neeraj Hatekar, a distinguished professor of econometrics, was suspended, the entire student and teaching community stood behind him and the university authorities had to step back and withdraw the suspension (Deshpande 2014). As mentioned earlier, scholarship of head of the institution has been found the common denominator for successful leadership in the 100 top universities of the world, and top Indian institutions of higher education, namely IITs, IIMs, IISc, BITS and all institutions supported by the Tata Foundation.

Understanding State of Development and Health of an Organization

We have discussed the various stages of the development of an institute—formative, rapid growth, steady state and decline. State of decay and decline is comparatively more difficult because it is clouded by subjective perceptions of the head of the institution. There are innumerable instances where a new incumbent fails to find quality and strength of the institution. He/she resorts 'to put the system on track, before I can take the institution to new level'. In most cases, by the time the system is 'put on track', the term of the incumbent vice chancellor or principal ends. The new person comes and begins to put the system on track. The game goes on.

One major reason is that, exceptions apart, Indian higher education institutions do not have either a well-articulated meaningful vision or a written and duly authenticated strategic plan to translate the vision into reality. Leadership for quality management demands not only short-, medium- and long-term vision, but also a strategic plan to translate them.

Understanding Tasks and People

As mentioned earlier, all leadership theories have flagged management of tasks and people as the two important leadership functions. Hence, it is extremely important to make clear judgment about tasks and people in the organization.

Tasks in an institution can be classified as routine and non-routine. Routine tasks include making timetable, conducting classes, conducting examination, evaluating examination papers, publishing results, maintaining the building and so on. A good idea would be to classify these routine tasks into at least two categories: easy and complex. Very often, the complexity of the tasks is not adequately understood. For example, conventional teaching may be easy but quality instruction is complex. Similarly, construction of buildings is comparatively easy than their maintenance.

Key to quality is management of innovation. The innovative practice can come from individual or from the systems initiative. Whenever a teacher innovates in his or her own instructional practices, this might be simple, but of limited effect on the system. Systemic innovation has greater impact on the institution due to participation of a large number of people, and the systemic innovation may comprise a large number of interrelated innovations. However, to create a culture of innovations, individual innovations need to be patronized. Since success is a necessary condition, leaders identify innovations and create strategic plans to implement.

The second dimension is understanding people. In the chapter on human resource management, we have discussed about the various roles of the academic staff and suggested competency mapping of each staff member. This will provide a clearer understanding of the staff. In that chapter, we primarily flagged competence and commitment or motivation on a matrix. We need to add two more dimensions, and these are ethics and values among the members of the staff and their change proneness or readiness to adapt innovations. This becomes necessary for bringing in innovation in the organization.

Graduation in Leadership

Leadership style and quality are not something fixed. These can be learnt. Graduating in leadership is learning to lead institutions for quality management and developing self-renewing capability as well. Self-renewal is possible only when an organization moves away from 'around the person approach' to collective leadership and delegation. Delegation is the key to institution building (Mukhopadhyay 2012a). Delegation is not allocation of responsibility. Delegation is devolving rights to decide with responsibilities. When initiatives and innovations emerge as a bottom-up process, when innovation and self-renewal become a culture of the institution, institution building would have happened. The journey begins from administration and management. The destination is L-5 or leadership invisible. Let us see the road map in Figure 13.6.

Figure 13.6:
Graduation in Leadership

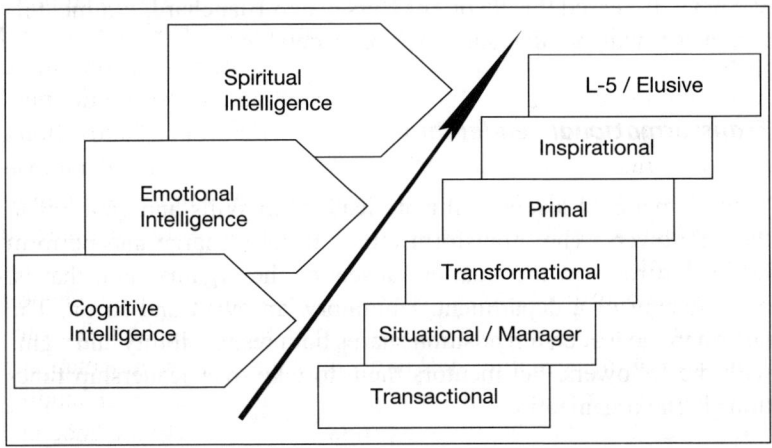

Source: Author.

Administration and management are two pre-leadership stages. Effect of leadership is change in the organization—change in human capabilities, tasks and organizational culture. Graduation in leadership is moving from transactional leadership to L-5 leadership through intermediate stages. Let us see the nature and styles of different levels of leadership.

Transactional Leaders

The concept of transactional leadership is founded on the principle that people work only for rewards. Hence, in this style there is a transaction—work transacted against material benefits. Transactional leadership expects work against compensation according to rules. Hence, there is veiled threat for non-performance as well as hope of reward for good performance. In this style, concern is almost exclusively about task and not people. To that extent, this resembles administrators.

Situational Leaders (Managers)

We have discussed this theory of Hersey and Blanchard. For me, this is management, another stage before leadership.

Transformational Leadership

Transformational leaders cultivate leadership skills and qualities in their followers. They transform others to take charge and perform leadership roles in the smaller subsets of the organization, that is, management of a department, laboratory, an event and so on. The person in the leadership position shares both responsibility and rights with the followers, but mentors them to take over leadership functions in the organization:[6]

> Transactional and transformational are the two modes of leadership that tend to be compared the most. James MacGregor Burns distinguished between transactional leaders and transformational by explaining that: transactional leaders are leaders who exchange tangible rewards for the work and loyalty of followers. Transformational leaders are leaders who

---

[6] www.mindtools.com

engage with followers, focus on higher order intrinsic needs, and raise consciousness about the significance of specific outcomes and new ways in which those outcomes might be achieved. Transactional leaders are more passive as transformational leaders demonstrate active behaviors that include providing a sense of mission.[7]

Primal Leadership

Goleman (2002) classified leadership styles into two broad categories: resonant and dissonant styles. In resonant style, the leader builds an emotional, rather empathic, relationship with the followers where they vibrate at the same wavelength, creating a symphony, though they may be engaged in different sets of activities. This style can be experienced in many of the well-led women's institutions. I experienced it in several of my workshops in women's colleges. In other words, women leaders create resonance more easily than their male counterpart.

In dissonant style, the leader and followers run into cross purposes. The leader and the competing groups set their own respective agenda often in cross purposes.

Inspirational Leadership

John Adair, Lance Secretan (1999) and others are the main contributors to the theory of inspirational leadership. The basic thesis is that when followers recognize their worth and potentiality, they would move on their own for personal and organizational self-actualization. They will lead themselves. The primary role of a leader is to create that inspiration among the followers to recognize their potential and move on their own. In one of my experiments in quality in rural primary education, I tried this model successfully (Mukhopadhyay 2013a) with 107 teachers working in 29 rural primary schools. Besides its effect on overall qualitative change in primary education, participating teachers concluded that they could achieve all that because they felt important, capable and strong enough to innovate.

---

[7] https://en.wikipedia.org/wiki/Transactional_leadership (accessed on 1 May 2014).

L-5 or Elusive Leadership

L-5 leadership was proposed by Jim Collins (2001) in his book *Good to Great*. L-5 leadership occurs when the leader becomes omnipresent without any visible presence. It is the stage where organizations learn to auto pilot themselves. This concept was also articulated by a Chinese scholar in 6th century BC—'Leader is good if his presence is felt, leader is better if his absence is perceived, and leader is best if his presence or absence does not matter'. I referred to the style of (late) Professor V.S. Vaidya of Jalgaon Polytechnic as a case in hand of this style (Mukhopadhyay 2005a).

Leader-Follower Positioning

While graduating in leadership, the position of the leader and the follower changes. At the transactional leadership level, leader is the boss and others are subordinates. The leader maintains great distance from the subordinates. In situational leadership, the gap reduces because there is a concern for people and relationships without conceding on task concerns. Yet, the leader stands taller than the followers. In transformational leadership, there is a qualitative shift in the relationship that between a mentor and mentee.

Primal leadership is about resonance at the same or complementary wavelengths. Hence, in this type of leadership, the leader and the follower come to the same level and share the same platform. They share the same height. Inspirational leadership is a complete turnaround, where instead of instructing followers, the leader asks, 'Can I help you?' Having developed the followers, the leader changes his/her position as an assisting person. Thus, in inspirational leadership, so-called followers stand taller than the designated leader. Secretan terms followers as 'Perceners'.

At the L-5 level, the leader becomes elusive where his/her presence or absence does not matter. In this model, followers become more visible than the designated leader everywhere. Ricardo Semler's *Maverick* (1993) provides an interesting case of this style.

It should be evident that as a leader moves up in the ladder of graduation, he/she reduces her visibility, relegating himself/herself to the background. Instead of leading from the front, he/she inspires from behind, allowing others to take charge.

Leadership Styles and Nature of Intelligence

Intelligence has been described in very many ways, starting with discriminating intelligence in Indian scriptures and by Alfred Binet and others. The latest descriptions are given by Gardner's multiple intelligence (1984), Goleman's (1995) emotional intelligence and spiritual intelligence by Dana Zohar and Marshall (2000). There is a guiding intelligence behind a style of leadership. At the lowest two levels, leadership decisions are taken logically that require algorithmic thinking or cognitive intelligence. As we move on to transformational leadership, along with cognitive intelligence comes emotional intelligence because of the affiliation of the leader with the follower. Primal leadership is predominantly guided by emotional intelligence.

Spiritual intelligence is still being debated—what is its nature? There are different definitions and descriptions forwarded by different scholars. From the Indian scriptural point of view, spirituality is awaking into the consciousness beyond self; recognizing self as a spec in the vast cosmic consciousness; perceiving the universe as a dream game of the omnipresent and omniscient consciousness called God. Since nature of inspirational leadership and L-5 leadership is rediscovering self by inspiring and promoting others putting self in the background, these styles of leadership are fuelled by spiritual intelligence.

Roadmap to Graduation

The first important step is to diagnose one's own leadership style and map it in the ladder, because the journey starts from there. I have seen how Dr Buch used his transformational style, and Professor Moonis

Raza or Professor Y Saran used inspirational leadership when I met them. The goal for every graduate student in leadership is the same—reaching L-5. If one is at transactional style, there are six steps to walk up; if one is at the resonant style, there are still several steps to reach the destination.

The process of leadership includes adopting measures to emotionally empower the followers to move from acting against rewards to affiliating with work, leading small activity groups, departments/units in the organization to take charge of large and complex functions in the organization. A simultaneous role of the leader is to slowly but definitely withdraw him/her to the backyard of organizational operations and position himself/herself to assist others. Something very obvious in this process of transition is reconstructing and reducing ego or 'I'-ness (that is spirituality), shifting from the limelight to behind the light. The best practical example of this leadership graduation is what an Indian mother does to her daughter.

Behavioural Determinism in Leadership Styles

Although many of the leadership theories profess strategic decisions for enhancing leadership effectiveness, style preference seems to be a semi-permanent, if not permanent, behaviour. Such behaviour gets repeated like habits. Hence, there is some kind of determinism in leader behaviour. They seem to be compelled to behave in a particular fashion repeatedly, though situations change.

Depending upon the stage of development of the organization, institutions need different kinds of visioning, power building, paternalization and so on. We come across people who headed more than one institution, but with differential impact on the institutions and success. Leaders with great reputation and success bring the same or similar set of skills and styles. Consequently, they make a differential impact. This consistency of behaviour, despite difference in situations, is what is construed as determinism in behaviour. Dr M.B. Buch successfully built CASE with young bright scholars, but not the well-established department of education in the university that he himself headed (Mukhopadhyay 2012a). My personal experience in

NOS versus NIEPA corroborates the same. Nurturant leaders can do a great job in a budding institution with young faculty.

Conclusion

A relatively new coinage of terms in leadership is 'Leaderful Practice' credited to Professor Joseph Raelin. In his own words:[8]

> Leaderful practice refers to the idea of leadership occurring collectively among people in social interaction rather than from individual action.... when asking students how they would refer to teams which were humming along as a single, cohesive unit, with everyone sharing the burden, supporting each other, and speaking for the entire team without any qualms. They would refer to it as a leader-'less' team. However, it is not a team devoid of leadership. Everybody is participating at the same time and all together. It is indeed 'full' of leadership!

Hence, it is Leaderful Practice. The four distinguished attributes of Leaderful Practices are concurrency, collaboration, collectivism and compassion. The classical model of one person leading the rest is an old story. As mentioned earlier, days of leaders are gone, it is time for leadership. We meant collective and collaborative leadership. We live in a networked world where we need to live collectively, collaboratively and compassionately. If these are the guiding factors of life at large, can there be a different way of living in the campus? Quality management in higher education demands and deserves a new leadership paradigm.

---

[8] http://www.damoremckimleadersatworkblog.com/professor-joseph-raelin-leaderful-practice/#sthash.CtFMpOob.dpuf (accessed on 2 May 2014).

14

ICT Integrated Education and Management[1]

Introduction

Indian higher education has accepted twin challenges of expansion and quality. It has shifted from its earlier stand of quantity first, quality then to quantity with quality. India has its declared agenda of reaching GER in higher education to 30 per cent by 2020. Unable to define quality parameters, it has decided to set up 15 'world-class universities'. Though a 'world-class university' has no *locus standi* in the research or professional literature, it indicates some kind of intention of quality. However, it misses the point—missing forest for the tree. Without quality for all or for many, quality for few is a non-starter. Without improving undergraduate education in the 36,000+ colleges, quality improvement in higher education will continue to be a mirage.

The main issue is how to reach out to such a huge number, and yet ensure quality. Should India reach out to the so far unreached through conventional mode by setting up many more colleges and universities? This is one of the recommendations of the National Knowledge Commission. This amounts to more of the same that has actually failed. Or, should India explore alternative ways of reaching

---

[1] I acknowledge with thanks the critical comments offered by Dr Sanjaya Mishra, education specialist (e-learning) in COL (Vancouver) on this chapter.

out to young women and men who are still outside the reach of the higher education system?

This twin challenge of quantity with quality is not unique to India alone. It is rather a global challenge. The case of India is complicated because of the sheer size of the population in the 18 to 23 age group. The problem is that young Indians have to be educated in as many as 18 languages. They belong to a wide diversity of cultural and religious groups. ICT offers a significant opportunity to respond to these twin challenges. There is a worldwide discourse on the role of ICT in enhancing the outreach and improving quality of higher education. UNESCO, OECD and the Commonwealth of Learning (COL) have taken the lead in this discourse with several studies and country cases. UNESCO makes a strong statement in this regard:

> Fundamental to the creation of qualified human resources is an accessible, effective and efficient higher education system, particularly when governments are counting on university graduates to be competitive in creating wealth for their respective countries. Universities are compelled to be innovative and lead by example in using cutting edge technology to meet these expectations. (UNESCO 2011)

With the support of Japanese Funds-in-Trust, UNESCO took the initiative of documenting case studies on innovative use of ICT in higher education in open and distance learning, blended learning, research and administration and management.

There are several major and minor studies undertaken by institutions and individual scholars on the role of ICT in higher education, especially for improving quality. The discourse is equally strong in India, and several major initiatives have been taken by the government as well as private enterprises in education. A school of thought in the government is considering changing the rules and regulations of the UGC to make ICT integrated education, TEL mandatory in higher education.

In this chapter, our focus will be on how ICT can be effectively utilized to enhance quality of higher education institutions. I shall submit my thesis under a few broad heads like contemporary theory of technology, ICT basics, ICT in teaching–learning processes, ICT in research, ICT in administration and management and ICT tools and techniques.

ICT Basics

ICT is a combination of information and communication technologies. Information technology logically means technology that can be used to access, process and store information. Communication technology means the technology that can be used to communicate with others either one to one, or one to many, or many to many. Together, it implies communication of information fed and archived in the systems of information technology.

There are five main issues that comprise the fundamentals or basics of ICT in higher education. These are technology or hardware, software, bandwidth and Internet connectivity, ICT literacy and digital contents. Let us briefly examine each of these issues before we get into their applications for quality management in higher education.

Technology or Hardware

Although ICT is often equated with computers, the technology development insists on a closer examination of the technology and the hardware. Conventionally, ICT has been interpreted in higher education institutions not only as computers but also almost invariably as desktop computers that are immovable. In the meanwhile, there have been a large number of developments, particularly in terms of miniaturization with increased processing speed and power, storage capacity, weight loss (light weight) and lowering of costs.

There is a wide range of options for the hardware like desktop computers, laptops, net books, tablets, smartphones and other hand-held devices that can simultaneously perform data processing, data management, Internet-based applications, social networking and the like. The new-generation devices not only are more powerful but also provide flexibility and user friendliness. For example, desktops are fixed on the classroom desks very often in a sequence with the jungle of cables that connect CPU to the VDU, keyboard, UPS and then UPS to the plug for power supply. Laptops with built-in batteries can survive anything between 2 and 4 hours without any power supply. Net books manage between 6 and 8 hours of working once charged. There are new devices developed by several companies where 24 or more net books can be charged at one go in a cabinet by connecting to only one plug point. Smartphones and iPads are still smarter devices because of their smaller size, light weight and power-packed features. These new compact devices provide flexibility for the users—students and teachers in higher education—to sit wherever they want and whichever way they want. For example, I have seen in several institutions where young students squat on the floor and work on their laptops sitting in a posture of their own preferences. Along with these main hardware computing systems, there comes a large number of accessories that facilitate use of hardware. Simple examples are attachable camera, sound box, cordless mouse, headphone for silent hearing and dictation with speech recognition software, portable device for temporary LAN and Internet connectivity. Although it is a function of the software, it is now possible to connect several technological devices like a laptop with a smartphone to create greater synergy of technology.

Important developments in terms of technology are miniaturization, making the devices lightweight and smaller in size for easy portability and 'work anywhere anytime' while reducing the cost dramatically.

Obviously, technology has not finished its journey. There are several major initiatives that are on the way for further miniaturization to the extent of building smartphones that can be folded like papers or pasted on the T-shirt and so on. On the other side, certain technology giants are working on inventing machines that can evaluate student learning, and not just processing the data like that on OMR. More and more developments will follow the path of miniaturization, improving the processing power and diversity at reduced cost.

For improvement of quality education with ICT, it is necessary to enhance personal access to computing and communicating devices. The developments in hardware are making things happen.

Software

The debate in the domain of software is largely between two issues: proprietary software and open-source software. I will add to the discourse the issue of digital content and digital evaluation tools. Although hard-core computer professionals define software only in terms of machine languages, and those programming languages that help us process information and data, educational technologists have defined the idea of software differently. According to educational technology, digital contents and digital educational material are the educational software.

Proprietary software prepared by particular companies, like Microsoft, Oracle and so on, does not allow access to the coding system and modify the programme to suit any specific need of an institution. Open-source software provides that flexibility; it allows accessing the codes to modify the software to suit the needs of application in a given situation. The revolution of open-source software had its beginning with LINUX, and then for specific applications like Ubuntu and Edubuntu. There is a raging debate between the protagonists of proprietary and open-source software. The issue is not of proprietary or open source, but what actually works, and what is the most smart and cost-effective. COL (2009) concludes the debate between proprietary and open-source software in the following words:

> *Open source or proprietary: What counts is what's most cost-effective!* There has been intense competition in some HEIs between Free Open Source Software (FOSS) and proprietary software. Strong interest groups on each side present this as an all-or-nothing choice, but the sensible approach is to use what is appropriate when it is appropriate. Free software is not free to run (free is used as in 'free speech' rather than 'free beer') and proprietary software may be suitable, but too expensive to buy. A total cost of ownership calculation, including the cost of servers, programming and IT support staff time, needs done when comparing the suitability of software. The ability to integrate data usage between multiple computer programmes without having to re-write the programming is important. Sometimes, proprietary packages that have integration in their design might be most appropriate. The stability of having a programme that works reliably may be paramount while the ability to have programmers rewrite the core program code might be most appropriate in other situations.

What is really important is to understand the implications and working facilities in the proprietary and open-source software.

ICT Literacy

ICT in education, especially in the teaching–learning process, is not a new issue, although its desirability and role are still to be resolved.

There are three fundamental issues with respect to ICT in the teaching–learning process. These are ICT literacy, ICT in the teaching–learning process and ICT in student assessment.

ICT literacy is the foundation for use of ICT in the teaching–learning process and student assessment. It is true for both students and teachers in higher education. The issue is what constitutes ICT literacy and how this can be developed. What is the mechanism of negotiation between conventionally known technology for ICT and the new-generation technology that has much larger penetration?

ICT literacy is no more demystification of either computers or information and communication technologies, nor is it knowledge of technology and theory of technology. Today, ICT literacy implies a set of skills that make a person able to use technology on the day-to-day business of the profession. For example, the ability to open a computer (hardware), open and save a file, enter data either in Word or on spreadsheet, browse the Internet to find academic resources in the form of written papers, PowerPoint presentations, videos and so on, use the Internet for connecting with others through email, social network software like Facebook and Twitter, create blogs and wikis and so on. The other dimension of literacy is to be able to use different types of technologies like desktops, laptops, iPads, tablet PC, smartphones and other such handheld devices to be able to access information and the Internet anytime, anywhere. Several agencies/companies like Microsoft, ECDL, Oracle and others offer ICT skill certification (Mukhopadhyay 2013b). These certificate courses are usually at three or four levels. Level one can be the benchmark for ICT literacy, especially the one offered by Microsoft.

This literacy is required by both the teachers and students in higher education institutions. There is a huge gap in ICT skills between teachers and students. Students being smarter continuously explore ICT in education, recreation and social media. It is the nature of the youth. In fact, a large number of college and university students, especially in the metropolitan cities and urban areas, are digital natives.[2] They have grown up with technology and, hence, are resilient to technology development and development of associated skill

---

[2] Marc Prensky coined the terms digital natives and digital immigrants in his seminal paper published in 2001; see http://www.marcprensky.com/writing/Prensky%20-%20Digital%20Natives,%20Digital%20Immigrants%20-%20Part1.pdf (accessed on 7 July 2014).

sets. Compared to the students, teachers are either digital migrants or even digital aborigines. By digital migrants, I mean teachers who make deliberate efforts to pick up ICT skills, learning and relearning the ICT skills for application in education. Digital aborigines are those who have resigned that either 'it is not possible to learn ICT skills at this age' or 'it is not necessary to learn ICT skills' to become a good teacher or a good researcher. However, the ICT literacy level among the teachers is also fast changing, especially among the younger teachers, and the proportion of digital aborigines is steadily reducing due to invasion of ICT in their personal life and family (mobile phones). Yet, the issue of the choice of application of ICT skills remains. Whereas a large number of teachers in universities are using ICT skills in personal life and work, it is still not common in the academic domain. For example, blogging by university professors is quite common in developed countries, but not in India. Very few professors, rather negligible few, in Indian colleges and universities maintain blogs. Similarly, the flipped classroom, which is becoming an order of the day in developed countries, is still to find any meaningful place in Indian higher education institutions.

The rather inadequate ICT skills among the teaching community are because of reluctance of teachers as well as policy deficits of the higher education system. For example, a large number of states are providing laptops to students at a significant cost to the state exchequer, but not to the teachers who are actually the gatekeepers of any innovation in education anywhere in the world. At a much lower cost, governments could provide laptops to teachers in colleges and universities; and that would have changed the ICT literacy scenario among the teachers in higher education and thereby enhanced the rate and quality of utilization of ICT facilities provided, at great costs, to the higher education institutions in India. However, the paradox is that homes of almost every higher education teacher have ICT facilities, provided at personal cost for their children, which they do not use themselves.

For the integration of ICT in the teaching–learning process as well as in other domains of ICT application in research, administration and management, ICT literacy is necessary. Some colleges and universities, especially in the private ones, have taken significant initiative in developing not only ICT literacy but also ICT skills among teachers. Although, conventionally it is believed that ICT literacy and skills can be developed through training, alternatives have not been explored. For example, mobile phones are almost reaching universal penetration.[3] Without going to any course on literacy and skill development, everyone learns to use the various features in a mobile phone. Most of the time, it is learnt through peer support and personal exploration. ICT literacy and skills can also be developed among the teaching community by creating provision for personal access to computing technology. In fact, this is a much sound alternative for not only creating ICT literacy and skills but also ensuring better utilization of ICT facilities in colleges and universities.

Digital Contents and Learning Material

The debate of proprietary versus open-source software continues in the domain of digital contents and learning material as well. There are tailor-made digital contents available off the shelf for a price. Such digital contents are often encrypted to prevent from copying and use for commercial purposes, causing revenue loss for the organization that produces the digital content. India has a large reservoir of digital contents in higher education originally produced for the Countrywide Classroom programme of the UGC by the 22 Educational Media Research Centres (EMRCs) and Audio-Visual Research Centres (AVRCs), coordinated by CEC.[4] These educational contents, originally in the video format ranging from low band to Betacam high band, have all been digitized. The new-generation educational contents are being produced by the same institutions in digital format with much more flexibility and variety, increasing better usability. However, not all the digital contents available from this official source relate directly to the curriculum transacted in Indian universities, nor is there any rigorous quality control on the production process and quality of content.

There is a huge amount of digital learning materials that are available in the open source. These are available either on different video-sharing platforms, such as YouTube, TeacherTube, or Ted, or

---

[3] 'Mobile-cellular subscriptions will reach almost 7 billion by end 2014': http://www.itu. int/net/pressoffice/press_releases/2014/23.aspx (accessed on 7 July 2014).
[4] See http://cec.nic.in/Pages/Home.aspx

on other open educational resource platforms (such as Connexions, Sylor, Open Learn, OER Commons and so on). Salman Khan's Khan Academy,[5] mostly on school educational content, has already stolen the limelight. The platform carries PowerPoint presentations, video lectures by the most authentic people, professionally developed programmes in two dimensions (2D), 3D video and animation.

Yet another possibility is for the innovative teachers to prepare their own digital content by recording their own commentary (based on a script built on a detailed content analysis) on the recorder on phone or laptop, and illustrate it with visuals drawn from open source, PowerPoint slides, field visuals shot with handy cams and video camera in the mobile phones (preferably android phones). We have done several programmes to train teachers in developing their own digital contents.

Another dimension is technology for student assessment. There are two issues in technology-assisted student assessment. One is an online test and on-demand test. The second is assessment through technology. Many institutions have created online tests. A student can take the test directly on the computer terminal with Internet connectivity. Usually, the computer calculates the score and provides the score sheet to the examinee immediately. Another technology-enabled testing is the on-demand test. In this case, the server houses a large question bank. Whenever a student applies for appearance in examination, by using a few coded commands, the computer generates test paper with the specifications using a blueprint. The student can take the test online, on-screen.

So far, technology has been used to scoring answer sheets by reading the bubbles through an OMR. Xerox Corporation, pioneer in photocopying, has developed a new machine, Xerox Ignite. 'Ignite is a web-based, teacher tool for printing, scanning and scoring a variety of assessments. The software provides frequent and specific feedback on what students are learning. Ignite's teacher tools also suggest ways to address each student's needs'.[6] Xerox Ignite is being adapted to suit the Indian learning environment and styles, including handwriting.

---

[5] See https://www.khanacademy.org/, which has many video resources for the school level.
[6] http://www.services.xerox.com/ignite/enus.html (accessed on 8 July 2014); http://www.techcircle.vccircle.com/2014/01/02/57949/ (accessed on 8 July 2014).

Bandwidth and Internet Connectivity

The final point about ICT relates to communication technology. Communication technology like wireless connectivity, cell phones, cable connectivity and so on significantly enhances the power of information technology, especially access to the Internet and the World Wide Web. These communication software platforms have stimulated the growth of software and cloud services (COL 2009). The dynamics of computer users change due to the increasing penetration of mobile phones and interactivity through the Internet.

According to the Telecom Regulatory Authority of India (TRAI; January 2013), there were 862.62 million mobile users in India. Adjusting use of two SIM cards, the effective number of users is 708 million serviced by about 13 network service providers, including two public sector undertakings, MTNL and BSNL. 'The number of *mobile phone* subscribers in *India* has almost touched the billion figure mark.... According to the latest report from TRAI, *mobile phone* subscriber base in *India* recorded ... growth to 980.81 million *users* in Q2 *2015*' (emphasis added).[7]

'The number of *internet users in India* has reached 354 million by the end of June 2015'.[8] According to another study, by 2015, India was expected to become home for second largest number of Internet users. In 2011, China had 480 million Internet users compared to 245 million in the United States and 120 million in India. This will change; India will have 330 to 370 million compared to China, maintaining the top position with 583 million users, and the United States sliding back to the third place with 279 million users.

Another important development initiative, namely ICT in research and library management, deserves mention. The National Knowledge Network (NKN) and the Information and Library Network (INFLIBNET) are two major initiatives. The NKN is a state-of-the-art multi-gigabyte pan-India network for providing a unified high-speed network, the backbone of all knowledge-related institutions in the country. The purpose of such a knowledge network goes to the

---

[7] dazeinfo.com/2015/.../number-mobile-phone-subscribers-india-q2-2015 (accessed on 4 September 2015).

[8] www.dazeinfo.com/2015/09/05/internet-users-in-india-number-mobile-iamai (accessed on 5 September 2015).

very core of the country's quest for building quality institutions with requisite research facilities and creating a pool of highly trained professionals. The NKN will enable scientists, researchers and students from different backgrounds and diverse geographies to work closely for advancing human development in critical and emerging areas.

Effective use of the bandwidth and Internet facilities, including INFLIBNET, will have significant impact on quality of higher education in every institution of higher education. The important issue will be making use of the penetration of mobile telephones with Internet connectivity.

Theory of Technology

The theory of technology adds an interesting new dimension to the discourse of ICT in higher education. The theory of technology is largely pioneered by Feenberg (2003, 2005). His fundamental argument is derived from a philosophical basis of the development of human civilization. In the process, he profusely refers to Karl Marx (*Das Capital*) and the neo-Marxist philosopher Herbart Marcuse (*One-Dimensional Man*). His basic thesis is contained in a matrix— between neutrality and value-ladenness of technology on one axis and autonomous process versus human control on the other axis.

According to Feenberg,[9] the value-neutral technology controlled by human beings is the 'standard modern view' where technology is used liberally for human progress. This, he calls, instrumentalism. Compared to instrumentalism, the deterministic view subscribes to the autonomy of technology along with the value neutrality. In other words, it proposes technology as the driving force of human development. The author argues that 'it is not up to us to adapt technology to our whims but on the contrary, we must adapt to technology as the most significant expression of our humanity'. Feenberg (2003) called the combination of value-laden and autonomous technology as substantivism. In substantivism, technology is attributed with substantive values in comparison to the value neutrality in the instrumentalist and

---

[9] Andrew Feenberg (undated), Critical Theory of Technology, https://www.researchgate. net/file.PostFileLoader.html?id...assetKey (accessed on 7 July 2014).

deterministic theories. The most important issue here is the combination of ends and means in using technology. Where the human control and value-laden technology intersects, it generates the critical theory of choice between ends and means, and alternative choices between ends–means systems.

Mlitwa (2012), after a detailed review of contemporary literature on ICT in higher education, concludes that there is a wide divide in the perspectives of ICT in higher education. He concludes that effective use of ICT can significantly benefit higher education. However, there are contextual issues that may either facilitate or hinder effective use of ICT in different settings, leading to differential impact on different audiences (cf. critical theory of technology as propounded by Andrew Feenberg). According to this critical theory of technology, the impact of ICT on teaching learning will vary according to the circumstances. He warns against 'one-size-fits-all' kind of solutions. Mlitwa emphasized on the need of openness and deeper engagement with technology development.

This theory of technology is not only relevant but also necessary in higher education because higher education is a system populated by distinguished scholars from various fields of studies and human knowledge. It is natural to question the role of technology and its positioning in the academic processes in the universities. Also, depending upon the theoretical convictions, the teaching community in higher education may choose to use and deploy technology in their academic functions.

ICT in Teaching Learning

ICT integration in the teaching–learning process can be seen from the deterministic as well as instrumentalist viewpoint. The instrumentalism, as mentioned earlier, believes technology to be value-neutral and under the control of human beings. Applied to teaching–learning processes, the instrumentalist viewpoint supports technology as an aid to instructivist approach to the teaching–learning process. In conventional and largely occurring classrooms in higher education institutions, lectures are delivered by teachers; some still follow the 'well-tested' and 'time-tested' model of dictating notes that teachers have inherited from their teachers and 'grand teachers'. ICT integration in the instructivist paradigm suggests use of technology tools to facilitate and improve the quality of lecture by the teacher. The most commonly used technology tools are the PowerPoint presentation and short video clippings. Some teachers, though not many, use digital contents pressed into DVDs. Very few use Internet-based resources in a classroom even where the classroom is equipped with Internet connectivity and access. The presentation of a lecture with such aids as PPT slides and videos reorients conventional lecture into a structured lecture format. Learning outcomes are better with structured lecture than the conventional free flow lecture. However, a structured lecture is not conditional to use of slides and videos. In fact, effective teachers in conventional format usually present a structured lecture. Importantly, aids such as PPT slides and videos automatically convert a free flow lecture into a structured lecture.

The deterministic viewpoint predicts that learning is a natural process for human beings. Technology facilitates that natural learning process with improved quality. Human learning is a self-organizing system, like many other fields of science and social science (Haken 2008). There is a lot of resemblance with the way search engines work in the Internet. In this value-neutral format of technology and autonomy, students are able to decide what they want to learn, when and how. Using rich resources available, such as OER, students can not only create their own learning but also create their own learning methods and styles. When knowledge is obsolete, whether attending classes to get knowledge is really smart or of any serious consequences for the future is a big question. On the contrary, when students design their own learning, they design their capability of learning to learn and incidentally pick up the knowledge which they would have otherwise caught in the classroom.

The emergence and dominance of open and distance education in the last couple of decades, and now the online education, are indications of strongly emerging deterministic mechanisms in human learning, especially in higher education. The best of the universities in the world have posted their courses and course materials on the web as OER. Students can now pick up courses as they wish from different universities and configure their own curriculum and be certified by accumulating credits. Similarly, a large number of universities have come up with MOOCs for students to enrol and learn wherever they are. Some scholars prefer to draw similarity of future education with health care practices. When a person is able to manage his/her health in the normal condition, he/she does not go to a hospital. However, when he/she gets some problem and unable to manage on his/her own, visits an outpatient department (OPD), takes the advice of the doctor, takes prescribed medicine and recovers to normal health. Only when this too does not help, a person is admitted to the hospital. Why should education be not left to the individual; he/she can visit a college or university, like an OPD, whenever he/she is in small difficulty. A student should go to the college or university regularly, like getting admitted in a hospital, when the learning difficulty and disability is far too serious for being treated by short-time advice of the teacher![10]

Between the two—instrumentalist and deterministic viewpoints—is the third alternative. And, that is of blended learning designs, where learning tools of instrumentalist and determinism can be brought together to create a synergy, facilitating a higher level of thinking and greater learning outcome for students. There have been a lot of research and discourse on blended learning designs (Bonk and Graham 2006, Garrison and Kanuka 2004, Mukhopadhyay et al. 2015). The most commonly articulated design is a mix of online education with face-to-face learning. ETMA worked with about 1,200 teachers to develop a situated model of blended learning design integrating ICT with selected learning tactics from a repertoire of more than 70 such tactics. This model of blended learning design has been presented in Chapter 9 (Mukhopadhyay et al. 2015).

In blended learning designs, the challenge is to blend different learning tactics to create a total impact on the learning of the students. Blended learning design warranted laying down the foundation (covering the course material) in a shorter period of time to generate space for activity-based learning. Carefully designed and professionally developed digital contents serve this purpose best. The contents covered in three or four periods of conventional lecture can be effectively captured in about 15-minute digital content.

For the sake of experiment, instead of digital content, teachers can use structured presentation with PPT slides and present in the fast-forward mode. But invariably, presentation using either digital

---

[10] Source: Personal discussion with Prof. M.M. Pant.

content or structured lecture must be followed by focused group discussion among the students around a few questions shared with them in advance. This form of blended learning design incorporates ICT to lay down the first foundation of learning; it complements different levels of human cognition and blends with a whole range of learning tactics.

There are several other associated issues and opportunities. Content generation and quality assurance of such digital contents is one of them. The National Programme of Technology Enhanced Learning (NPTEL) is one such effort where lectures by IIT professors are posted on the web that engineering students can access and benefit from. This is a very important initiative. However, video recording of live lectures is not effective means of communication, although it serves a major purpose of creating access for the highly motivated engineering students to virtual IIT professors, especially when Indian engineering education runs with chronic and perennial staff deficiency. Second, what applies to technology or engineering education may not hold good for the undergraduate students of arts, science and commerce. First, a large majority of undergraduate students do not have the same enthusiasm and motivation as their counterparts in engineering education. Second, there is wide divergence on quality of teachers. Exception apart, good teachers in undergraduate courses and colleges move up to university teaching. The solution is to access and evaluate digital contents from the CEC sources already available online.

There is also a need to adopt flipped classroom techniques where a teacher can create her/his own digital content and post it on either YouTube or on his/her own blog encouraging students to access, utilize and discuss amongst them guided by the questions raised by the teacher.

Students' engagement in laboratories is another important issue for quality learning. As such, there is a skewed distribution of science courses in the 36,000 colleges in the country. Wherever it is there, the quality of education suffers due to poor provision of laboratories. ICT provides an important opportunity of creating digital laboratories (iLabs) where students can experiment in virtual reality condition. For a variety of experiments, they can alter the value of the variables and see their impact on the dependent condition/ variable. MIT took a major initiative in creating iLabs, especially in engineering education.[11] MIT is collaborating on this innovative initiative with several Indian institutions like IITs, BITS and others. Several Indian organizations like NIIT are also actively engaged in developing iLabs. Under the National Mission on Education through Information and Communication Technology (NMEICT), several vlabs[12] have been developed by a group of private and public institutions in the country.

Given the developments of communication technologies from desktop to handheld devices, it has made videoconferencing and audio conferencing fairly easy and within reach. Many international conferences today resort to videoconferencing, saving the cost and time of international travel. I have been successfully using videoconferencing through Skype and Google for reaching out to my experimental site in Udang, a village in Howrah district, for capacity building of teachers. This also helps us to increase access to technology and access to distinguished teachers located at a distance. Yet again, under the support of NMEICT funding, software called A-VIEW[13] has been developed in India to support two-way videoconferencing over the Internet.

Facebook, blogs and wikis are the other social network devices that can substantially enrich quality of curriculum transaction in higher education (Pittenger 2013). There are several instances where teachers post their lectures, lecture notes on their blogs with a set of questions for students to comment and post it on the blog. Slowly and steadily it develops into a serious discourse on the subject. The teacher posts lecture notes several days in advance. So, by the time students attend the class, there has already been a serious discussion among students on the subject. Now the classroom discourse reaches a completely different level.

Libraries are the richest resource for students and specially the teachers in higher education. The budgetary allocation for the library is far too scanty for any meaningful stock of scholarly material, especially in college libraries. Journals, especially the reputed peer-reviewed journals, are extremely expensive for colleges and universities to subscribe. With the spread of technology and the connectivity

---

[11] http://icampus.mit.edu/projects/ilabs/ (accessed on 12 July 2014).
[12] See http://www.vlab.co.in/
[13] See http://aview.in/

in and among the universities and colleges through library networks, for example, Inflibnet,[14] libraries can subscribe to e-journals, e-books and centralized repository of theses and dissertations. This reduces the cost while increasing the access to resources for large number of students.

Teaching–learning is the central core of higher education. ICT can substantially change the face of this core process in colleges and universities. By taking charge or complementing the 'covering of curriculum' component of the teaching–learning process, ICT releases time for the teachers to be creative in curriculum transaction and self-enrichment.

ICT in Research

Two important requirements of research are access to books, journals, research reports in the concerned field and computing power for large data management and complex calculations. Both these facilities are now available relatively easily through applications of ICT. Also, application of ICTs is particularly powerful and uncontroversial in higher education's research function (COL 2009). With the availability of e-books and online journals, access to research literature has substantially increased with a dramatic reduction in the cost and time. Even about two decades ago, Indian researchers had to move from one university library to another in different parts of the country for collecting 'related literature' for review.

Today, it is available at the doorstep. 'The combination of communications and digital libraries is equalizing access to academic resources, greatly enriching research possibilities for smaller institutions and those outside the big cities' (COL 2009). Similarly, the kind of data analysis that had to be done using the huge computers after card punching can today be carried out on the desktops with far more ease and speed. One other important development is the process of consultation of experts through communication technology. Today, research student or a senior research professional, for example, a professor, can access expert for consultation from any part of the world,

---

[14] See http://www.inflibnet.ac.in/

which was not possible earlier. And this consultation substantially increases the quality of research.

An interesting development is collaborative research and documentation across the country and across the world. Collaborative research conducted by CASE at the M.S. University of Baroda as early as in the 1970s was a nightmare; just handling of the correspondence between the members of the research team in different states of the country was humongous. The situation was equally difficult when I conducted an Evaluation of Educational Technology Scheme of the Government of India in 1992–1993, and a National Project on Management of Change in Education in the late 1980s involving almost 25 professors from different universities and institutions in the country. The absence of modern communication technology was the biggest stumbling block.

Every page—letter or report—had to be typed on a typewriter or cut stencils often by ourselves. Today, the developments in communication technology have made it possible for research teams to work together from across the world. Personally, when I edited a book, *Educational Technology: Knowledge Assessment* (Mukhopadhyay, 2004b), I invited some of the best-known experts, including Colin Latchem, Wellesley Foshay, Charles Reigeluth, David Tiedmann and others, from different countries in the world. I had not met anyone but was quite familiar with their academic contribution and reputation in the concerned field. Similarly, when I contributed to international volumes. I hardly knew the editors personally, though I could verify their academic credentials and developed respect for them (Mukhopadhyay 2001 in Latchem and Hanna 2001; Mukhopadhyay and Parhar 2014). We worked on a national project on the assessment of teacher employability spread over 12 states of India from Jammu and Kashmir to Tamil Nadu and Meghalaya to Gujarat involving 12 professors as co-investigators and 4,300+ respondents all through electronic communication (Mukhopadhyay et al. 2015).

The ICT in research needs policy support, especially for creating a collective information system. Familiar with this requirement, the Indian policymaking system initiated connecting libraries and institutions through a national network. As pointed out in the document by COL (2009), high bandwidth is the necessary condition for such applications to allow computing power to be enhanced and aggregated by linking these equipments together.

ICT in Administration and Management

Our chapter (Mukhopadhyay and Parhar 2014) on ICT in Higher Education Administration and Management in India in a book edited by Huang Ronghuai, Kinshuk and Jon K. Price deals with the issue extensively. Applications of ICT in administration and management in higher education began in the early 1970s in certain countries. In India, application of ICT in educational administration and management began in the mid-1980s. ICT was applied mainly for student admission and management of records, examination result processing and certification, personal administration and human resource management, financial management and a bunch of other areas like inventory management, library management and so on. However, the application of ICT in administration and management in higher education was not common in all the universities and colleges. In some of the higher education institutions that took the leadership in this area, maintained a parallel process of manual and computerized administration and management, especially in finance management. Another area was library management where the old card catalogues continued along with computerized information system; the same is true about issuing of books. ICT application in administration and management in higher education today is rather common across colleges and universities in India. However, the institutions differ widely in choice of areas of application in administration and management and also the sophistication of ICT application.

One of the reasons for ICT application in administration and management in higher education is the sudden spurt in enrolment in higher education. COL (2009) refers to an OECD study that indicated that the rate of transition of students from school graduation to higher education stuck 57 per cent in 2006 compared to 37 per cent in 1995, a growth of 20 per cent within a decade. The spurt in enrolment in higher education is much stormier in India. The gross enrolment ratio (GER) in Indian higher education was 4.30 per cent in 1991–1992; it rose to 11.61 per cent in 2005–2006 and 20.8 per cent in 2011–2012 (MHRD 2014). In real terms, there were 10.5 million students in 2005–2006 in the Indian higher education system. This number rose to 29.2 million in 2011–2012 (MHRD 2014). Along with the growth of enrolment of students in higher education, there was growth in the number of colleges and universities, number of teaching and non-teaching staff and budget allocation to higher education. Also, there has been a shift in the qualitative nature of expansion that includes private initiatives, cross-border delivery of education through twinning arrangements, opening campuses in India and the like. ICT has been found a handy tool for management of sudden expansion with a huge diversity.

This necessity of use of ICT in the administration and management of higher education was also facilitated due to certain developments and benefits, especially ICT's increased power of massive data management (Middlehurst 2003). One major agenda is to harness technology for developing a comprehensive higher education management system with enrolment projection covering all the diversities that help better planning and standards setting. Similarly, ICT has been found as a useful device for monitoring academic processes and results, which are the core functions of colleges and universities. Further, colleges and universities are using ICT for facilitating strategic decision making through improved quality of management information system, flow of information on a more regular basis without obstruction, and to tune up with the demands and culture of the younger generation for better and improved access to university services and information through online connectivity.

Institutions of higher education have come to recognize and utilize ICT

- to process large data with meticulous and impeccable accuracy;
- to archive large data and records in digital format to save space that costs very high to the institutes;
- to generate reliable and consistent records from the data archive;
- to quickly search relevant data and records from the data archive; and
- to save human cost of data entry and data analysis by machine-enabled processing, like OMR and others.

Most universities and colleges have created their own dedicated websites that help them connect not only to the world but also with the prospective students. These websites are helping students to compare courses (quality and costs) and decide the choice of universities and courses.[15] Many colleges and universities are using ICT for e-governance, online admission and online payment of fees by the students, online access to course outlines and study materials, even online discussion forums and examinations. In fact, relatively complex organizations like open and distance education institutions, where students are spread all over India and several other countries, find ICT as an important tool for the administration and management. IGNOU, state open universities, All India Management Association, the Indian Society for Training and Development (ISTD) and many other organizations that are offering courses through open and distance education in the conventional mode as well as online have extensively been using ICT, including Moodle and other LMS software. The use of ICT, especially in student admission and payment of fees and online access to the course design and course material, has been extremely helpful for students in difficult areas. For example, a student who had to travel by boat to reach his college in the Sunderbans area of ex-Kolkata is now able to seek admission online, pay fees online and retrieve the course outline.

IGNOU has been using Enterprise Resource Planning (ERP) software for personal and financial management. With the staff distributed all over India at various regional centres, study centres as well as in the headquarters, ERP has been found a useful administrative device.

A majority of the university libraries, though not a majority of the colleges, use ICT for library management. As mentioned earlier, through UGC-sponsored Inflibnet, universities are able to access information from all libraries connected through the network.

ICT in administration and management in higher education has caught the imagination of policymakers and leadership at the institutional level. More and more institutions are adapting ICT enabled administration and management or e-governance. Now that application of ICT in the administration and management of higher education has spread to almost all colleges and universities, it is time to set national standards for ICT enabled administration and management.

---

[15] I had a personal discussion with Binay Kumar Pathak of JNU who worked on this issue for his doctoral study under the guidance of Professor Soumendranath Chattopadhyay.

ICT Facilities

The major issue at hand is the creation and effective utilization of ICT facilities. As mentioned earlier, there are five issues related to the use of ICT in colleges and universities. These are hardware, software, digital content, ICT literacy skills among the teaching and non-teaching staff, and bandwidth and connectivity.

Under various schemes in higher education, most colleges and universities are now equipped with computer labs and other communication hardware. Similarly, some proprietary software is also available with these institutions of higher education, and they are free to access open-source software. Digital contents are accessible from the CEC, although all of them may not be of satisfactory quality. Though not all, but a majority of teaching and non-teaching staff in higher education institutions are ICT literate and have some skills of using ICT. However, the ICT skill of the teaching and non-teaching staff is not equally backed by attitudinal transformation for making effective use of ICT in academic processes.

There are a few serious concerns.

- First, steady power supply, especially in the rural areas, is a challenge. The problem is not unique to the rural areas alone. The erratic power supply in urban areas, especially during summer, is equally problematic. The issue has been discussed in many forums without any meaningful solution.
- Second, connectivity and bandwidth of the Internet are still poor, which reduces the effectiveness of ICT in colleges and universities to a very significant extent. However, this problem can be partially solved by colleges and universities by adapting to certain mechanisms boosting the bandwidth. With NKN, connectivity in colleges and universities has slightly improved.
- Third, maintenance of ICT facilities is a major problem. Although it is recommended that ICT hardware should be seen to have a limited time span, in reality that does not happen. The long-drawn-out complicated write-off procedure does not allow the removal of obsolescence in ICT in colleges and universities.

- Fourth, the issue of e-waste management is a much bigger concern nationally[16] and internationally.[17] Though this issue figures in every serious discourse on ICT in education, it has still remained at the level of discussion without any serious policy decision and action. Government rules and guidelines are still not clear on the issue of e-waste management.

Conclusion

ICT application in higher education has matured enough to merit further arguments. The important issue is making effective use of ICT in all aspects of higher education for quality improvement. ICT in administration and management can make student services more efficient, leaving lasting impression on the students. Integrating ICT in the academic process has all the potential for enhancing effectiveness in the teaching–learning process and improved learning outcome by the students. ICT in research has been changing quality of research by the teachers. Communication technology enhances opportunities of collaboration among the professional community across the universities within India as well as across the world.

Despite all the potentials of ICT changing the face of higher education and improving quality, there are several unresolved issues that need attention and resolution.

Full implications of ICT are still not known since ICT is evolving with greater power, flexibility, lowering cost and deeper penetration while Indian higher education is expanding with growing ambition for quality much faster than ever before.

---

[16] See the occasional paper on the topic by Rajya Sabha at http://rajyasabha.nic.in/rsnew/publication_electronic/E-Waste_in_india.pdf (accessed on 12 July 2014).
[17] See UNEP at http://www.unep.org/gpwm/FocalAreas/E-WasteManagement/tabid/56458/Default.aspx (accessed on 12 July 2014).

End Piece

15

Quality Culture in Higher Education

Introduction

We began this book with a philosophical underpinning of quality in higher education, focusing on all-round development of students, happy, satisfied and inspired teachers, dynamic leadership and an ambiance with positive vibrations in the campus. We conclude our presentations on quality management in the 14 previous chapters. Hence, there would be summarizations and occasional repetitions to emphasize and draw home certain important points.

There are three anchoring points for quality culture in higher education. These are 'concept or nature of a university', 'quality' and 'quality culture'. Any discourse on quality in higher education must be anchored in the idea of a university. The most distinguished and most often referred to idea, quoted in Chapter 1, is provided by John Henry Newman in 1854. We quote again, for facility of reading:[1]

> If I were asked to describe as briefly and popularly as I could, what a University was, I should draw my answer from its ancient designation of a *Studium Generale*, or 'School of Universal Learning.' This description implies the assemblage of strangers from all parts in one spot; – from all parts; else, how will you find professors and students for every department of knowledge? And in one spot; else, how can there be any school at all? Accordingly, in its simple and rudimental form, it is a school of

---

[1] http://www.bartleby.com/28/2.html (accessed on 5 August 2014).

knowledge of every kind, consisting of teachers and learners from every quarter. Many things are requisite to complete and satisfy the idea embodied in this description; but such as this a University seems to be in its essence, a place for the communication and circulation of thought, by means of personal intercourse, through a wide extent of country. (*The Harvard Classics* 1909–1914)

Kenaw (2003) used the Newman model to argue about the idea of a university, as can be applied to Addis Ababa University. From this theoretical but all-comprehensive concept of a university, a new generation of concepts emerged, especially in recent years—universities as knowledge enterprises (Crow 2009, Mitra and Mandke 2004), though opinion is divided on which kind of a university is a knowledge enterprise. Some define research universities as knowledge enterprise; for the other group of thinkers, all universities must be a knowledge enterprise to be qualified to be called a university. Universities cannot be classified as teaching and research universities. The debate can be brought to an acceptable position by adopting reductionism of the concept of knowledge enterprise. In the changing Indian scenario in higher education, an educational knowledge enterprise has three attributes:

1. Knowledge creation (research),
2. Knowledge archiving (print and digital archiving) and
3. Knowledge dissemination (printed and e-publications, teaching–learning process).

Concept of Quality

Although there have been some efforts to define quality, these are largely restricted to the compulsions of dictionaries. Scholars who worked on quality in education have bypassed the issue saying, 'Quality is a dynamic idea and exact definitions are not particularly helpful. However, its range of meanings does cause confusion. Important practical consequences flow from these different meanings' (Sallis 2002), or leaving it a mystery, "Quality is something that stares at you, something you do not fail to recognize but find it difficult to define' (Mukhopadhyay 2005a). Or, quality is described something positive (while analysing the concept of quality as propounded by Deming). From the various descriptions and discussions on the subject, quality is, as referred to earlier:

- Perceptual (as perceived by the consumer)
- Both process and product (product carries manifest quality, and process provides the intrinsic support)
- Exceptional (something special; in operational terms, you have scale or steps of its achievement and a cut-off point)
- Perfection (or consistent; in other words, it identifies a specification to be met absolutely)
- Fitness for purpose (satisfying specified intentions)
- Value for money (self-explanatory)
- Transformative (captured by the terms like 'qualitative change' or 'continuous improvement' (Harvey and Green 1993)

Quality Culture

If defining quality was difficult, defining quality culture is still more challenging. 'Culture' derives its concept from a whole range of disciplines like sociology, psychology, anthropology, history, philosophy and so on. In fact, there is a history of evolution of the concept of culture. According to the *Digital Dictionary*, 'Culture of a particular organization or group consists of the habits of the people in the way they generally behave'. Metaphorically, culture is what 'emits out of a diamond' but not the diamond itself. Culture, like the personality, is the style of the organization—a brand that represents an organization.

Harvey and Stensaker (2008) provided a detailed account of quality culture in higher education. Higher education has developed its own internal quality management system, especially during the past few decades. Recommendations of various committees and commissions appointed by the UGC and their expressed concerns about quality laid down the basis of quality management systems in higher education. Though quality assurance and quality assessment have found a stable place in the discourse in Indian higher education, especially after NAAC found its way through the Indian higher education system, 'quality culture' in higher education is still to become a subject of discourse. This, according to Yorke (2000), is a paradox. 'Part of the paradox, as far as learning and teaching are concerned, can be attributed to external demands which are homeostatic, when the future of higher education seems to be needing a radical commitment to curricular development' (Yorke 2000). In this discourse, institutional autonomy and accountability appear to be two major issues. During the last few decades, there has been an increasing pressure for accountability in many regions of the world.

> The growth of a higher education market has raised expectations among the 'clients' of HEIs (students, employers, other stakeholders). Obviously, globalization of higher education with mobility of students and graduates in the job market has also become an important factor. For instance, it is clear that in the Bologna Process in Europe Higher Education[2] (currently involving 46 countries and intended to increase mobility) quality is a cornerstone of the transformation processes. (Lanares 2011)

Article 51A of the Indian Constitution (Fundamental Duties of Indian Citizens) exhorts 'striving for excellence', echoing the same sentiment. In India, the issue of accountability has remained confined mostly to wishful thinking; autonomy has continued to dominate the scene. Ehlers (2010) argued that quality development in higher education is to 'go beyond implementation of rules and processes for quality manager'. In fact, quality improvement inspired by innovation and creativity cannot be rule bound. My fundamental argument is that promotion of quality culture should aim at enabling every member of the academic community to improve their profession.

Although this concept of holistic and inclusive quality culture is increasingly gaining ground, there is a definite dearth of meaningful research to provide a comprehensive understanding and framework of quality culture in higher education. Probably because of this missing link, some took recourse to coining 'world-class universities' to decipher the meaning of quality culture in higher education.

World-class Universities

World-class universities has emerged to be a catchword; an easy vision statement by even small-time universities. What do world-class universities mean (Levin and Dongshu 2006)? In the absence

---

[2] www.ec.europa.eu/education/policy/higher.../bologna-process_en.htm/ (accessed on 9 August 2014).

of any viable and agreed upon definition, most scholars have taken recourse to the attributes of top 100 or 200 universities in the world as ranked by Times Higher Education Supplement (THES), Shanghai Jiao Tong University (SJTU) and Quacquarelli Symonds (QS) to define 'world class'.

The first issue in this discourse is who defines world-class universities? According to UNESCO and OEC, the International Association of University Presidents (IAUP) is to establish a worldwide quality register (Eaton 2004). According to Philip Altbach (2003b), world-class universities are ones 'ranking among the foremost in the world; of an international standard of excellence'; for Lang (2005), world class must have a system dimension. Robinson (2005) derives from industrial definition of world class to conclude 'industrial definition of quality means a guarantee that something meets a certain basic standard' – 'top of the world rankings'. Yet, a good number of scholars consider 'world class' as a tautology. Mohrman's (2005) and Niland's (2000) comments are worthwhile: For universities, world-class standing is built on reputation and perception—often seen as subjective and uncertain—and it requires outstanding performance in many events'.

Levin and Ou (2006) found 'wide agreement' converging into three major roles in all 'great universities'. These are:

1. Excellence in education of their students;
2. Research, development and dissemination of knowledge; and
3. Activities contributing to the cultural, scientific and civic life of society.

Levin and Ou made a meaningful effort in defining world-class universities with the help of certain quality benchmarks based on analyses of contemporary contributions by a large number of scholars. These are as follows:

- Excellence in research (i.e., top-quality faculty)
- Academic freedom and an atmosphere of intellectual excitement
- Self-governance
- Adequate facilities and funding
- Diversity
- Internationalization
- Democratic leadership
- A talented undergraduate body

- Use of ICT, efficiency of management and library
- Quality of teaching
- Connection with society/community need
- Within institutional collaboration for collaborative research

We may now examine how the universities are rated by the three rating systems, and whether these criteria can match the benchmarks mentioned above (Table 15.1).

Table 15.1:
Criteria for Rating Universities by SJTU, THES and QS

SJTU	THES	QS Star Rating System
1. Award score: The total number of staff winning Nobel Prizes in physics, chemistry, medicine and economics and Fields Medal in mathematics (20 per cent)	International faculty score: percentage of international staff (5 per cent)	Academic peer review (40 per cent)
2. Alumni score: The total number of the alumni winning Nobel Prizes and Fields Medals (10 per cent)	Faculty/student score: staff-to-student ratio (20 per cent)	Faculty–student ratio (20 per cent)
3. Nature and sciences score: The number of articles published in *Nature* and *Science* between 2000 and 2004 (20 per cent)	Citation/faculty score: The number of citations for academic papers generated by each staff member (20 per cent)	Citations per faculty (20 per cent)
4. HiCi score: The number of highly cited researchers in broad subject categories in life sciences, medicine, physical sciences, engineering and social sciences (20 per cent)	International student score: percentage of international students (5 per cent)	International orientation (10 per cent)
5. SCI score: The total number of articles indexed in Science Citation Index-expanded, Social Science Citation Index and Arts and Humanities Citation Index (20 per cent)	Peer/recruiter review score: A scale from 1 to 5 (distinguished) to rate peer schools' academic programmes (40 per cent/10 per cent	Recruiter review (10 per cent)
6. Size: The weighted scores of five indicators divided by the number of full-time equivalent academic staff (10 per cent)		

Source: http://en.wikipedia.org/%20%20%20"http://en.wikipedia.org/

For SJTU, a 90 per cent score is assigned to research reputation; even remaining 10 per cent is also on research reputation but on the alumni. The THES criteria relate to institutional and instructional characteristics, research reputation, student characteristics and others. Whereas SJTU criteria are exclusively output oriented or product based, THES criteria are more systemic incorporating the input–process–output model.

Our fundamental question is whether analysis of definitions and benchmarks indicates quality culture. The THES format seems closer to promote quality culture in higher education. It should be obvious that SJTU criteria are too output focused to meet the requirements of the benchmarks of quality culture derived out of the wisdom of a large number of scholars. Some interesting questions have been raised with respect to these frameworks of rating. A few most important ones are as follows:

- Why are the top-ranking universities centred on the American Continent with the exceptions of the UK, and one or two from Japan and China?
- Whether these ratings have Anglo-phone bias?
- Whether politics, policies and governance matter?

For a detailed treatment, we may refer to Harvey and Stensaker's (2008) nine caveats. Important amongst them are:

1. Quality culture is not mechanistic or codified, a system produced by specialists for adoption by others but an iterative, indeed dialectical, process of evolution that does not just focus on internal processes but relates them to a wider appreciation of social and political forces and locates them historically and understand that quality culture is not a panacea;
2. The dialectical evolution is compatible with a democratic notion of quality culture as a lived, learned experience that itself generates knowledge, rather than simply processes it;
3. Quality culture is not just about checking outputs at each stage but is also a frame of mind, as much of the management literature implies;
4. A quality culture is an ideological construct, a fact that cannot be glossed over by a set of prescriptions or recipes for implementation;
5. Quality culture is not likely to be constructed irrespective of the context in which it is located, which again limits the possibilities for knowledge transfer.

On the basis of styles of response to quality initiatives, Levin and Ou (2006) proposed typologies of quality culture, namely responsive, reactive, regenerative and reproductive quality culture. In one of the earlier chapters on strategic planning, we classified institution in terms of quality as basic and niche. Carrying that framework further, my preferred configuration is the following.

Basic Quality Culture: Focused on quality culture on all programmes and courses of the university;

Niche Quality Culture: Focused on selective programmes and courses for meeting the external demands in those areas alone.

We argue, then, that quality culture can be globally conceptualized but locally configured that is acceptable to the culture of Indian society in general and Indian higher education in particular, yet with a caveat that such localized or Indianized culture would have enough space to reflect global culture. We need to take a closer look at the planning model of education prevalent in India (Figure 15.1).

Figure 15.1:
Planning Parameters for Higher Education

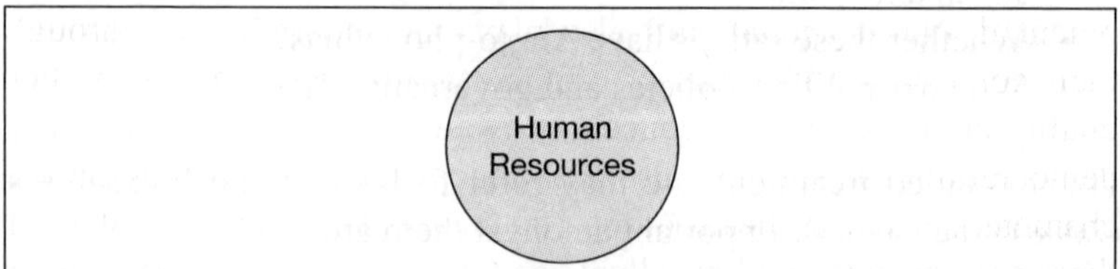

Source: Author.

The model is systemic. The vision and goals form the nucleus of the planning model. Quality culture in such a model derives its inspiration from the vision and goals—the vision and goals that are shared and collective; vision and goals that have been owned by the members of the academic community.

Academic inputs and processes comprise curriculum, textbooks and other print and digital learning material, and the instructional process. The demand of quality culture in this context is the state-of-the-art curriculum in every subject (a basic quality culture), access to high-quality instructional material, for example, web-based resources, dedicated university web portals, blogs, digital and printed books, and so on. A special focus is on high-quality instructional processes that help students to think at higher levels rather than treating the brain as a warehouse of huge amount of unfiltered and unverified information. It helps students to create flexible brain maps than rigid ones. From the standpoint of criteria of the evaluation of quality, this refers to instructional processes of the THES.

The second unit comprises human resources, especially people in the leadership position and teachers who help students to realize their potential. Non-teaching staff also plays an important role through their contribution in terms of efficiency, attitudes and values. For quality culture in higher education institutions, it implies not only democratic leadership but also academic leadership. A study on the characteristics of the heads of top 100 universities revealed that all of them are dedicated and excellent scholars, equal to the best in their institutions, if not the best. Here comes the role of research and knowledge creation. This involves creating knowledge through research that is easily comparable with the best in the world as indicated by the patenting and publications—"ranking among the foremost in the world; of an international standard of excellence" (Altbach 2003b). Research has been the most important criterion for the evaluation of quality culture by both SJTU and THES.

The third element of the planning model is infrastructure—classrooms, laboratories, libraries, ICT facilities and other associated infrastructure for games and sports, cultivation of art and culture, recreation and so on. There are three sets of criteria for examining infrastructures: adequacy, adequate enough for the users; functional, everything in working order; aesthetics, everything is beautiful, inspiring and tasteful. Quality culture in institutions of higher education demands care and development of infrastructure in all the three dimensions and not just adequacy.

The fourth element is finance, implying availability of adequate amount of funds transferred on time. It also implies flexibility: not only guarantee of salaries on time and minimum basic facilities (and budget), but also access to funds for research and development projects (budgeted and non-budgeted). Quality culture would also demand appropriate, efficient and just-in-time use of financial resources. A critical analysis of this planning model will indicate that it includes all the elements and concerns of quality culture in higher education.

Few Issues

A major issue is how to develop quality culture in our existing or upcoming universities in the country.

1. Though there is a commitment of funds by the Government of India, especially for the new central universities and proposed innovation universities, these are not adequate or comparable to unit costs of education in some of the top 200/500 universities in the world. The new universities are still struggling to find their feet in terms of land and space, architectural designs and buildings and other academic infrastructures. During the 12th Five-Year Plan, the Government of India decided to set up 14 'world-class universities'. However, the concept of funding is totally misplaced, and its approach to selection of universities are guided more by non-educational (probably political) than educational considerations.
2. The students are important partners in the whole process of quality culture in higher education. Because of sheer enormity of the student market, there is enough opportunity of selecting the best quality students in the selected institutions and universities. As of now, the GER is just above 20 per cent which is to be raised to 30 per cent in phases.[3]

---

[3] The plan documents project 30 per cent GER by 2020. The minister for HRD, in his address on 24 August 2013, as reported by the *Times of India*, projected 30 per cent GER

3. It is necessary to understand that higher education is in a bind since the quality of students entering higher education is a function of the quality of school education. The secondary and senior secondary education sector has been perennially neglected in post independent India's planning and financing. Quality culture in higher education would continue to be a distant dream as long as school education continues to suffer from neglect and non-attention of the government(s).

4. Educational planners need to change their planning processes, incorporating the meaning and implications of intra-sectoral dependence. Further, Indian universities are still less than cosmopolite, or at best nationally cosmopolite without adequate number of international students to bring in a global cosmopoliteness in the campus. Indian higher education attracted 22,521 foreign students (2011–12) (UNESCO and GOI 2014)—about 0.1 per cent of the total strength of students in higher education.

Many studies have indicated cosmopoliteness and campus diversity as important determinants of quality culture. India needs to make special efforts to attract international students in the campuses.

Another issue is student involvement in the management of quality in institutions of higher education dealt in details in Chapter 12. Unlike in Australian and American universities, students are yet to be integrated into the system as an equal partner in quality management.

There are a few issues related to teachers. The first issue is their entry quality and professional preparation. In the SET, the success rate of candidates for college job is less than 3 per cent. Generally, quality-deficient teachers do not produce high-quality graduates. Then, having the first preference not being teaching, exceptions apart, higher education is left with the opportunity of 'selecting from the rest'. As revealed by several studies by NASSCOM and Aspiring Minds, Indian graduates lack employability skills. Higher education as an employment domain is not free from this employability

---

by 2020. That GER is already at about 18 per cent, chances are high that the minister's projection may come true.

skill-deficit. This is compounded by the lack of professional preparation of teachers, their continuing education and their own employability skills. Academic Staff Colleges set up after the National Policy on Education started with the limited understanding of what constitutes teacher preparation. In the absence of any positive agenda, it defined it 'not to be like B.Ed'. Hence, higher education continues to miss the science of human learning and instructional processes. Quality instructional processes are no more restricted to good lectures or even good-quality critical discourses. The new science of pedagogy for higher education can be seen embedded into

Acarya Purva-Rupam, Antevasy Uttara-Rupam,
Vidya Sandhi, Pravachanas Samdhanam, Ity Adhividyam.
(*Taittiriya Upanishad*, I.4.1)

'The teacher is the prior form; the pupil is the later form, knowledge is their junction; instruction is the connection' (rendering by Radhakrishnan 1998). By implication, a teacher is also a student, just a senior one; teacher is a perennial learner compared to the prevailing perception of being a 'learned' person.

An important shift in the pedagogy is taking place globally, changing teaching to learning. The second important emphasis is on ICT-integrated learning. The ICT-integrated blended learning design (Mukhopadhyay 2014) offers a unique opportunity to blend ICT in the instructional processes, mentioned in Chapter 7 on Teaching–Learning Processes and again briefly in Chapter 14.

The second dimension is research. We cannot say the same good words about the IITs and IIMs. There have been enough controversies on this issue based on comments by certain individuals of good standing, like Infosys-famed Sri Narayana Murthy and Minister Jairam Ramesh. This has also been the contention of some of the architects and institution builders in technical education (Mitra 2007). Instead of personal opinion, a better option is to create data and information on research output and their publication in high-quality indexed journals. Nobel Prizes and Field Medals, publications in exclusive journals like *Nature* and *Science* by the professors of these leading Indian institutions are rare. A natural question is if certain institutes can be world class in undergraduate programmes, what stands in their way to become a world-class research institution? Research has been given some special space in higher education by including research and publication as a set of criteria in CAS. This 'confirmed promotion' compared to earlier practice of best among the equals for promotion has not helped in either developing inclusiveness or improving quality in research. This hesitant step to research has not compelled the laggards among the academicians, nor has it inspired the early adopters. Who continue to struggle and survive in such an unchallenging ambience are the 'innovators' who are indomitable any way.

One of the major issues in this context is how teachers could be much more responsive and creative agents for change. What incentive system would work for teachers? The present system of salary and promotion has been treated in India so much as a matter of right. How can research be prioritized and how should handholding be the responsibility of the state? Can American rigorous tenure system be practiced in India, too? What kind of architecture can be built for it?

This question of quality culture is the issue of change management. Chin and Bennis' (1969) classical three models of management of change, namely empirical–rational, normative–reeducative, power–coercive, deserve consideration. Nichols (2010) added one more strategy, namely environmental–adaptive.

Biggest demands for quality culture in higher education are on the instructional processes and research. It is a case of systemic change management. There is no single formula for change management.

Change is also culturally embedded process. Hence, response to the issues raised here needs careful consideration; and factored within the cultural setting of India. Because of the dynamics of the employment market, very few brilliant people join teaching profession. Universities and professional institutions are working with significant staff deficiency, and the government is extending the year of retirement without any meaningful performance evaluation. In a situation characterized by a dearth of qualified and quality teachers, the tenure system may jeopardize the basic operations in the institutes of higher education. Yet, it is a fact that in Indian higher education, salary, compensations, though low compared to teachers in developed countries and professional in corporate sectors, and nominal promotions are taken for granted. Accountability is often overshadowed by autonomy.

The recent promotional policy of the UGC is relatively more stringent, offering some hope. These strategies resemble the 'power–coercive' strategy of change management. At the same breath, it is fraught with the danger because of personalization of administration—'around-the-man' approach to change. Its implementation depends upon the leadership in the university. Also, these strategies of performance assessment based on peer-group evaluation have not yielded many dividends. It can be seen in case of statutory bodies like National Council for Teacher Education (NCTE), AICTE, then Distance Education Council (DEC) and so on. All of them are plagued with complaints for irregularities.

A fresh initiative for inspiring teachers in higher education to take to quality journey through normative–reeducative processes may yield results. It must be linked to competition and incentives of a different order. For example, in India a performing and a non-performing professor superannuates at the end of the same prescribed age limit. In a few developed countries, based upon the research and academic productivity, a distinguished professor is entitled to decide his/her time to retire. This is significant since academic community in India is ageing while in good health. There are innumerable examples where competent and capable scholars switchover to alternative channels of paid or voluntary engagement. IITs are losing some of their faculty members to the private institutions.

A second dimension is supporting and promoting research. The proposals submitted by the distinguished and not-so-distinguished scholars are evaluated in the same manner. As a member of the committee to evaluate RFP of the Illinois Board of Education, I experienced how the weightages were distributed to the quality of the research proposal and the credential of the researcher. Instead of seeking funding for every project, the government and the institutions should create a format for RFP and invite distinguished scholars to respond. This should help in creating a proactive research ambience that will help teachers to be responsive. Funded research projects can also build in financial incentive to the scholars by adding a portion of the research project to the personal incentive.

A majority of the projects undertaken by university teachers are often miniscule and have a very limited impact. On the one hand, the funding agencies are far too conservative; on the other hand, the university professor has been conditioned to think small. This must change. University academicians must be encouraged to take larger projects that will have major social impact or lead to scientific discoveries. This will also develop self-concept and capability to match their counterparts in the world outside.

Another important requirement is the de-bureaucratization of research funding. In contemporary India, research funding is decided by people in the administrative hierarchy who are remotely familiar with, if at all, the nuances and demands of major research projects. Universities should be provided with a block research grant and freedom to make use of these through internal processes.

University Leadership

The final point is about the leadership in higher education institutions. There are innumerable studies across civilizations and countries that isolate leadership quality and style as the single most determining factor for developing quality culture. Developing quality culture is institution building. According to experience, out of hundreds of people occupying leadership position in higher education institutions, only a small fragment of these build institution and quality culture (Mukhopadhyay 2012a). One of the common characteristics of all institution builders is their academic distinction (Latchem and Hanna 2001). In terms of research findings, distinguished academicians as head of institutions enjoy source credibility, which is necessary for inspiring colleagues. This proposition is in tune with shift in the science of leadership towards inspirational and elusive leadership. In order to build quality culture in institutions of higher education, the government must formulate certain policy options. The contemporary emphasis on political and bureaucratic connectivity as the criterion for selection of heads of higher education institutions must change. This largely is a decade-and-half-old phenomenon when there was a significant change in the governance of education, higher education in particular, with political convictions. However, this aberration in leadership was meticulously followed by successive governments (Mukhopadhyay and Parhar 2007). The mass scale elevation of the known and unknown institution into deemed universities and the consequent sweeping recruitment of vice chancellors are some of the important concerns in the context of developing quality culture in higher education institutions.

Conclusion

As we know, the teaching community can be divided into four groups on the basis of their willingness and competence. There is a small minority who are willing and also competent; another minority who are neither competent nor willing to learn. A large majority of teachers in our institutions of higher education belong to two categories, namely competent but not willing, and willing but not competent. The competent and willing group of teachers does not require any specific management strategy; they need facilitation and organizational support. These are innovators and/or early adopters. The second minority group—neither willing nor competent is almost a lost case—they are the laggards. Power–coercion seems to be the only way out to get their minimum contribution in the system, at least to carry on the routine works. Between the other two majority groups, those are competent but not willing are threat to the system because they are capable. They require special care for attitudinal transformation, relocating the locus of their motivation. The other majority group, namely those who are willing but not competent, offers an important 'opportunity' for the institution. It is relatively easy to develop the competencies among those who are willing. This would simply require a blueprint for human resource development in higher education. When teachers receive such individualized attention and care, things may fall into places. In various other fields, for example, space science, India has proven its style of resilience to challenging circumstances. Our hope is that teachers in higher education will not fall short of this environmental-adaptive resilience.

Bibliography

Abou-Elgheit, Emad. 2012. 'Brain-Based Learning Design: Fundamentals of Brain-Based Learning'. ISM, Doctoral Assignment. Available at: http://www.talkingpage.org/artic011.html (accessed on 20 November 2014).

Abrahamowicz, D. 1988. 'College Involvement, Perceptions, and Satisfaction: A Study of Membership in Student Organizations'. *Journal of College Student Development*, 29(3): 233–38.

Adair, John. 2003. *The Inspirational Leader: How to Motivate, Encourage and Achieve Success*. London: Kogan Page.

Allen, Roger. 2009. *The 3 Stages of Organizational Development*. Littleton, Colorado: Centre for Organizational Design.

Altbach, Philip G. 2003a. 'Globalization and the University: Myths and Realities in an Unequal World'. *Journal of Educational Planning and Administration*, 17(2): 227–47.

———. 2003b. 'The Costs and Benefits of World-class Universities: An American's Perspective'. *International Higher Education*, 33(Fall): 5–8.

Altbach, Philip G. (ed.). 1999. *Private Prometheus: Private Higher Education and Development in the 21st Century*. Westport: Greenwood Press.

Altbach, Philip. G. 2005. 'A World Class Country Without World Class Higher Education: India's 21st Century Dilemma'. *International Higher Education*, Summer: 81–89.

Ameny-Dixon, Gloria M. 2010. *Why Multicultural Education is More Important in Higher Education Now than Ever: A Global Perspective*. Available at: http://www.nationalforum.com/Electronic%20Journal%20Volumes/Ameny-Dixon,%20Gloria%20M.%20Why%20Multicultural%20Education%20is%20More%20Important%20in%20Higher%20Education%20Now%20than%20Ever.pdf (accessed on 12 June 2014).

Anaya, G. 1996. 'College Experiences and Student Learning: The Influence of Active Learning, College Environments and Co-curricular Activities'. *Journal of College Student Development*, 37(60): 611–22.

Anderson, L.W., D.R. Krathwohl, P.W. Airasian, K.A. Cruikshank, R.E. Mayer, P.R. Pintrich, J. Raths and M.C. Wittrock. 2001. *A Taxonomy for Learning, Teaching, and Assessing: A Revision of Bloom's Taxonomy of Educational Objectives*. New York: Longman.

Anzalone, S. (ed.). 1995. 'The Case for Multi-channel Learning'. In *Multi-channel Learning: Connecting All to Education*. Washington DC: EDC.

Anzalone, S. 1995. 'The Case for Multi-channel Learning'. In *Multi-channel Learning: Connecting All to Education*, edited by S. Anzalone. Washington, DC: EDC.

―――. 2004. 'Multi-channel Learning'. In *Educational Technology: Knowledge Assessment*, edited by Marmar Mukhopadhyay, pp. 63–82. New Delhi: Shipra.

Aspiring Minds. 2010, 2013. 'National Employability Study: IT/ITeS Sector'. Available at: http://www.aspiringminds.in (accessed on 26 April 2016).

―――. 2013. 'National Employability of Graduates, 2013'. A Report. Available at: http://www.aspiringminds.in/researchcell/whitepapers/ national_employ-ability_report_graduates_2013.html (accessed on 7 April 2016).

Astin, A.W. 1993. *What Matters in College? Four Critical Years Revisited.* San Francisco, CA: Jossey-Bass.

Ausubel, D. 1962. 'A Subsumption Theory of Meaningful Verbal Learning and Retention'. *The Journal of General Psychology*, 66(2): 213–24.

―――. 1963. *The Psychology of Meaningful Verbal Learning.* Oxford, England: Grune & Stratton.

Author Unknown. 2011. 'An Overview of Brain-based Learning, its Core Principles'. Available at http://www.educatorstechnology.com and also at http://www.funderstanding.com/theory/brain-based-learning/brain-based-learning/ (accessed on 7 April 2015).

Bailey, D.M. 2012. 'How to Use Baldrige for Strategic Planning and Raise Health Status and Employee Engagement at the Same Time'. Available at: http://nistbaldrige.blogs.govdelivery.com/2012/04/20/ (accessed on 26 April 2016).

Barrie, Simon C. 2004. 'A Research-based Approach to Generic Graduate Attributes Policy'. *Australia Higher Education Research and Development*, 23(3): 261–75.

Berk, L.E., and B.L. Goebel. 1987. 'Patterns of Extracurricular Participation from High School to College'. *American Journal of Education*, 95(3): 468–85.

Bhushan, S. 2004. 'Managing Tertiary Education for Integrated Knowledge Economy'. New Delhi: NIEPA (unpublished manuscript).

Biggs, J, and Kevin Collis, 1982, *Evaluating Quality of Learning: The SOLO Taxonomy.* New York: Academic Press.

Blake, R., and J. Mouton. 1985. *The Managerial Grid III: The Key to Leadership Excellence.* Houston: Gulf Publishing Co.

―――. 1964. *The Managerial Grid: The Key to Leadership Excellence.* Houston: Gulf Publishing Co.

Blanchard, K., and S. Bowles. 1997. *Gung Ho! Turn On the People in Any Organization.* New York: William Morrow & Co.

Bloom, B.S. et al. 1956. *Taxonomy of Educational Objectives: Classification of Educational Goals, Handbook I: Cognitive Domain.* New York: David McKay Company.

Bloom's Taxonomy Action Verbs. Available at http://www.clemson.edu/ assessment/assessmentpractices/referencematerials/documents/Blooms%20 Taxonomy%20Action%20Verbs.pdf (accessed on 7 January 2014).

Bonk, C.J., and C.R. Graham (eds). 2006. *The Handbook of Blended Learning*: *Global Perspectives, Local Designs*. San Francisco, CA: John Wiley & Sons, Inc.

Botkin, J.W., M. Elmandjra, and M. Malitza. 1979. *No Limits to Learning: Bridging the Human Gap: A Report to the Club of Rome*. Oxford: Pergamon.

Brendon, Rigvy. 2009. 'Review of Graduate Skills: Critical Thinking, Teamwork, Ethical Practice and Sustainability'. Australian Learning and Teaching Council Project. Available at: http://graduateskills.edu.au/literature-review/ (accessed on 26 April 2016).

Broatch, Alistair. 2007. *A Brief Guide to the (O)ADRI Cycle*. Available at: http:// www.utas.edu.au/provost/quality/documents/A-brief-guide-to-OADRI.pdf (accessed on 12 May 2014).

Bryson, John M. 1995. *Strategic Planning for Public and Non-profit Organizations: A Guide to Strengthening and Sustaining Organizational Achievement*. Revised Edition. San Francisco, CA: Jossey-Bass.

Buch, P.M. 1972. 'An Inquiry into Conditions Promoting Adaptability in Indian Schools'. Unpublished Doctoral Thesis, M.S. University, Baroda.

Burke, G., and P. Mckenzie. 2009. 'Economics of Quality Schooling'. In *Quality School Education for All*, edited by Marmar Mukhopadhyay, pp. 179–98. New Delhi: ETMA.

Burton, M.D. 1981. 'Identifying Potential Participants for College Extracurricular Activities'. *College Student Journal*, 15(3): 251–54.

Chapman, J. 2002. *System Failure, Why Governments Must Learn to Think Differently*. London: Demos. Available at: http://www.demos.co.uk/files/systemfailure2.pdf/ (accessed on 8 April 2016).

Checkland, P. 1985. *Systems Theory and Management Thinking*. London: SAGE.

———. 1990. *Soft Systems Methodology in Action*. Chichester: John Wiley & Sons.

———. 1998. *Systems Thinking, Systems Practice*. Chichester: John Wiley & Sons Ltd.

———. 2000. 'Soft Systems Methodology: A Thirty-year Retrospective'. *Systems Research and Behavioral Science*, 17, S11–S58.

Chin, R., and K.D. Benne. 1969. 'General Strategies for Effecting Changes in Human Systems'. In *The Planning of Change*, second edition, edited by W.G. Bennis, K.D. Benne, and R. Chin, pp. 32–59. New York: Holt, Rinehart & Winston.

Chowdhry, Kamla. 1977. 'Institution Building: Two Approaches in Contrast'. In *Institution Building in Education and Research: From Stagnation to Self Renewal*, edited by Ravi Mathai, Udai Pareek, and T.V. Rao, pp. 12–18. New Delhi: All India Management Association.

Cohen, L. 1983. 'Made-in-USA Quality Circles Become People-building Tool'. *Community and Junior College Journal*, 52: 34–35.

COL. 2009. 'ICTs for Higher Education'. Background paper for the UNESCO World Conference on Higher Education', 5–8 July, Paris. Available at: http://www.col.org/PublicationDocuments/pub_ICTs_for_Higher_Education_Unesco_July2009.pdf (accessed on 10 April 2016).

Collins, Jim. 2001. *Good to Great*. New York: Harper Collins.

Collis, K., and J. Biggs. 1982. *Evaluating the Quality of Learning: The SOLO Taxonomy*. New York: Academic Press.

Cooperrider, David L., and Diana Whitney. 2005. *Appreciative Inquiry: A Positive Revolution in Change*. San Francisco, CA: Berrett-Koehler Publishers.

Craig, D.H., and T.R. Warner. 1991. 'Working Together: The 'Forgotten Majority' of Student Organizations and Campus Activities'. *Campus Activities Programming*, 23(9): 42–46.

Crebert, G. 2000. 'A Snapshot of Generic Skills Development at Griffith University'. Available at: http://www.citeseerx.ist.psu.edu/viewdoc/download? doi=10.1.1.202.2581&rep=rep1&type=pdf (accessed on 12 April 2016).

Crosby, P.B. 1979. *Quality Is Free: Art of Making Quality Certain*. New York: McGraw Hill.

Crow, Michael M. 2009. 'The Research University as Comprehensive Knowledge Enterprise: The Reconceptualization of Arizona State University as a Prototype for a New American University'. Tempe, AZ: Arizona State University. Available at: www.curriculumreform.org (accessed on 26 April 2016).

De Bono, Edward. 1970. *Lateral Thinking: Creativity Step by Step*. New York: Harper & Row.

Delors, J., et al. 1996. *Learning: The Treasure Within*. Paris: UNESCO.

Deming, W.E. 1986. *Out of the Crisis*. Cambridge: Cambridge University Press.

Deshpande, Alok. 2014, 19 January. 'Mumbai University Professor Reinstated', *The Hindu*.

DST. 'Technology Information, Forecasting Assessment Council Reports'. New Delhi: Department of Science and Technology. Available at: http://www.tifac.org.in/index.php?option=com_content&view=article&id=34&Itemid=46 (accessed on 5 August 2014).

Drucker, Peter. 1954. *The Practice of Management*. New York: Harper Collins.

Eaton, Judith. 2004. 'The Opportunity Cost of the Pursuit of International Quality Standards'. *International Higher Education*, 36: 3–5.

Eaton, Sarah. 2011. '21 Characteristics of 21st Century Learners'. Available at: https://drsaraheaton.wordpress.com/2011/12/07/21st-century-learners/ (accessed on 15 October 2014).

ECDL. 2011. 'Promoting Inclusive Economic Growth and Employment through Enhanced ICT Skills and Knowledge'. Report by ECDL Foundation. Available at:

http://www.ecdl.org/media/ECDLPositionPaper-e-Productivity1.pdf (accessed on 14 July 2014).

Ehlers, Ulf-Daniel (ed.). 2010. 'Moving from Control to Culture in Higher Education Quality'. In *Changing Cultures in Higher Education: Moving Ahead to Future Learning*. New York: Springer.

Elton, S.E. 2011. Characteristics of 21st Century Learners. Available at: http://drsaraheaton.wordpress.com/ (accessed on 26 April 2016).

ERIC Digest. 1984. Quality Circles in the Community College. ERIC Digest Identifier: ED353008. Available at: www.ericdigests.org/1993/quality.htm (accessed on 26 February 2014).

ETMA. 2015. 'Baseline Survey of Technology Enabled Learning in Asian Commonwealth Countries'. Vancouver: COL. Available at: oasis.col.org/bitstream/handle/.../2015_COL_TEL_Baseline_Asia.pdf? (accessed on 23 December 2015).

Farahbakhsh, S. 2006. 'Leadership in Educational Administration: Concepts, Theories and Perspectives'. *Academic Leadership*, 4(1): 85–110.

Feenberg, A. 2003. 'What Is Philosophy of Technology?' Lecture for the Komaba Undergraduates, June. Available at: http://www.sfu.ca/~andrewf/komaba.html (accessed on 22 April 2015).

———. 2005. 'Critical Theory of Technology: An Overview'. *Tailoring Biotechnologies*, 1(1): 47–64.

Feigenbaum, A.V. 1951. *Quality Control: Principles, Practice, and Administration*. New York: McGraw Hill.

———. 1983. *Total Quality Control*. New York: McGraw Hill.

Flavell, J.H. 1976. 'Metacognitive Aspects of Problem Solving'. In *The Nature of Intelligence*, edited by L.B. Resnick, pp. 231–36. Hillsdale, NJ: Erlbaum.

Fletcher, Adam. 2004. *Meaningful Student Involvement: Resource Guide*. Olympia, WA: SoundOut. Available at: www.sparkaction.org/node/27348 (accessed on 27 October 2014).

Forbes, Scott, H., and R. Ann Martin. 2004. *An Analysis of Holistic Schools' Literature*. Portland, OR: Holistic Education. Available at: www.holistic-education.net/articles/research04.pdf (accessed on 12 September 2014).

Foshay, A.W. 2000. *The Curriculum*. New York: Teachers College, Columbia University.

Frazier, A. 1997. *Roadmap for Quality Transformation in Education*. Florida: St. Lucie Press.

Gagné, R. 1985. *The Conditions of Learning and the Theory of Instruction*. Fourth edition. New York: Holt, Rinehart, and Winston.

Gardner, Howard. 1983. *Frames of Mind: The Theory of Multiple Intelligence*. New York: Basic Books.

———. 2010. *Multiple Intelligences*. Available at: http://www.howardgardner.com/MI/mi.html (accessed on 26 April 2016).

Garrison, D.R., and H. Kanuka. 2004. 'Blended Learning: Uncovering Its Transformative Potential in Higher Education'. *The Internet and Higher Education*, 7(2): 95–105.

Gibran, Kahlil. 1923. *The Prophet*. New York: Alfred A. Knopf.

Gilmore, H.L. 1974. 'Product Conformance Cost'. *Quality Progress*, 7(5): 16–19.

George, Michael L. 2003. *Lean Six Sigma*. New Delhi: Tata McGraw Hill.

Glatthorn, Allan A. 2000. 'Aligning the Curriculum'. In *The Principal as Curriculum Leader: Shaping What Is Taught and Tested*, second edition, edited by A.A. Glatthorn, pp. 83–91. Thousand Oaks, CA: Corwin Press.

Gnanam, A., David Bradbury, and Anthony Stella (eds). 2003. *Benchmarking Quality in Higher Education: Indo-UK Perspectives*. New Delhi: Sterling.

Goleman, D. 1995. *Emotional Intelligence: Why It Can Matter More than IQ*. Bantam Books, 10th Anniversary edition.

Goleman, D. et al. 2002. *The New Leaders: Transforming Art of Leadership into Science of Results*. London: Little Brown.

GOI, Ministry of Education. 1948. 'The Report of the University Education Commission (Radhakrishnan Commission), December 1948–August 1949'. New Delhi: GOI, Ministry of Education.

———. 1953. 'Report of the Committee on Implementation of the Recommendations of the University Education Commission (Humayun Kabir Committee)'. New Delhi: GOI, Ministry of Education.

———. 1958. 'Report of the National Committee on Women's Education (C.D. Deshmukh Committee)'. New Delhi: GOI, Ministry of Education.

———. 1961. 'Report of the Committee on the Model Act for the Universities'. New Delhi: GOI, Ministry of Education.

———. 1966. 'Education and National Development, Report of the Education Commission (Kothari Commission), 1964–66'. New Delhi: GOI, Ministry of Education.

———. 1985. 'National Commission on Teachers for Higher Education (Rais Ahmad Committee)'. New Delhi: GOI, Ministry of Education.

GOI, Ministry of Human Resource Development. 2009a. 'Report of the Committee to Advise on Renovation and Rejuvenation of Higher Education (Yashpal Committee)'. New Delhi: GOI, Ministry of Education.

———. 2009b. 'Report of the Committee for Review of Existing Institutions Deemed to be Universities (Tandon Committee)'. New Delhi: GOI, Ministry of Education.

GOI. 2010. 'National Knowledge Commission: Reports'. New Delhi: GOI. Available at: www.knowledgecommission.gov.in/ (accessed on 14 August 2014).

Habibullah, A.H.M., and Jai B.P. Sinha. 1980. 'Motivational Climate and Leadership Styles'. *Vikalpa*, 5(2): 85–93.

Hager, P., S. Holland, and D. Beckett. 2002. *Enhancing the Learning and Employability of Graduates: The Role of Generic Skills*. Melbourne: Business/Higher Education Round Table. Available at: http://www.bhert.

com/publications/position-papers/B-HERTPositionPaper09 (accessed on 27 August 2015).

Haken, Herman. 2008. 'Self-Organization', *Scholarpedia*, 3(8): 1401. Available at www.scholarpedia.org/article/Self-organization (accessed on 3 May 2014).

Halpin, A.W., and D.B. Croft. 1963. 'The Organizational Climate of Schools'. *Administrator's Notebook*, 11(7): 1–22.

Harris, R.W. 1990. 'The CNAA Accreditation and Quality Assurance'. *Higher Education Review*, 23(3): 34–53.

Harvey, L. 2002. 'The End of Quality?' *Quality in Higher Education,* 8(1): 5–21.

Harvey, L. and D. Green. 1993. 'Defining Quality'. *Assessment and Evaluation in Higher Education: An International Journal*, 18(1): 1–29.

Harvey, L., and J. Newton. 2004. 'Transforming Quality Evaluation'. *Quality in Higher Education*, 10(2): 149–65.

Harvey, Lee, and Bjørn Stensaker. 2008. 'Quality Culture: Understandings, Boundaries and Linkages'. *European Journal of Education*, 43(4): 427–41.

Hase, S., and C. Kenyon. 2000. 'From Andragogy to Heutagogy'. Ulti-BASE In-Site. Available at: http://epubs.scu.edu.au/gcm_pubs/99/ (accessed on 17 March 2014).

Hay, Richard. 2015. *Professionalization of Teachers and Institutions*. New Delhi: Shipra.

Hensens, Erica. 2007. 'Student Participation in Quality Enhancement: the Scottish Perspective'. In *International Perspectives on Student Participation in Quality Enhancement*, edited by V.S. Prasad and J. Patil, pp. 62–65. Bangalore: NAAC. Proceedings of International Conference on Student Participation in Quality Enhancement (SPQE) held on 16–17 September 2006 at Bangalore, India. Available at: http://naac.gov.in/docs/International%20 Perspectives%20on%20Student%20Participation%20in%20Quality%20 Enhancement.pdf (accessed on 26 April 2016).

Hersey, P., and K.H. Blanchard. 1977. *Management of Organizational Behavior: Utilizing Human Resources*, third edition. New Jersey: Prentice Hall.

———. 1992. *Management of Organizational Behaviour.* New Delhi: Prentice Hall of India.

Heyel, C. 1982. *The Encyclopedia of Management.* Third edition. New York: Van Nostrand.

Hirsch, J.E. 2005. 'An Index To Quantify An Individual's Scientific Research Output'. Available at www.pnas.org/content/102/46/16569.full (accessed on 26 April 2016).

Hirshfield, C. 1983. 'Quality Circles in the Classroom: An Experiment in the Pedagogical Uses of Japanese Management Methods'. Paper Presented at the Annual Conference of the Eastern Community College Social Science Association, Williamsburg, Virginia, 23–26 March.

Holec, Stanislav, Martin Hruška, and Jana Raganová. 2004. 'Integrated Science Through Computer-aided Experiments'. *Informatics in Education*, 3(2): 219–28.

Holt, M. 2000. 'The Concept of Quality in Education'. In *Improving Quality in Education*, edited by C. Hoy, C. Bayne-Jardine, and M. Wood. London: Falmer Press.

House, Robert J. 1996. 'Path–Goal Theory of Leadership: Lessons, Legacy, and a Reformulated Theory'. *Leadership Quarterly*, 7(3): 323–52. Available at: http://d1c25a6gwz7q5e.cloudfront.net/papers/674.pdf (accessed on 26 April 2016).

House, R.J. and G. Dressler. 1974. 'The Path Goal Theory of Leadership'. In *Contingency Approaches to Leadership*, edited by J.G. Hunt and L.L. Larson. South Illinois: University Press.

Hunter, J.E., and R.H. Hannah. 1987. 'Application of Meta-analysis'. *Industrial and Organizational Psychology*, Vol. 2.

Idrus, Rozhan, M. 2008. Transforming Engineering Learning via Technogogy, 5th WSEAS/IASME International Conference on Engineering Education, Heraklion, Greece, 22–24 July. Available at: http://www.wseas.us/e-library/conferences/2008/crete/education/education02.pdf (accessed on 8 August 2014).

Ishikawa, K. 1985. *What is Total Quality Control*. New Jersey: Prentice Hall.

Ison, R.L. 2008. 'Systems Thinking and Practice for Action Research'. In *The Sage Handbook of Action Research Participative Inquiry and Practice*, second edition, edited by Peter W. Reason and Hilary Bradbury, pp. 139–58. London: SAGE.

Jay, G., and E. Jones. 2005. 'Whiteness Studies and the Multicultural Literature Classroom'. *Melus: The Journal of Society for the Study of Multi-Ethnic Literature of the United States*, 30(2): 99–121.

Jenkins, A. 1995. 'The Research Assessment Exercise, Funding and Teaching Quality'. *Quality Assurance in Education*, 3: 4–12.

Jensen, Eric. 2007. *Brain-based Learning*. Cheltenham, Australia: Hawker Brownlow Education.

Jeskova, Z., and L. Onderova. 2004. 'Computer-Aided Laboratory Exercises in Physics Teaching'. Available at: http://physedu.science.upjs.sk/odf/www_kega/media/04.pdf (accessed on 29 May 2014).

Johnson, R., and A. Onwuegbuzie. 2004. 'Mixed Methods Research: A Research Paradigm Whose Time Has Come'. *Educational Researcher*, 33(7): 14–26.

Jones, P.K. 1989. 'Report on the 1989 Research Assessment Exercise'. University Funding Council, London.

Judge, T.A., R.F. Piccolo, and R. Ilies. 2004. 'The Forgotten Ones? The Validity of Consideration and Initiating Structure in Leadership Research'. *Journal of Applied Psychology*, 89(1): 36–51.

Juran, J.M., and F.M. Gryna, Jr. (eds). 1988. *Juran's Quality Control Handbook*. Fourth edition. New York: McGraw Hill.

Kahn, M. 2008. 'Multicultural Education in the United States: Reflections'. *Intercultural Education*, 19(6): 527–36.

Kalam, Abdul A.P.J. 2002. *Ignited Minds: Unleashing the Power within India*. New Delhi: Penguin.

Kalam, Abdul A.P.J., and A.S. Pillai. 2004. *Envisioning an Empowered Nation: Technology for Societal Transformation*. New Delhi: Tata McGraw Hill.

Karim, Sanaz. 2009. 'Applying Systems Approach to Educational—Organizational Change—Improvement of an Interdisciplinary Program'. Dissertation: Upsala Universitet.

Kaufman, R. 1992. *Mapping Educational Success*. California: Corwin.

Kaufman, R., and D. Zahn. 1993. *Quality Management Plus: The Continuous Improvement of Education*. California: Corwin.

Kenaw, S. 2003. 'The Idea of a University and the Increasing Pressures of Utilitarianism: A Critical Reflection on Addis Ababa University'. *The Ethiopian Journal of the Social Sciences and Humanities*, 1(1): 35–61.

Kerlinger, F.N. 1973. *Foundations of Behavioral Research*, Third Edition. New York: Holt, Rinehart and Winston, Inc., American Problem Series.

Kitano, Margie K. 1977. 'A Rationale and Framework for Course Change'. In *Multicultural Course Transformation in Higher Education: A Broader Truth*, edited by A.I. Morey and Margie K. Kitano, pp. 1–11. Needham Heights, MA: Allyn and Bacon.

Klepper, S. 1997. 'Industry Life Cycles'. *Industrial and Corporate Change*, 6(1): 145–82.

Knowles, M.K., E.F. Holton, and R.A. Swanson. 2005. *The Adult Learner: The Definitive Classic in Adult Education and Human Resource Development*. Amsterdam: Elsevier.

Konana, Prabhudev. 2015. 'The Difference Alumni can Make'. *The Hindu*, 31 December.

Kotter, John. 2005. *Our Iceberg Is Melting*. New York: St. Martin Press.

Krathwohl, David R. 2002. 'A Revision of Bloom's Taxonomy: An Overview'. *Theory into Practice*, 41(4): 212–18.

Krause, Kerri-Lee, and Lisa Armitage. 2014. *Australian Student Engagement, Belonging, Retention and Success: A Synthesis of the Literature*. Heslington York: The Higher Education Academy.

Kumar, M. Jagadesh. 2011. 'Evaluating Scientists: Citations, Impact Factor, h-Index, Online Page Hits and What Else?' Available at: http://mamidala.wordpress.com/2011/07/10/25/# (accessed on 26 April 2016).

Ladwig, D.J. 1983. 'Determining the Effectiveness and Evaluating the Implementation Process of a Quality/Performance Circles System Model to Assist in Institutional Decision Making and Problem Solving at Lakeshore Technical Institute'. EdD Dissertation: Nova University.

Lanares, Jacques. 2011. 'Enhancing Quality through Internationalization', Keynote Address, Salão Nobre.

Lang, Daniel, W. 2005. '"World Class" or The Curse of Comparison?' *The Canadian Journal of Higher Education*, 35(3): 27–55.

Latchem, C., and D. Hanna. 2001. *Leadership for 21st-Century Learning: Global Perspectives from Educational Innovators*. London: Kogan Page.

Levin, Henry M., and Dongshu Ou. 2006. 'What Is a World-Class University?' Conference of the Comparative and International Education Society, Honolulu, Hawaii, 16 March. Available at http://www.tc.columbia.edu (accessed on 5 April 2016).

Lewin, K. 1951. *Field Theory in Social Science*. New York: Harper & Row.

Lewin, K., R. Lippit, and R.K. White. 1939. 'Patterns of Aggressive Behavior in Experimentally Created Social Climates'. *Journal of Social Psychology*, 10: 271–99.

Lewis, David, and Ruth Goodison. 2004. 'Enhancing Learning with Information and Communication Technology (ICT) in Higher Education'. Research Report #533, University of Wolverhampton, Wulfruna St, UK.

MacGregor, J. 2004. 'Foreword'. In *Ethics: The Heart of Leadership*, edited by Joanne B. Ciulla, pp. ix to xii. Westport: Praeger.

Mansour, M., and W. Schaufelberger. 1989. 'Software and Laboratory Experiments Using Computers in Control Education'. *iEEE Systems Magazine*, 9(19): 19–24.

Martin, Ben R. 2011. 'The Research Excellence Framework and the "Impact Agenda": Are We Creating a Frankenstein Monster?' *Research Evaluation*, 20(3): 247–54.

Mitra, C.R., and P. Mandke. 2004. *The Knowledge Enterprise: Redefining Higher Education*. New Delhi: Samskriti.

Mayo, Sandra, and Patricia J. Larke. (n.d.). 'Multicultural Education Transformation in Higher Education: Getting Faculty to "Buy in"'. *Journal of Case Studies in Education,* 1: 1–9. Available at: http://www.aabri.com/manu-scripts/09337.pdf (accessed on 25 July 2014).

McGregor, D. 1960. *The Human Side of Enterprise*. New York: McGraw Hill.

Merrill, D. 1983. 'Component Display Theory'. In *Instructional Design Theories and Models: An Overview of Their Current States*, edited by C.M. Reigeluth, pp. 279–334. Hillsdale, NJ: Lawrence Erlbaum.

Merrill, M.D. 1994. *Instructional Design Theory*. Englewood Cliffs, NJ: Educational.

MHRD. 2009. Report of 'The Committee to Advise on Renovation and Rejuvenation of Higher Education'. New Delhi: MHRD.

———. 2014. *All India Survey on Higher Education (2011–12)*. New Delhi: Ministry of Human Resource Development, Government of India.

Middlehurst, R. 2003. *Competition, Collaboration and ICT: Challenges and Choices for Higher Education Institutions*. UK: University of Surrey.

Miller, A. 2002. *Mentoring Students and Young People. A Handbook for Effective Practice*. London: Routledge.

Miller, R. 2000. 'A Brief Introduction to Holistic Education'. *The Encyclopaedia of Informal Education*. Available at: http://infed.org/mobi/a-brief-introduc-tion-to-holistic-education/ (accessed on 23 February 2015).

Ministry of Education and Culture. 1985. *National Commission on Teachers in Higher Education* 1983. New Delhi: Mimeo. Also available in Raza, Moonis, and Nirmal Malhotra. 1991. *Higher Education in India: A Comprehensive Bibliography*. New Delhi: Concept Publishing Company.

Ministry of Human Resource Development and Confederation of Indian Industries, ASHE. 2013. Annual Status of Higher Education of States and UTs in India, 2013 Page 11, Deloitte Touche Tohmatsu India Private Limited. Available at: http://ciihighereducation.in/pdf/ASHE%20Report%202013.pdf (accessed on 14 October 2014).

Mitra, C.R. 2007. 'Technical Education'. In *Indian Education: Dynamics of Development*, edited by Marmar Mukhopadhyay and Madhu Parhar, pp. 174–85. New Delhi: Shipra.

Mitra, C.R., and P. Mandke. 2004. *The Knowledge Enterprise: Redefining Higher Education*. New Delhi: Samskriti.

Mitra, Sugata. 2006. *The Hole in the Wall: Self-Organising System in Education*. New York: University of Michigan.

Mlitwa, N. 2012. Global Perspectives on Higher Education and the Role of ICT. Lecture delivered at the Cape Higher Education Consortium Conference, University of the Western Cape (UWC), Bellville, South Africa, 8 September. Available at: http://eprints.rclis.org/6716/1/Global_Perspective_on_Higher_Education_and_the_Role_of_ICT%E2%80%A6.pdf (accessed on 23 April 2014).

Mohrman, Kathryn. 2005. 'World-class Universities and Chinese Higher Education Reform'. *International Higher Education*, 39 (Spring): 22–23. Also available at: https://ejournals.bc.edu/ojs/index.php/ihe/article/view-File/7475/6670 (accessed on 26 April 2016).

Montelongo, Ricardo. 2002. Student Participation in College Students' Organizations: A Review of Literature. *Journal of Indiana University Student Personnel Association*, 50–63 Also available at: http://portal.education.indi-ana.edu/Portals/32/Student%20Participation.pdf (accessed on 26 April 2016).

Moretz, H.L. 1983. Quality Circles in Education. Final Report. Charlotte, NC: Central Piedmont Community College (ED 231 479).

Morgan, C., Valerie Hall, and Hugh Mackay. 1983. *The Selection of Secondary Head Teachers*. Milton Keynes: OUP.

Moy, J. 1999. *The Impact of Generic Competencies on Workplace Performance. Review of Research Monograph Series*. Adelaide, Australia: National Centre for Vocational Education Research. Available at: www.bhert.com/publica-tions/position.../B-HERTPositionPaper09.pdf (accessed on 16 July 2014).

Mukhopadhyay, Marmar. 1981. *Barriers to Change in Secondary Education*. Udang (Howrah): Udang Books.

———. 1989a. Interview—A Component of Total Selection System. NIEPA, New Delhi.

———. 1989b. Management of Change in Education: In Search of Indian Model. NIEPA, New Delhi (mimeo).

Mukhopadhyay, Marmar. 1990. 'Recruitment in Education: Need for Modernization'. *Journal of Educational Planning and Administration*, 3(1): 69–79.

———. 1995. 'Multi-Channel Learning: Case of National Open School'. In *Multi-Channel Learning: Connecting All to Education*, edited by S. Anzalone. Washington, DC: EDC.

———. 1997. 'Globalisation of Education: Implications for India'. *University News*, 35(18), May.

———. 1999. 'Taxonomy of Educatedness'. *University News*, 37(26): 1–4.

———. 2001. *Total Quality Management in Education*, First edition. New Delhi: SAGE.

———. 2002. *Educating the Nation: Need for a Dedicated Satellite*. Ahmedabad: ISRO.

Mukhopadhyay, Marmar (ed.). 2004a. *Value Development in Higher Education*. New Delhi: Viva Books.

———. 2004b. *Educational Technology: Knowledge Assessment*. New Delhi: Shipra.

———. 2005a. *Total Quality Management in Education*. New Delhi: SAGE Publications.

———. 2005b. 'Organizational Micro Analysis'. In *Total Quality Management in Education*, second edition, pp. 50–62. New Delhi: SAGE.

Mukhopadhyay, Marmar. 2006a. *Educational Technology: Knowledge Assessment*. New Delhi: Shipra.

———. 2006b. *Story of EDUSAT*. New Delhi: Shipra.

———. 2007. 'Secondary Education: Victim of Perennial Neglect'. In *Indian Education: Dynamics of Development*, edited by M. Mukhopadhyay and M. Parhar, pp. 119–44. New Delhi: Shipra.

———. 2012a. *Leadership for Institution Building in Education*. New Delhi: Shipra.

———. 2012b. *ICT in Education Policy Toolkit*. New Delhi: UNESCO-INTEL.

———. 2013a. 'Education for Rural Transformation: A Case of Udang Forum'. In V. Chinapah (ed.). 2013. *Education for Rural Transformation (ERT) Good Practices from National and International Perspectives The 3rd ERT International Symposium, 2012 Vadodara, India*, pp. 133–60. Stockholm: Stockholm University.

———. 2013b. 'ICT Skill Certification for Employability and National Economic Growth. For Microsoft Corporation'. Gurgaon: ETMA.

———. 2014. 'Indian Higher Education: Shine versus Substance'. Unpublished paper for limited/private circulation.

Mukhopadhyay, Marmar, Madhu Parhar, Paushalee Dutta, and K. Khanna. 2014. *ICT Integrated Blended Learning Designs*. Gurgaon: ETMA (unpublished manuscript).

Mukhopadhyay, Marmar, and Madhu Parhar (eds). 1999. 'Open and Distance Education'. In *Indian Education: Developments since Independence.* New Delhi: Vikas Publishing House.

Mukhopadhyay, Marmar, and S. Bhushan. 2004. Access and Quality in Higher Education: Role of Private Participation. *University News*, February.

Mukhopadhyay, Marmar, and Madhu Parhar (eds). 2007. *Indian Education: Dynamics of Development.* New Delhi: Shipra.

Mukhopadhyay, Marmar, and Madhu Parhar. 2014. 'ICT in Indian Higher Education Administration and Management'. In *Education in Global Context: Emerging Trends Report 2013–2014*, edited by Huang Ronghuai, Kinshuk and Jon K. Price, pp. 263–83. New York: Springer.

Mukhopadhyay, M., P. Dutta, M. Parhar, and T. Agarwal. 2015. *Employability Skills of Teachers* Gurgaon: ETMA (Study sponsored by Indian Council of Social Science Research).

Murgatroyd, S., and C. Morgan. 1993. *Total Quality Management and the School.* Buckingham, UK: Open University.

Murray, P. 1983. The Quality Circle and the American Survey: What to Do When You Can't Have Lunch. Unpublished paper (ED 233 770).

Navaratnam, K.K. 1997. 'Quality Management in Education Must Be a Never-ending Journey'. In *Educational Dilemmas: Debate and Diversity. Vol. VI: Quality in Education*, edited by K. Watson, C. Modgal and S. Modgol, pp. 3–20. London: Cassell.

Nayak, S. 2005. 'The Campus Diversity Initiative: A Case Study'. *Higher Education Policy*, 18: 419–28.

Newell, W.H. 1990. 'Interdisciplinary Curriculum Development, Oxford, Ohio'. *Issues in Integrative Studies*, 8: 69–86.

Newman, J.H. 1854. *The Idea of a University.* Modern History Sourcebook. Available at: http://www.fordham.edu/halsall/mod/newman/newman-university.html (accessed on 30 March 2014)

Newton, J. 2002. 'Views from Below: Academic Coping with Quality'. *Quality in Higher Education*, 8(1): 39–61.

Nichols, Fred. 2016. 'Four Strategies for Managing Change'. Available at: http://www.nickols.us/four_strategies.pdf (accessed on 2 February 2016).

Nicholson, R. (ed.). 1989. 'The Person at the Helm'. In *School Management: The Role of the Secondary Head Teacher.* London: Kogan Page.

Nicol, D., and D. Macfarlane-Dick. 2006. 'Rethinking Formative Assessment in HE: A Theoretical Model and Seven Principles of Good Feedback Practice'. *Studies in Higher Education*, 31(2): 199–218.

Niland, John. 2000. 'The Challenge of Building World Class Universities in the Asian Region. On Line Opinion' (Australia's e-journal of social and political debate). Available at: www.onlineopinion.com.au/view.asp?article=997 (accessed on 3 May 2014).

Nisbette, R.E. 2003. *Geography of Thought.* London: Nicholas Brealey.
————. 2009. *Intelligence and How to Get It: Why Schools and Cultures Count.* New York: W.W. Norton & Co. Inc.
NRC Report. 2010. 'The National Research Council's Assessment of Research-Doctoral Programs'. Available at: http://www.gsas.harvard.edu/faculty/national_ research_council_report_2010.php (accessed on 17 June 2013).
Oakland, J.S. 1988. 'Quality Assurance'. In *The Gower Handbook of Management,* Second edition, edited by D. Lock and N. Farrow. Hauts: Gower Publishing.
OECD. 2006. OECD Information Technology Outlook 2006. Available at http://www.oecd.org/sti/oecdinformationtechnologyoutlook2006.htm (accessed on 14 April 2016).
Office of Research and Postgraduate Studies. 2004. 'Definition of Research Office of Research and Postgraduate Studies'. The University of Queensland. Available at: www.uq.edu.au.research/orps/?id=5718 (accessed on 5 August 2014).
Olaewe, O.O. 2006. *Educational Research Methods: An Analytic.* Nigeria: Nig. Ltd.
Olaewe, O.O., and K.A. Bashiru. 2009. 'The Place of Non-Parametric Statistics in the Conduct of Research in the Millennium Age (21st Century)'. *The Pacific Journal of Science and Technology,* 10(2): 211–16. Available at www.akamaiuniversity.us/PJST10_2_211.doc (accessed April 2016).
Oliva, P.F. 2009. *Developing the Curriculum.* Seventh edition. Boston, MA: Pearson/Allyn and Bacon.
O'Neil, H.F. Jr. 1979. *Issues in Instructional Systems Development.* Second edition. New York: Academic.
Orr, Leonard. 1998. *Breaking the Death Habit: The Science of Everlasting Life.* Berkeley, California: Frog Books.
Page, G.T., and J.B. Thomas. 1977. *The International Dictionary of Education.* London: Kogan Page.
Pant, M.M. 2012. 'Conversation with Prof. M.M. Pant on Matters Educational'. *Learning 221,* Issue 0006, 6th August 2012.
Parasuraman, A., V.A. Zeithaml, and L.L. Berry. 1985. 'A Conceptual Model of Service Quality and its Implications for Future Research'. *Journal of Marketing,* 49(4): 41–50.
Pareek, Udai. 2012. 'Self Regulation: The Key to Institution Building—IIMA'. In *Leadership for Institution Building in Education,* edited by Marmar Mukhopadhyay, pp. 178–90. New Delhi: Shipra.
Parhar, Madhu. 2002a. 'Access in Higher Education'. *University News,* 40(45), New Delhi.
————. 2002b. Enrolment Projection in Higher Education. *University News,* 40(27): 1–4.

Parhar, Madhu, G. Mythili, and P. Unnikrishnan. 2010. 'Student Satisfaction Survey at Indira Gandhi National Open University'. *EduComm Asia* (Commonwealth Educational Media Centre for Asia), 15(1): 16–21.

Partnership for 21st Century Skills. 2002. *Learning for the 21st Century: A Report and Mile Guide for 21st Century Skills*. Tuscan, AZ. Available at: http://www.21stcenturyskills.org/images/stories/otherdocs/p21up_Report. pdf (accessed on 16 July 2014).

Pascarella, E., and P.T. Terenzini. 1991. *How College Affects Students*. San Francisco, CA: Jossey-Bass.

Paton, Robert A., and James McCalman. 2000. *Change Management: A Guide to Effective Implementation*. London: SAGE.

Peters, T.J., and R.H. Jr. Waterman. 1982. *In Search of Excellence*. New York: Harper and Row.

Pittenger, Amy L. 2013. 'The Use of Social Networking to Improve the Quality of Interprofessional Education'. *The American Journal of Pharmaceutical Education*, 77(8): 174.

Planning Commission. 2001. 'India as Knowledge Super Power: Strategy for Transformation', Task Force Report. New Delhi: Planning Commission. Available at: http://planningcommission.nic.in/aboutus/ taskforce/tk_know. pdf (accessed on 16 July 2014).

———. 2013. *Twelfth Five Year Plan*. New Delhi: GOI. Available at: http://plan-ningcommission.gov.in/plans/planrel/12thplan/pdf/12fyp_vol1.pdf (accessed on 27 September 2015).

Porter, Michael E. 1990. *The Competitive Advantage of Nations*. New York: Free Press.

Postlethwaite, T.N. and Torsten Husen (eds). 1994. *The International Encyclopedia of Education*. Second edition. London: Pergamon.

Powar, K.B. 2001a. 'Quality of Research'. In *Supervision of Research in Universities*, edited by K.B. Powar and Z.S. Shafi, pp. 47–56. New Delhi: Association of Indian Universities.

———. 2001b. 'Research in Indian Universities'. In *Supervision of Research in Universities*, edited by K.B. Powar and Z.S. Shafi, pp. 213–21. New Delhi: Association of Indian Universities.

———. 2002. *Indian Higher Education: A Conglomerate of Concepts, Facts and Practices*. New Delhi: Concept Publishing.

———. 2003. 'Quality Assurance through Performance Indicators and Benchmarking'. In *Benchmarking Quality in Higher Education: The Indo--UK Perspectives*, edited by A. Gnanam, David Bradbury and Antony Stella. New Delhi: Sterling Publishers Pvt. Ltd.

Powar, K.B., and Z.S. Shafi (eds). 2001. *Supervision of Research in Universities*. New Delhi: Association of Indian Universities.

Prasad, V.S., and J. Patil (eds). 2007. *International Perspectives on Student Participation on Quality Enhancement*. Bangalore: NAAC

QNC. 1986. *Development of Education in Qatar in 1984/85186,* International Conference in Geneva.

Radhakrishnan, S. 1998. *The Principal Upanisads.* New Delhi: Harper Collins Publisher.

RAE. 2001. Research Assessment Exercise. Available at: http://webcache.google usercontent.com/search?q=cache:http://www.gla.ac.uk/media/media_196744 _en.pdf&gws_rd=cr&ei=byOAVpSKG5SjuQT1z7agAg (last accessed 26 April 2016).

Raelin, Joe. 2004. 'Preparing for Leaderful Practice'. *TD March.* Available at: http://www.leaderful.org/pdf/RaelinTD.pdf (accessed 7 December 2015).

Ramsden, P., and I. Moses. 1992. 'Associations between Research and Teaching in Australian Higher Education'. *Higher Education,* 23: 273–95.

Ratcliff, J.L. 2003. *Dynamic and Communicative Aspects of Quality Assurance.* London: Taylor & Francis.

Reigeluth, C.M. 2004. 'Instructional Systems Design'. In *Educational Technology: Knowledge Assessment,* edited by M. Mukhopadhyay, pp. 33–54. New Delhi: Shipra.

Reigeluth, C.M. (ed.). 1999. *Instructional Design: Theories and Models,* Vol. 2. New Jersey, NJ: Lawrence Erlbaum Associates.

Rigby, B. 2009. *The Assessment of Graduate Skills: Orientating Students and Standards for an Uncertain Future.* Available at: file:///C:/Users/isachdeva/ Downloads/GraduateSkills_ReviewOfAssessment.pdf (accessed on 14 June 2014).

Robinson, David. 2005. GATS and the OECD/UNESCO Guidelines and the Academic Profession, *International Higher Education,* 39: 6.

Robson, Mike. 1985. *Quality Circles: A Practical Guide.* London: Gower.

Romiszowaski, A.J. 1994. 'Systems Approach to Design and Development'. In *The International Encyclopedia of Education,* edited by H. Torsten and T.M. Postlethwaite, pp. 5895–5901. Oxford: Pergamon.

Rouse, Margaret. 2005. 'Definition of Systems Thinking'. *Techtarget.* Available at http://searchcio.techtarget.com/definition/systems-thinking (accessed on 23 December 2015).

Sallis, E. 2002. *Total Quality Management in Education.* Second edition. London: Kogan Page.

Sanders, J.O. 2007. *Spiritual Leadership: Principles of Excellence for Every Believer.* Kindle edition. Chicago, IL: Moody Publishers.

Schuller, R. 2006. *Tough Time Never Last, But Tough People Do.* New York: Bantam Books.

Science Watch. 2011. 'Sci-bytes: Journals Ranked by Impact: Education & Educational Research, Week of January 2, 2011'. Available at http://archive. sciencewatch.com/dr/sci/11/jan2-11_1/ (accessed on 25 April 2016).

Secretan, Lance. 1999. *Inspirational Leadership: Destiny, Calling and Cause.* Toronto: Macmillan Canada.

Semler, R. 1993. *Maverick.* New York: Warner.

Sharma, Deepa. 2006. *Quality in Education: The Quality Circle Way*. New Delhi: Gyan Publishing House.

Singh, Karan. 2003. 'Inter-faith Values for Education for a Global Society'. In *Education for a Global Society: Interfaith Dimensions*, edited by M. Mukhopadhyay, pp. 1–8. New Delhi: Shipra Publications.

Sleeter, C.E., and C. Grant. 2006. *Making Choices for Multicultural Education: Five Approaches to Race, Class, and Gender*, fifth edition. Hoboken, NJ: Wiley.

Smith, S.O., Ward, V. and House, A. 2011. '"Impact" in the Proposals for the UK's Research Excellence Framework: Shifting the Boundaries of Academic Autonomy', *Research Policy*, 40(10): 1369–79.

Somaiah, Malathi. 2007. 'Student Feedback Systems for Quality Enhancement in Higher Education: IIMs' Experience'. In *International Perspectives on Student Participation in Quality Enhancement*, edited by V.S. Prasad and J. Patil, pp. 42–51. Bangalore: NAAC.

Space Management Group. 2006. *UK Higher Education Space Management: Project Review of space norms*. UK: Space Management Group. Available at: http://www.smg.ac.uk/documents/spacenorms.pdf (accessed on 17 October 2014).

Stella, Antony. 2007. 'Student Participation in Quality Assurance'. In *International Perspectives on Student Participation in Quality Enhancement*, edited by V.S. Prasad and J. Patil, pp. 4–18. Bangalore: NAAC. Available at: http://naac.gov.in/docs/International%20Perspectives%20on%20Student%20Participation%20in%20Quality%20Enhancement.pdf (accessed on 26 April 2016).

Stephenson, S.L. 2003. 'Saving Quality from Quality Assurance'. Paper Presented at the 15th International Conference: Assessing Quality in Higher Education, Cape Town.

Streuner, J.N. and A.C. Tuijnman. 1994. 'Curriculum in Adult Education'. In *The International Encyclopedia of Education*, Second edition, edited by T. Husen and T.N. Postlethwaite, Vol. 3, pp. 1308–15. Oxford: Pergamon.

The University of Sydney Project. *Teaching and Learning, Academic Support and Graduate Attributes*. Sydney: The University of Sydney. Available at: http://sydney.edu.au/arts/teaching_learning/academic_support/graduate_attributes.shtml (accessed on 9 September 2014).

Think: College Pty Ltd. *Approach, Deployment, Results and Improvement (ADRI) Quality Circle as the Strategic Plan Model*. Australia: Think: College Pty Ltd. Available at: http://www.equella.think.eduthink.edu.au/ (accessed on 12 February 2014).

Tim, Turpin, and S.G. Jones. 2001. 'Innovation Networks in Australia and China'. In *Universities and the Global Knowledge Economy: A Triple Helix of University–Industry–Government Relations*, edited by Etzkowitz Henry and L. Loet. London: Continuum.

Torrance, E.P. 1962. *Guiding Creative Talent*. Englewood Cliffs, NJ: Prentice Hall.

Truckman, B.W., and M.A.C. Jensen. 1977. 'Stages of Small Group Development Revisited'. *Groups and Organizational Studies*, 2: 419–27.

Udpa, S.R. 2001. *Quality Circles: Progress through Participation*. New Delhi: Tata McGraw-Hill.

UGC. 1967. 'Committee on Colleges'. Report of the Mahajani Committee.

————. 1984. 'Committee to Enquire into the Working of Central Universities'. Report of the Madhuri Shah Committee.

UGC. 1990. 'UGC towards New Educational Management'. Report of the Gnanam Committee.

————. 2012. *Annual Report 2011–12*. New Delhi: UGC.

UIC. 2014. 'Measuring Your Impact: Impact Factor, Citation Analysis, and other Metrics'. Available at http://researchguides.uic.edu/c. php?g=252299&p=1683205 (accessed on 25 April 2016).

UNDP. 2011. 'World Education Report'. New York: UNDP.

UNESCO. 1979. *Planning Standards for Higher Education Facilities: Examples from National Practices*. Paris: UNESCO. Available at: www.unesdoc. unesco.org/images/0003/000363/036371EB.pdf (accessed on 18 July 2014).

————. 1996. *Learning: The Treasure Within*. Paris: UNESCO.

————. 2011. *ICT in Higher Education: Case Studies from Asia and the Pacific*. Bangkok: UNESCO. Available at: http://unesdoc.unesco.org/ images/0021/002141/214143E.pdf (accessed on 15 November 2015).

UNESCO and GOI. 2014. *Status of International Students in India for Higher Education*. New Delhi: MHRD. Available at: http://mhrd.gov.in/sites/upload_ files/mhrd/files/statistics/FSI2014_0.pdf (accessed on 10 November 2015).

Verma, Y. 2007. 'Teachers Perceptions about Ensuring Students Participation in Enhancing Quality in Higher Education'. In *International Perspectives on Student Participation in Quality Enhancement*, edited by V.S. Prasad and J. Patil, pp. 19–33. Bangalore: NAAC. (Proceedings of International Conference on Student Participation in Quality Enhancement (SPQE) held on 16–17 September 2006 at Bangalore, India.

Verspoor, Adriaan M. 1994. 'Introduction: Improvement and Innovation in Higher Education'. In *Revitalising Higher Education*, edited by J. Salmi and A.M. Verspoor. Oxford: Pergamon.

Vroeijenstijn, T. 1992. 'External Quality Assessment, Servant of Two Masters? The Netherlands University Perspective'. In *Quality Assurance in Higher Education: Proceedings of an International Conference, Hong Kong, 1991*, edited by A. Craft, pp. 97–108. London: Falmer Press.

Walpole, MaryBeth, and R.J. Noeth. 2002. 'The Promise of Baldrige for K-12 Education: ACT'. ACT Policy Report. Available at: http://files.eric.ed.gov/ fulltext/ED499905.pdf (accessed on 25 April 2016).

Watty, K. 2003. 'When Will Academics Learn About Quality?' *Quality in Higher Education*, 9(3): 213–21.

Weismer, W.H., and S.F. Cronshaw. 1988. 'The Moderating Impact of Interview Format and Degree of Structure on Interview Validity'. *International Journal of Selection and Assessment*, 7: 26–34.

Wiesnerf, W.H., and S.F. Cronshaw. 1988. A meta-analytic Investigation of the Impact of Interview Format and Degree of Structure on the Validity of the Employment Interview. *Journal of Occupational Psychology,* 61: 275–290. Also available at: http://webcache.googleusercontent.com/ search?q=cache:http://boardoptions.govws.com/jobinterviewpredictiveva-lidity.pdf&gws_rd=cr&ei=rqKCVr6OMpCUuAS61JbgDQ (accessed on 26 April 2016).

Westley, F., B. Zimmerman, and M. Patton. 2009. *Getting to May Be: How the World Is Changed.* Canada: Random House LLC.

Williams, J. 2002. 'Publish and be Damned? Publicising Student Feedback and the Quality Process'. Available at: http://citeseerx.ist.psu.edu/viewdoc/dow nload?doi=10.1.1.195.7148&rep=rep1&type=pdf (accessed on 17 February 2014).

Wilson, K.K., and G.E.B. Morren. 1990. *Systems Approaches for Improvement in Agriculture and Resource Management.* London: MacMillan.

World Bank. 2000. *Higher Education in Developing Countries: Peril and Promise.* Washington, DC: World Bank (Published for the Task Force on Higher Education and Society).

———. 2002. *Constructing Knowledge Societies: New challenges for Tertiary Education.* Washington, DC: World Bank.

Yorke, Mantz. 2000. 'Developing a Quality Culture in Higher Education'. *Tertiary Education and Management,* 6(3): 209–25.

Zohar, D., and I. Marshall. 2000. *Spiritual Intelligence: The Ultimate Intelligence.* London: Bloomsberrry.

Index

About the Author

A topper and gold medallist from Calcutta University and Rabindra Bharati University, Kolkata, in MSc (Education) and Tagore Literature, respectively, Professor Marmar Mukhopadhyay did his PhD from Maharaja Sayajirao University, Vadodara, and post-doctoral work from the University of Illinois, Urbana-Champaign, USA. He has provided leadership as joint director and director (i/c) of the National Institute of Educational Planning and Administration (NIEPA), New Delhi, chairman of the National Open School (NOS), vice president of the International Council of Distance Education (ICDE), Oslo, and member of the Steering Committee of International Multichannel Action Group on Education (Washington, DC).

He has been involved in educational policy making since 1986. He chaired the CABE subcommittee on the universalization of secondary education. He has been a member of various working committees of the Planning Commission.

Professor Mukhopadhyay specializes in (educational) management, educational and training technology, and open and distance education. He has conducted a large number of capacity-building programmes for college principals, university registrars and other senior officials. Mukhopadhyay uniquely combines experience as a teacher in higher education with expertise in management science, educational management training and institution building. His case of institution building—NOS—has been published in *Leadership for Institution Building*, an award-winning book on leadership.

British Council, UNESCO, UNICEF, the World Bank, Common wealth of Learning, Department for International Development (DFID), IBM, Intel, Microsoft, GESCI, KPMG, Institute of Human Settlement, the Indian Space Research Organisation (ISRO), NIIT and so on have consulted Professor Mukhopadhyay.

Professor Mukhopadhyay represented India in many important international forums, including International Conference in Education (ICE) in Geneva, UNESCO (Reconstruction of Post-war Afghanistan), Regional Quality Forum (Beijing) and so on.

Professor Mukhopadhyay has contributed 24 books and more than 250 book chapters, addresses to learned gatherings, research papers, thematic articles and conference papers published from India and abroad. Some of his important titles include: *Open Schooling: Selected Experience, Education in India: Dynamics of Development, Leadership for Institution Building in Education, Value Development in Higher Education, Educational Technology: Knowledge Assessment, Story of EDUSAT* and so on. His book *Total Quality Management in Education* (SAGE, 2005) is globally acclaimed and has been rendered into several Indian languages.

Professor Mukhopadhyay has been involved in the production and direction of more than 40 educational films as a script writer, actor, producer and director. Some of his educational films have been repeatedly telecast.

He has travelled widely on professional assignments to Europe, America, the Middle East, Africa, China and South Asia.

With all these activities, he anchors himself to the rural community. His 'Udang Experiment' on arresting primary school dropouts was flagged by the Government of India's Education for All (EFA) document for the high level group (HLG) meeting in Brazil in 2005, which attracted attention of the international media. His information technology intervention in rural areas received extensive coverage in Western news media drawing attention of the United States Agency for International Development (USAID) team.